READING HUIZINGA

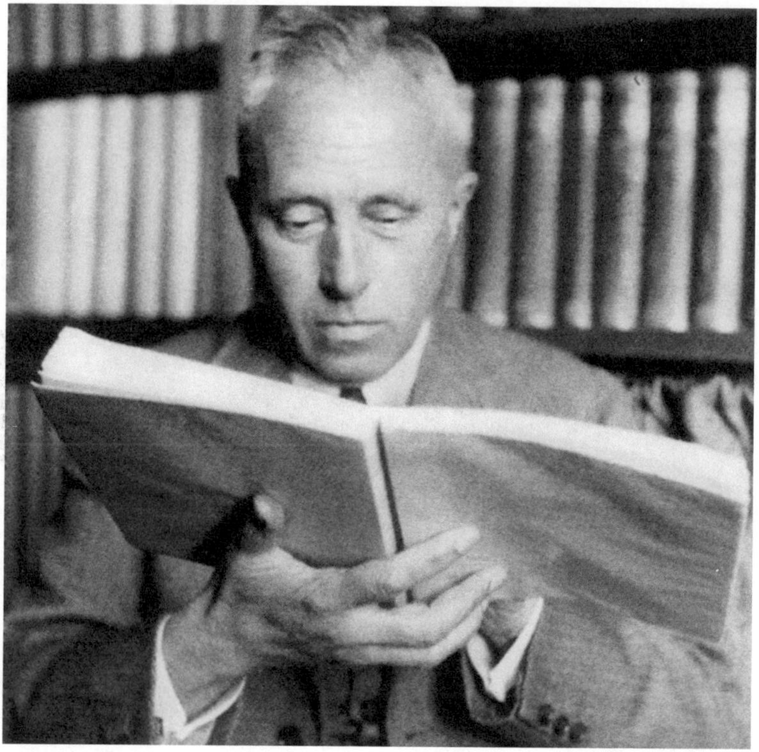

READING HUIZINGA

WILLEM OTTERSPEER

TRANSLATED FROM THE DUTCH
BY BEVERLEY JACKSON

Amsterdam University Press

The publication of this book was made possible by a grant from Leiden University Fund.

Cover illustration: Jan van Eyck, *The Arnolfini Marriage*, 1434 (detail)
Cover design and layout: Suzan Beijer, Amersfoort
Photo author: Erik Borst, Amsterdam

ISBN   978 90 8964 180 9
e-ISBN   978 90 4851 148 8
NUR   612

© W. Otterspeer / Amsterdam University Press, Amsterdam 2010

All rights reserved. Without limiting the rights under copyright reserved above, no part of this book may be reproduced, stored in or introduced into a retrieval system, or transmitted, in any form or by any means (electronic, mechanical, photocopying, recording or otherwise) without the written permission of both the copyright owner and the author of the book.

A serious house on serious earth it is,

In whose blent air all our compulsions meet,

Are recognised, and robed as destinies.

And that much never can be obsolete,

Since someone will forever be surprising

A hunger in himself to be more serious,

And gravitating with it to this ground,

Which, he once heard, was proper to grow wise in,

If only that so many dead lie round.

From Philip Larkin, *Church Going*

To the memory of Michaël Zeeman

CONTENTS

Preface 11
Introduction: A classic author 13

LIFE AND WORK 19
1 Life 21
2 Work 41

READING AND WRITING 59
3 Reading 61
4 Writing 78

CONTRAST AND HARMONY 95
5 Contrast 97
6 Harmony 113

PASSION AND SYNAESTHESIA 129
7 Passion 131
8 Synaesthesia 148

METHOD AND MYSTICISM 167
9 Method 169
10 Mysticism 186

EXTRAPOLATION AND METAMORPHOSIS 203
11 Extrapolation 205
12 Metamorphosis 220

CODA 235
13 Historical greatness 237

Select bibliography 245
Notes 247

PREFACE

It was from Huizinga that I learned how to read, and Huizinga was the subject of my first publication; it was a foregone conclusion that I would some day write a book about him. The genesis of this particular book arose from a period in residence at Harvard University as Erasmus Professor in 2003. My duties there included lecturing on Huizinga, a task that gave me an opportunity to arrange my thoughts about him. When I returned to Leiden, I set about gathering the hours and days to write the book that I had had in mind for so many years.

In doing so, I had a formidable arsenal of literature at my disposal. Given the Netherlands' customary lack of largesse in relation to its classical authors, Huizinga has little reason to complain. A handsome edition of his collected works was published soon after his death (9 vols., 1948-1953), and recently an equally handsome edition of his correspondence (3 vols., 1989-1991) has been added to this. Huizinga is still read and commented on today. In the Netherlands, the editors of this correspondence, Léon Hanssen, Wessel Krul, and Anton van der Lem, have provided the impetus for a modern approach to his work. The new bibliography published by Van der Lem

(*Inventaris van het archief van Johan Huizinga*, Leiden 1998) proves that the work is still being translated. And new studies are still being written in other countries: not so long ago, Christoph Strupp published *Johan Huizinga. Geschichtswissenschaft als Kulturgeschichte* (2000).

These books list all the literature that has been published on Huizinga. I therefore judged it unnecessary to duplicate all that material in an extensive bibliography for this book. I have seen it all, and I have used it all. In that sense, there is nothing original about this book. At most, any claim to originality would come from my own reading of Huizinga. That is why this book bears the title *Reading Huizinga*, in that fine tradition in which Janet Malcolm wrote *Reading Chekhov* (2004), or in the equally fine tradition of William Trevor's *Reading Turgenev*.

Writing this book brought back many happy memories of discussions with my students, in Cambridge most notably with Edward Wouk and in Leiden with Theodor Dunkelgrün. And I would not have wanted to forego the enthusiasm of Hugo van der Velden, the Hollander at Harvard. The collaboration with Beverley Jackson, who translated the book into English, proved to be an enriching experience. The translation has benefited from her meticulousness and sense of style. Huizinga himself has not always been fortunate with his translators. It would be a great boon if this book helped to create an awareness that many of his works still await discovery by the English-speaking world.

INTRODUCTION

A CLASSIC AUTHOR

Given that Dutch culture has no classic authors, no Pléiade serving as its literary pantheon, no living collective memory nourished by a curriculum, it is remarkable how persistently Johan Huizinga continues to be read. By his own simple definition, 'to be classic means still to be read', Huizinga is one of the Netherlands' few classic authors. Dutch culture does have a few classic books, although their numbers are dwindling, but in the sense of a classic author, Huizinga's only competition comes from writers such as Multatuli and Louis Couperus, Willem Elsschot and Willem Frederik Hermans.[1]

Johan Huizinga, the most famous Dutch historian, certainly lends himself to comparison with writers more readily than with other historians. His work is far better read as a series of parables than as a historiographical oeuvre. In fact, those who read him as a historian will scarcely discover any cohesiveness in his work. In his best-known books, *The Waning of the Middle Ages* (1919), *Erasmus* (1924), *In the Shadow of Tomorrow* (1935), and *Homo Ludens* (1938), the authorial voice is that of a historian, a biographer, a cultural critic and an anthropologist, in that order. His work does possess cohesiveness –

more so, perhaps, than in the case of any other historian – but it is to be found less in his subject-matter than in themes addressed in his writing. To date, Huizinga is the only Dutch author who has ever had a realistic chance of being awarded the Nobel Prize for literature. Only those who read him as a writer will appreciate the enduring value of his work.

With the aversion to heights that is indigenous to the Low Countries, his reputation was soon cropped, like Multatuli's, for instance, to more manageable proportions. Immediately after his death, Jan Romein and others, even his friend C.T. van Valkenburg, denied that he had been a genius. Another friend, Gerrit Jan Heering, granted him 'a stroke of genius', but no more than that. And adepts of all the sub-disciplines into which history has branched since he was writing assure us that Huizinga has nothing more to teach us, and imply that on the contrary, his reputation is an obstacle blocking the path to greater and more anonymous progress in historiography.

An amusing chapter might be written on 'Huizinga as a career', on the way in which not only historians like Romein, and even Pieter Geyl, but also later historians proclaimed him dead to advance their own immortality. Romein is a perfect example, in his case of 'socialist criticism': of the conviction that Huizinga was a spokesman for 'those bourgeois circles that "apportion" glory'. He writes, 'Even so, I feel that the remarkable esteem, indeed, I may say veneration, that he has attracted both at home and abroad, calls for some explanation of this emphasis, without wishing to condone it.' He surely did not come to praise Caesar.[2]

Huizinga's definition of the word 'classic' appeared in a newspaper article he wrote about the great German historian Ranke. He had just returned from a conference on philology in Germany, and had felt at home there. He himself had been trained as a philologist, and the hospitality of that field of scholarship remained dear to him, although he had been appointed to a chair in history and wrote primarily about historical subjects. But that was not all. He had rediscovered the Germany he had once known, with its taste of 'mild Rhenish'. One after-dinner speaker had pointed out that no fewer than six of Ranke's descendants and kinsmen were seated around the table that evening, as well as the publisher of Ranke's collected works. 'I was witness to the existence of an intellectual hagiolatry of a pure and sincere kind.'[3]

Saints and heroes – history was full of them, at least in Huizinga's eyes. His work is populated by people he admired, events he celebrated, and phenomena with which he identified. He was the Cassandra of culture, but at the same time he called himself an optimist. He knew the dark side of history, but saw it as the reverse side of the light. He liked to divide the world according to virtues and vices. We will find in Huizinga no description without prescription, no history without contrasts.

That is precisely what drew him to Ranke. At the heart of Ranke's work was the contrast between Latin and Teutonic in European society. As Huizinga summarised Ranke's proposition, 'This society could come forth only from the secular-ecclesiastical universalism of the Middle Ages. The Teutonic nation embodies the opposition to that universal state, first in the emperor's opposition to the Pope, and subsequently in the Reformation that severed the ancient unity.' What appealed to Huizinga was Ranke's description of the unity of the old Europe shattering into fierce antagonism, a clash of opposing values. From this arose the multicoloured vision of Ranke's thesis, the fullness of his narrative.

At the same time, the conservative, or rather conservationist, approach of Ranke's work appealed to him, his desire to contribute, with his work, to the renewal of the old, the restoration of the *Romanitas*, the harmonic unity of Roman-Christian Europe. From

Ranke's youthful writings Huizinga quotes a vision of the great minds of antiquity and the modern age joining to express their most profound ideas. 'Would that not be a concert of the most marvellous harmony, of one tone, one breath, a single word!,'[4] adding, 'but in all that consciousness of the infinite variety and multifaceted nature of human thought and action, that Ranke who surveys worlds is already present.'

Finally, he praises Ranke's ability to see the great in the small, what Ranke himself called 'Gestaltung des Moments': eternity in a moment. According to Huizinga, Ranke's historical personages were 'figures, in the fullest sense of the word'. He depicted them in a few words, sometimes in a single gesture – Charles IV waving off flies with a maple twig he has nonchalantly peeled during an audience.

Huizinga was not uncritical of Ranke, whose style struck him as too smooth and made him impatient. 'It is an endless adagio. There is motion, and colour, and pomp, but never pace. Even acts of war progress in an Olympic or academic mode. Ranke is the utter antithesis of his two contemporaries in historiography, the feverish-possessed Carlyle and Michelet. Without a doubt he is greater than both, not only as a researcher. Michelet shoots bolts of lightning, and Carlyle unleashes hurricanes. Ranke creates, orders, and rules. He is above passion.'[5]

In all this, Huizinga was writing – quite inadvertently it seems – a self-portrait. In the qualities he ascribes to Ranke he defined the quintessence of his own authorship. Oppositions and their dissolution, contrast and harmony, these were the warp and weft of his work. The rhythm embedded in this was a feature of both history and culture. In his historiography, Huizinga mixed passion and receptivity, mysticism and method. Better than anyone, he knew how to invest historical truth with the excitement of fiction. That which was gone – gone, forever – remained of value in the present, that which appeared to be a small detail contained a world of significance. 'In all things lies the supreme miracle', he once wrote about one of his favourite writers, Nathaniel Hawthorne.

Writing of that same Hawthorne, the American critic Edmund Wilson once noted that the relative lack of movement that characterises his books corresponded to the pace of his secluded existence. At the heart of the traditional and stable world evoked by Hawthorne was a tendency 'to idealize historical episodes, to weave fantasies out of their dreams; to reflect upon human life, upon Man's relation to nature, to God and the Universe; to speculate philosophically or euphorically, to burst into impetuous prophecy on the meaning and the promise of the United States.' Replace the United States with the Netherlands, and all this applies to Huizinga.

At the same time, that is precisely the criticism that may be levelled at his work. But that is not what this book is about. On that subject, a great deal – far too much – has already been written. Nor is this book about Huizinga the historian. On that subject too, many fine books and cartloads of articles have been written. My focus here is on Huizinga the writer. I shall base myself on the best things he wrote. The weaknesses in some of his writing – his often surprising inconsistency, his sometimes rather ponderous style – are not what made him a classic. And that is what this book is about, about what makes Huizinga a classic author, a writer who is still read today.

LIFE AND WORK

1

LIFE

Johan Huizinga was reserved by temperament. 'In a scholar, so much of his individual personality is left unspoken,' he wrote of his teacher, the orientalist Hendrik Kern. He might have been describing himself. But he was also passionate. This passion could easily be concealed beneath the mantle of learning. Even so, the essence of his life, the lion's share of which was spent in a study, was embedded in that passion, in the fundamental contradictions of that life and the form in which he kept them in check.[1]

The first and perhaps most important of those contradictions relates to the place where Huizinga was born. There is no other writer in Dutch literature, and certainly no historian, whose thinking is so dominated by a sense of place. Mediaeval serfs are sometimes described, in a wonderfully vivid phrase, as *glaeba adstricti*, chained to the land. This image applies both to the young boy known as 'Han' and the older Huizinga. His view of reality and the world was determined in the first place by Groningen and the surrounding region – the Ommelanden. That opposition between city and land also raises wider contrasts, such as old versus new, and centre versus periphery. From a still broader perspective, the essential subject of his work, the contrast between permanence and mutability, might well be traced to that initial local opposition.

Huizinga's family came from the Ommelanden. When the children played in their grandfather's house with the cousins from Friesland, local pride would frequently spark heated exchanges. He and his brother felt a hearty contempt whenever they heard their guests' dialectal *jou* and *jimme* for 'you'. Still, it did not escape the boys' attention that these cousins felt Frisian 'in a higher sense than we felt ourselves to be Groningers ... I was probably not yet aware that my own name was of proud old Frisian stock, and even if I did know, it had not yet become clear to me that my provincial sense of Groningen identity was a recent product of a long and complex political development, in which an original local character had been submerged and lost, whereas in every Frisian boy, the remains endured of a primeval tribal consciousness.'[2]

The contrast between Groningen and Friesland, which was both exacerbated and attenuated by the fact that the Ommelanden were originally Frisian, imparted to his local pride the fervour of a bond and the nostalgia of loss. 'They are truly venerable, those Frisians between Vlie and Lauwers,' he would write as a professor in Groningen. 'They are the only Germanic tribe to have owned their old land – or some of it – with the same old names, from Caesar's time down to the present day.' But ownership and loss were connected. In the early Middle Ages, the Frisian character of the Ommelanden withered away, and Huizinga has called this a cultural loss. The new Saxon population adopted little of Frisian culture and brought little to put in its place. 'These parts acquired a dry and prosaic quality to their popular culture' he wrote, and it filled him with melancholy.[3]

Johan himself was born on 7 December 1872 in Groningen, then a small town with a population of about 42,000, where modernity announced itself with the levelling of ramparts. Groningen was only accessible by way of a single-track railway line, and within the town people moved about by horse-drawn tram. Neither gas nor electricity had yet arrived, and society was rigidly divided into its separate estates. The city had its own university, and professors belonged to the élite. This included the family in which Johan was raised, since his father was professor of physiology at Groningen University.[4]

The dominant presence in his early boyhood, however, was not his father but his grandfather, Jakob Huizinga (1809-1894), a Mennonite minister, richly endowed with the 'holy sentiments' that were appropriate to his Church. Profound self-scrutiny and a Biblical renewal of life were the beating heart of his faith. Jakob's account of this lifelong process took the form of a diary, which he kept faithfully for sixty years. With great tenacity and stifling love he continued to impress upon his grandchildren the need to remain close to God. At the same time, he was obliged to watch his sons deviating from his footsteps, and lived in the constant awareness that those around him heard him but did not listen. 'Ah, who is there who can feel with me? Who can I regard as one with me in mind and soul?'

His eldest son, Dirk (1840-1903), Johan's father, was the greatest renegade of the family. Although he did set off to study at the Mennonite Seminary in Amsterdam, once there he was bewitched by modern theology and the natural sciences, old port and young actresses. Three weeks before his first-year examinations he took to his heels and wrote letters from Germany threatening foreign legion and suicide. When his father tracked him down in Strasbourg, the two had a conversation that was undoubtedly as mortifying to the father as it was a relief to the son, and Dirk was left with student debts and syphilis. He paid off the debts but never managed to shake off the disease, though he tried everything from hydropathy to the local quack. He embarked on a new course of studies – medicine in Groningen – which resulted in the irreversible collapse of his faith, prompting bitter diary entries from his father. 'He whom once I idolized, I now see cast down in the grimiest dust', this time an allusion not to licentious conduct but to a materialist philosophy of life. For Dirk had traded in his faith for phosphorus, and religious introspection for empirical research. The exchange yielded an early professorship and a respectable career, but the syphilis remained. The attacks of pain and migraine suffered by his father would cast an occasional cloud over Johan's childhood.

But no more than that. Neither he nor his two-year-older brother Jakob (1870-1948) seems to have been badly affected. The list Johan made of the presents he would like for his eleventh birthday, and that he assured his father would be 'graciously received' – a watch, a steam engine, a box of tin soldiers, atlas, books – are not suggestive of parsimony or worries and illustrate his father's generosity. They contrast with the frugality of the diarist grandfather, who grumbled that his old volume of the *Kindercourant* – a kind of *Boy's Own* – could not compete with a toy fortress or a box of magic tricks. They show the carefree side of a childhood that seems to have been filled with outings and journeys that opened the young boy's eyes to the beauty of his country. 'I have a lively memory,' Huizinga wrote shortly before his death, in *Dutch Civilization in the Seventeenth Century*, 'of a day in 1880 when my father showed me that looking out of the train near Amsterdam, towards the river Zaan, you could see some hundred windmills.'[5]

The grandfather and the father both made their influence felt. In one of his many attempts to keep his grandson on the straight and narrow, seventy-five-year-old Jakob gave twelve-year-old Han a medallion for his coin collection. The message or 'Commemoration' he wrote to accompany the gift contained the following admonitions: 'Foremost among all virtues is the truth. Therefore have the courage always to be true; you will then be great and good. Never deal in wrath. What you lose in time you will gain in strength, prudence, and wisdom. If you wish to find the right key to someone's mind, ask him boldly who his best friends are. If you want to find a faithful servant who will be pleasing to you, be your own servant. It is good to be praised, but it is better to be praiseworthy. Men of character are not born, but formed by effort, struggle and prayer. Crush whatsoever breaks the peace, and nurture whatsoever nurtures love.' Without this document, Huizinga's life cannot be fully understood.

The father imparted to his son a different kind of truth, that of science. His father's efforts in original research focused on the origins of life, the spontaneous generation of life from dead matter. Although his theories were shot down soon after they were launched, they brought him a brief moment of fame and an honorary doctorate from Leiden University. In this respect he set a clear example to his son: research was about both meticulousness and breadth.

These two legacies were as influential as they were contradictory. Early on, they settled into a framework of contrasts that would determine Huizinga's thinking for the rest of his life: science versus religion, reason versus feeling, individual versus community, change versus permanence. Those are concepts scarcely digestible for a secondary-school pupil, but that he was gradually absorbing them – beneath the surface as it were – is demonstrated by his decision to be baptized. Through baptism, eighteen-year-old Johan joined the religious congregation of his grandfather, but the affirmation of faith he wrote to accompany it rather reflected his father's enlightened spirit. His grandfather, both uplifted and disappointed, saw the document rather as 'a treatise of philosophical enquiry into the origins of the concepts of Religion and morality among different peoples'. Jesus and the Mennonites were discussed in respectful terms, 'but an affirmation of faith such as I would wish to see from a fledgling Mennonite was entirely absent.'

Meanwhile, neither religion nor philosophy sufficed to channel the intense passion that Johan had inherited from both his grandfather and his father. This passion initially made him a melancholy boy with the associated fierce mood swings. A contributory factor was the fear that his father's disease had also taken root in his sons. His brother's mental instability and the fact that both brothers were deaf in one ear seemed to point that way. Their half-brother Herman (1885-1903), born into their father's second marriage, became so obsessed with this notion that he committed suicide by drinking photographic developer.

There was something else. Both the boys' grandfather and their father had been widowed quite young: Jakob after the birth of their seventh child, and Dirk after only four years of marriage. Their grandfather had reacted by completely idealizing his wife, their father by completely sublimating his loss. Jakob would never remarry: in his mind his deceased wife became a perfect being, an example who inspired him to lead a pious life. Dirk remarried two years after losing his wife, put himself up for election to the city council, and switched from fundamental research to popular science. While one sought isolation with God, the other found the sociability of the Enlightenment.

The early images of women that became impressed on Johan's retina were thus dominated by the categories of holiness and absence. The ethereal concept of women that was evidently ingrained in him from an early age was reinforced by the stamp of doom that his father's disease had impressed on sexuality. It became the concrete embodiment of the tension he felt between passion and fulfilment. In 1897, in a notebook in which he wrote down passages from his reading, he quoted the following words from Nietzsche's *Genealogy of Morals*: 'Sensuality and chastity are not necessarily opposed; every good marriage, every true love, transcends any such contrast'.

And yet, while Johan Huizinga was no ordinary boy, he certainly did not have an unhappy childhood. In Manna de Cock (1847-1910) his father had found a good second wife, and someone who 'surrounded the children with matchless loving care'. Han liked being at home and was an avid reader. His favourite books were historical adventure novels and fairy tales. And these tales and adventures were not just for reading, they were also to be performed. From one perspective Huizinga's boyhood days might be seen as one long fancy-dress party. One of his favourite memories dated from the late summer of 1879, when Groningen's student fraternity staged a re-enactment of the *joyeuse entrée* of Count Edzard of East Friesland into the city of Groningen in 1506. He later recalled the tiniest details: how windy it had been, that a flagstaff had snapped, the glittering metal of Count Edzard's armour. He wrote in his memoirs that in this spectacle he had forged his first link with the past, 'and it was deep and enduring'.[6]

True, Han was rather an odd boy, or at least, that was how his friends saw him. They were allowed to join in when he was arranging his castle and putting his army of tin soldiers in battle array, but then he would confuse his visitors, who were used to Floris V and Muiden Castle, with the fanciful names he gave his knights and their castle, and the extraordinary adventures he dreamed up. He had a better rapport with his brother, with whom he studied the arcane details of heraldry and argued about crests, cantons and cotises, while his classmates played with their spinning-tops or marbles.[7]

This game with the past, this amalgam of fairy tales and history, acquired an added dimension when his own past was involved, as in the copper anniversary of his father and stepmother. First printed songs were handed out and sung. Then, Johan – 'in the most old-fashioned of garments and make-up' according to his grandfather – acted out a scene from the life of Pieter Huisinga Bakker, an eighteenth-century merchant from Amsterdam who was supposedly compiling a genealogical register of the Huizinga family. His brother and a female cousin played the family's progenitors. The grandfather was adorned with a wreath, the bridal couple were given presents from antiquity, and the festivities concluded with Homer (Jakob) and Anacreon (Johan), together with one of their Muses (the cousin) singing an appropriate song, which Johan had undoubtedly written for the occasion.

This special relationship with the past is also reflected in the coin collection that Johan built up with his brother. 'How it grew I can't remember' wrote Huizinga in his memoirs, 'but it included *scheepjesschellingen* [6-stuyver pieces] and silver riders, with some coins even dating from 1500 and earlier. We had a lead Beggar Medal inscribed "better Turkish than Papist", emergency paper coins issued during the siege of 1672, and a medallion struck to mark the second anniversary of Groningen's university in 1814, with the motto "dummodo monumentum adsit" ["May this endure in commemoration"]'. The finest piece in the collection was given to them by an uncle on the occasion of yet another masquerade, this time in 1884: a *denarius* dating from the time of Louis the Pious, excavated from a terp in Hunsingo. The Middle Ages and Groningen, united in an obole of the dream!⁸

Werner Kaegi attributes this denarius story to 'an inclination to name magic' in Huizinga. Names, whether of families or places, certainly enchanted the young Han. He called his partiality to aristocratic roots and names two of his secret transgressions, 'with disdain for my own all too blatant plebeian descent from Mennonite preachers and small farmers from the Ommelanden'. The magical effect of names also applied to dikes and canals, towns and villages. Huizinga could recite them as Homer recited the names of ships.

The same applied to words and their etymology. At secondary school Johan acquired a special fascination for linguistics. His teacher Jan te Winkel, perhaps a little too much of a scholar to make a good teacher, proved willing to respond to a question on the possible kinship between the Dutch word *hebben* [to have] with the Latin *habeo* by dishing up the principles of Grimm's Law, the First Germanic Sound Shift. So Johan learned how *pater* [father] had become *vader* and *caput* [head] had developed into *hovet* and subsequently into *hoofd*. 'I found this knowledge riveting, and from then on I determined to study linguistics.'

In this way a new contrast was born: that between philology and history. For his passion for linguistics did not supersede that for history. 'My heart and imagination were with the Middle Ages, about which I knew very little, but of which I had a kind of luxuriant and at the same time vague vision, not primarily filled with knights and plumes. I recall a fantasized drawing of a port in a Hanseatic city, which I probably made at the age of fourteen.' The historian could no longer recall which reading had fired his imagination; more important is the combination of reading and drawing that the image displayed. His unmistakeable gift for drawing, with which he entertained classmates and fellow students, and would later enchant colleagues and queens, would make him one of the most visual of Dutch historians.[9]

In the meantime, the student Huizinga resolved the contrast between philology and history in the same way, and just as effortlessly, as the primary-school boy had mixed fairy tales and history and the secondary-school pupil had mixed reason and religion. He had wanted to study Semitic languages in Leiden, but in the end he stayed in Groningen to study Dutch literature. Still, the lectures in comparative linguistics and historical grammar, mythology and Arabic – which he sometimes had to seek out in other faculties

– satisfied his emerging thirst for scholarship. The lectures in Sanskrit, a standard part of the curriculum, taught at Groningen by the great master of that subject, Jacob Samuel Speyer, would instil in him an enduring love of linguistics. So engrossed did he become in the 'beautiful poetic form' of holy Sanskrit that he threw himself into the ardent study of Buddhism.

At the same time he took an active part in student life, albeit with a certain distance. He joined the student fraternity, but almost immediately set up an exclusive club with a few fellow-students in his year, which he called, in typical Huizinga style, 'The Northern Stable or the Knights of the Blue Horse', including the troubadour 'Marie brise le coeur, l'irrésistible' – a role that he is unlikely to have claimed for himself. He probably preferred to style himself 'the knight with the burning heart, the king's clerk'. It was in this period that he wrote his dramatic sketch, 'The black knight', of which only the list of *dramatis personae* has been preserved. He also devoted a great deal of time to the many committees that were part and parcel of student life, the most important one being that for the masquerade of the anniversary year of 1894. The response among the student body was disappointingly feeble, and some suggested that the whole idea was outmoded. Huizinga reacted in characteristic style. 'And nonetheless we are proud, gentlemen,' he is said to have proclaimed at dinner that evening, 'to be the bearers, the last bearers, of a fine thing that is nearing extinction.'

But it was above all in literature that he found the past. In his student days he became acquainted with the greatest author of his reading life, Dante: 'Nessun maggior dolore che ricordarsi,' he wrote in the margin of one of his notebooks – 'No greater suffering than to remember'. But he also read Shakespeare and the other great Renaissance writers of Britain and Italy. At the same time, he was a 'passionate devotee' of the Movement of 1880, a group of innovative poets, prose writers and artists whose principles included 'art for art's sake' and whose chosen styles included impressionism. 'They taught us,' he wrote in his memoirs, 'to place science well below the arts, to seek our true life in the depths of our being (which was a great blessing), and also, not to worry about politics and suchlike (which was a great mistake).'[10]

The debate that was pursued within the Movement of 1880 between art and society, avant-garde and socialism, also played itself out in his own heart. However hard it may be to see in the later (liberal) conservative Huizinga the early aesthetically-minded socialist, anyone who wants to understand him must try to do so. What is needed is an eye for that special whole that Huizinga was able to forge from ostensibly incompatible parts: an art rooted in society, an élite willing to serve. His mentor in this amalgamation was Jan Veth.

Jan Veth (1864-1925) was eight years older than Huizinga and the most important portrait painter of his generation. He was also the most important art critic brought forth by *De Nieuwe Gids*,[11] but above all he excelled in converting the tensions harboured within the Movement of 1880 into a harmonious artistic and social ideal. In that sense he truly served as 'a new guide' for Huizinga – as the latter would later write in his biography of Veth – a 'signpost', pointing away from the Generation of 1880. 'He confirmed to me, what my heart told me, that impressionism was not the only way to innovation, and that it was not necessary to renounce the old in order to embrace the new.... It was as if someone had grasped your shoulders and set you on your feet, with an encouraging pat on the back and a firm push, and said, "That way".'[12]

Huizinga himself provided what was to be the standard description of that new direction, again in the form of opposites:

The intellectual sea-change that started to make itself felt in the life of the arts and literature in the Netherlands around 1890 was based partly on a reaction against the excessive individualism and impressionism of the first exponents of the Movement of 1880, and arose from a need for more style and certainty, a bolder sense of direction and belief. It was no coincidence that while the earlier period had been dominated by literature, and poetry in particular, in this decade it was the visual artists and architects, the musicians, the social and historical thinkers, who came to the fore. The initiative lay with the constructive minds. Yet the efforts ... were far from monolithic or focused on a single point. They reached out to two poles, socialism and mysticism. But for both, the slogan was art and society, monumental art.[13]

This implied that the young Huizinga had seriously embraced the aesthetic socialism familiar from the work of Henriëtte Roland Holst.[14] In his retrospective look at forty years of the Netherlands under the reign of Queen Wilhelmina (Terugblik; 1938), he wrote that socialism acquired influence among the late nineteenth-century Dutch intelligentsia in two separate guises: a practical and political form and a more theoretical and aesthetic version. It was the latter form to which Huizinga too inclined. And what applied to the young queen applied to him as well: 'What hope and expectation must have filled her young head!' Even after that hope had been shot to smithereens in the First World War, his friendship with the Roland Holsts remained intact. Even when the politics of socialism and economic liberalism parted company, the 'inner predisposition' that united them continued to exist.

After graduation, Huizinga took up a position as a history teacher at a secondary school in Haarlem, where he worked from 1897 to 1905. In the last two years of his time there, he combined this work with a post as a private lecturer in Ancient Indian literature and cultural history at the University of Amsterdam. He would later describe this period as 'those years of clarity'. It was then that this Dante reader found his Virgil in Jan Veth, and his Beatrice in Maria Vincentia Schorer, who was known as Mary. He had met this burgomaster's daughter from Middelburg in 1892 through his stepmother, who was a friend of her mother's. Just fifteen years old, she had a gift for music, and she possessed everything that the student dreamed of, and lacked. She could give him the trappings of an upper-middle-class lifestyle and the warmth of a cultivated milieu. The Schorers had been elevated to the nobility by King Willem I at the beginning of the nineteenth century, and owned a splendid mansion, Toornvliet, just outside Middelburg. Music and painting, urban architecture and rural idyll, it all merged in a *Gesammtkunst* that revolved around Mary, and the two were married in 1902. That same year he and Mary visited Dante's Ravenna together, of which he wrote that 'it gave me a better understanding of the concept of Majesty', and they also saw the major exhibition of Flemish Primitives in Bruges.

These were also years of clarity in terms of religious and philosophical outlook. 'From about 1900 onwards,' wrote Huizinga to his cousin Menno ter Braak in 1938, 'I acquired a firmer awareness, though without the acceptance of any denomination, of Christian morality as the supreme guiding principle of human life.' Whatever had once appealed to him in the ancient Indian religions, in their beauty and ritual, ultimately struck him as too insubstantial, too vague, too unworldly and divorced from reality. In the manuscript of 'Mijn weg tot de historie' ('My Path to History') he refers to 'the realization that the world of Ancient India was actually far too remote for me, and appealed to me far less than the Western Middle Ages, which for me were dominated by Dante, by Gothic, by

St Francis.' Thus Huizinga shifted his gaze from the East to the West, from glitter to beauty, from an emphasis on form to simplicity. In the meantime, he had become the custodian of his own happiness. 'In those years of clarity, in which our five children were born, my spirit lived above all in the music of Bach and Schubert, and to a lesser extent also that of Mozart, Beethoven and Brahms, and in every kind of visual art that came within our ambit.'

His son Leonhard has described this life, most notably the part that took place in Toornvliet. His father had explained the origin of the country house's name. It had nothing to do with the mansion's tower (*toren*) or the little brook (*vliet*) that ran along the back of the grounds, but with the flight (*vlieden*) of wrath (*toorn*). It was the place where life knew no anger. He sketches a picture of his father there: 'I see him with his top hat and whip, playing the ringmaster for us children, who circled all around him in the hall, as roaring lions or unmanageable horses ... I see him only cheerful: with mother and ourselves in the blossoming garden, at the table making endless jokes, *maître de plaisir* at parties and birthday celebrations.' As for his mother, he mostly *heard* her. 'The piano-playing coming from the music room, when Peter van Anrooy came to make music with my mother and we stayed awake or even crept stealthily downstairs to listen; and the sounds of crystal and conversation whenever there was a dinner-party. I can still see us children at the windows of the playroom that overlooked the great hall, our noses pressed flat against the glass so that we would miss nothing of the grand spectacle. Father and mother after receiving the guests in the music room, ceremoniously filing into the dining-room with them in pairs. We used to sing softly: "Arm in arm, and see how warm", but that by no means diminished the sense of awe with which we watched these events.'[15]

For Huizinga, his personal idyll was reflected in a political one.

'There was a time, and curiously, it was not so long ago,' he wrote in 1938, looking back at Wilhelmina's jubilee year, 'that the Dutch people, always inclined towards a certain intellectualism of attitude, were rather too willing to lull themselves into the illusory belief in the better, safer system of states that seemed to be in the offing. The Netherlands had been privileged to host the first and second Peace Conferences. In The Hague, first the Court of Arbitration, then the Peace Palace, and then the Permanent International Court of Justice were established. The spirit of Hugo de Groot had flowered once more in Tobias Asser and Cornelis van Vollenhoven. Though the country's armed forces were too small, it had been spared the storms of the century (in a deceptive proof of the safety of pacifism), along with the wealth of its coveted overseas possessions. And then the League of Nations arrived to cast all its most hopeful expectations into an enduring, robust mould. No wonder the League of Nations found and retained no stouter champion than the Netherlands.'[16]

In that one year of 1914, which saw a world war shatter his vision of peace and security, and the death of his wife curtail his earthly term of happiness, all this would be dashed from Huizinga's hands. In April 1913, not long after the birth of their youngest child, Mary was diagnosed with cancer, and after a period that swung cruelly between hope and despair, she died, not yet thirty-eight years of age. In Huizinga's entire correspondence, there is not a single letter so brief and heart-rending as the note to Peter van Anrooy and his wife, dated 21 July 1914: 'The end came this evening, without consciousness or suffering.'[17]

Before or after the world war, before or after Mary's death: this seems to be the clearest watershed in a life that was built of contrasts. But even here, the contrasts mingled. Certainly, the great work on which Huizinga had already been working for ten years by then, *The Waning of the Middle Ages*, had become 'darker and less serene' than he had initially intended; 'too much of the shadow of death' had been cast over the book, as he wrote in the preface. And certainly, he distanced himself physically, almost immediately, from the place where he had known such happiness: in 1915 he left Groningen, where he had been appointed professor of general and Dutch history ten years earlier, and accepted a chair in Leiden, this time only in general history.

Yet the post-1914 Huizinga was essentially unchanged. He remained the same father, who threw himself into birthday and St Nicholas celebrations with gusto, producing grandiloquent doggerel and satirical verse. He wrote and directed plays for his children: 'The lapdog, or Cornelis with the keen memory; a comedy in three acts' (Christmas holiday, 1915), 'Whirlman can make three wishes; folly based on an old theme, in five scenes' (winter 1916, not performed), 'The Miracle of St Nicholas', 'The magician who fell on hard times'. He also wrote more serious plays, like 'After the war', written in 1916, which tells the story of an old English captain in the merchant navy who makes peace with a German U-boat officer who had been instrumental in his son's death. A 'tear-jerker of the purest sort' according to his son Leonhard, but one in which the writer was both child and dreamer. At the same time, just how difficult he found all this is clear from other parts of Leonhard's narrative: when his friend's daughter Bine de Sitter came to run the household after Mary's death, Huizinga sent her home again, for fear that she might cause the children's memories of their mother to fade.[18]

And although he stopped writing plays after the death of his eldest son, Dirk, in 1920 – 'the blow that for a second time...' – he remained a master of language who played unique games with his four other children, such as his cities word game. The game went roughly like this. Take the town girl who goes to the countryside and sits on a rick, not noticing the wasps buzzing around it. Suddenly she jumps up in pain, and now she's convinced that... [Hastings]. Or... Pa ate an entire cake that had been baked for the guests. So what did [Marseille]? Huizinga was always a man of great friendships: Jan Veth, Peter van Anrooy, Richard and Henriëtte Roland Holst, the 'magician' André Jolles, that other magician, the anthropologist Bronisław Malinowski, the Erasmus scholar P.S. Allen, the Sanskrit scholar Sylvain Lévi, the economist and politician Luigi Einaudi, the psychiatrist C.T. van Valkenburg, and the jurist Cornelis van Vollenhoven ('Mr Kees'). Leonhard recalled the sparkling dinner parties, the damask, the crystal, the conversation, discussions shifting from English to Russian, an anecdote starting off in French and ending with a punch-line in Arabic.[19]

Of all these friends, the most extraordinary was Jolles. 'The man who was as precocious as he was gifted', Huizinga calls him in his memoirs. Well travelled and well read, with a knowledge of art and literature stretching from the Middle Ages to his own time, this artist *manqué* drank the beaker of failure to the last drop. Possessed of a rabid brilliance – Leonhard recalls the collective hangover that settled over the Huizinga home after a visit from Jolles – he was unable to secure a chair at a Dutch university, even with Huizinga's support. He whiled away his days in Germany, where as time went on he started to wonder if he had become a 'kraut' himself, and he ended up embracing National Socialism. He was too arrogant to write down his masterpiece himself – the *Einfache Formen*, a work of some considerable influence on Huizinga – and it did not reach its structuralist readership until after his death, in French translation. Yet his interests paralleled those of Huizinga, so much so that he rightly referred to their 'parallel lives'. Even so, in 1933 he broke off this friendship, which dated from 1896 – *he* broke it off, not Huizinga, for whom loyalty to a friend took precedence over his abhorrence of the Nazis.

Huizinga had expressed this abhorrence in no uncertain terms that very year – the year in which he became rector of Leiden University. In his capacity as rector, he had made the university premises available to a conference organized by the International Student Service, until he learned that the German delegation was to be headed by one Johann von Leers, the author of a pamphlet entitled *Forderung der Stunde: Juden raus!*, a diatribe worthy of Julius Streicher. He summoned Von Leers to the Senate room, asked him if he was the author of the work in question, and upon receiving the affirmative answer, told him to leave the university grounds, without so much as a handshake. It led to a diplomatic scandal, a row with his own board of governors, and most notably, and most painfully for Huizinga, it provoked a feud with German historians, who allowed their devotion to what they called 'national honour' to prevail over an opportunity to show a modicum of courage.

These turbulent years were also the period that witnessed the construction of that unique oeuvre, which grew from the late Middle Ages back to the twelfth century and forwards to the Renaissance, which linked cultural theory to cultural criticism, and which brought Huizinga fame both in the Netherlands (membership of the Royal Academy of Arts and Sciences, editor of the prestigious journal *De Gids*, tutor to the princess) and in the international arena (an honorary doctorate from Oxford University, membership of the International Commission on Intellectual Cooperation, candidacy for the Nobel Prize). Yet he travelled little ('travelling does not broaden the mind') and read sparingly ('my literary knowledge consists solely of gaps'). He lived by the clock: he wrote in the morning, lectured (or attended meetings) in the afternoon, and read or browsed through grammar textbooks in the evening. In this way he learned a dozen or more languages: besides French, German and English, he spoke – with varying degrees of ease – Italian, Spanish, Portuguese, and Russian, and could read Latin and Greek, Hebrew and Old Norse, Sanskrit and Arabic.

And then, as if by magic, love returned to his life. Auguste Schölvinck, a Catholic merchant's daughter from Amsterdam, came to live in the Huizinga home in 1937 in the all-encompassing capacity of housekeeper and secretary, but two weeks after the arrival of Guste – a delightful young woman, just twenty-eight years of age – Huizinga asked her if she might see fit to extend her 'duties' to that of 'driver and indispensable manager, and also to some extent a sweet daughter, but most of all to be my greatest love for ever'. Of the passion that was kindled in the sixty-five-year-old scholar's breast for his sweetheart, his lionheart, his dearest Goes, his 'great and sweet little beloved', his 'dear, dear, child', the letters he wrote her provide the sweltering proof.

And once again we encounter the familiar combination of passion and propriety, eroticism and self-control. Scarcely had Guste informed the professor – who was away in Paris – of her decision to join her life to his, when it occurred to him, as he was dressing in his hotel room, that it would only be nine days until he returned in Leiden and could go to her room, 'to find ... there is no word for it, since I do not wish to say the fragrance of your being'. He did not wish to say it, but a few months later, at the St Nicholas celebrations, he wrote a few lines of doggerel to accompany a hoped-for gift of 'powder for use after bathing': 'Sprinkle fragrant powder on and around, I'll come to you and drink in the scent.' At the same time, he wrote, 'My dearest child, I hold you in my arms, and kiss you more intimately, but also with more purity – more holiness? I know no word for it – than ever.'[20]

And while those around him were cutting predictable jokes at his expense ('Mating of the Middle Ages'), and crisis and the threat of war loomed all around, Huizinga's books of cultural criticism were taking shape, and he was 'simply happy' [J.C. Bloem] in Leidse Hout. Although the outbreak of the Second World War convinced him that he was living in the most calamitous century of human history, the war also brought him the birth of his daughter Laura, his 'sweet little Loortje'. His stay in St Michielsgestel failed to dent his spirits, nor indeed did his banishment to De Steeg, where he spent the last eighteen months of his life, living and working on his *Geschonden wereld* ('Shattered world'), which was dedicated, as was his *Homo Ludens*, 'to the woman who has now filled almost seven of my late years with the radiance of happiness, and who enables me to make light of the exile imposed on me by my country's enemies'. He died in the expectation of the country's liberation, fortified by an ethical belief that he set down in eleven brief prayers, on 1 February 1945.

2

WORK

What makes Huizinga a 'classic' writer is the harmony of his work. It is as if the unmistakeable unity of this oeuvre projects itself back into his life. Of course Huizinga went through a certain development. Politically he changed from a species of socialist into a species of liberal, the aesthetic cast of his work appears gradually to have been superseded by the ethical, his quest for a religious habitat was eventually stilled by what he called 'taking delight in the world'. Yet there is essentially no development in Huizinga's life – at least not in a linear sense. It is far better to speak in terms of 'pupations', an analogy drawn by Jacob Burckhardt, the cultural historian for whom Huizinga had such great admiration. 'History is and remains, for me, poetry, in the highest sense of the word,' Burckhardt wrote to a friend while at university. 'I see it as a miraculous process of successive pupations and new, perpetually new revelations of mind. I stay here on this edge of the world and stretch out my arms to the source of all things, and that's why to me history is pure poetry, which one may appropriate simply by looking.'[1]

This quotation holds the key to the profound unity of Huizinga's oeuvre. A close look shows how naturally the philologist emerged from the linguist, the historian from the philologist, the cultural critic from the historian. An attentive eye will see that the critic was latent in the linguist, and that the historian always remained a philologist. In essence, the core of both *The Waning of the Middle Ages* and *Homo Ludens* can be found in his early work on Ancient Indian literature. *The Waning of the Middle Ages* and *Man and the Masses in America* are pendants; *The Waning of the Middle Ages* and *Dutch Civilization in the Seventeenth Century* are mirror images. *Homo Ludens* is just as much a kind of cultural criticism as *In the Shadow of Tomorrow*. This cohesiveness in his work is best illustrated by examining its two primary themes: the contrast between old and new, and the concept of rebirth, or renaissance.

OLD AND NEW

The nucleus of Huizinga's oeuvre, the seed from which everything else grew, can be found in the 'Introduction and Proposal for a Study of Light and Sound',[2] a plan for a dissertation that he submitted to the Groningen linguist B. Sijmons in 1896. He had prepared it in Leipzig, where he had been enrolled for six months – the winter semester of 1895-1896 – after graduating from Groningen University. The dissertation would never materialize: the supervising professor saw no academic merit in it and Huizinga himself later conceded that the subject had been overly ambitious. Nonetheless, the proposal contained a number of brilliant ideas about nothing less than the origins of language. In Huizinga's view, language came into being in the same way as poetry: as a lyrical mixture of sensory impressions. Synaesthesia was the cradle of language.

Still, this directly felt, sensory language had a tendency towards erosion. In his proposal, Huizinga quotes the nineteenth-century German novelist Jean Paul, who calls language 'a dictionary of faded metaphors'. Born in poetry, language became utilitarian. Only in literature did it regain its old splendour. But from those eroded forms you could still deduce the earliest associations: amid those dusty cinders, the original spark still burned. 'I therefore consider it justifiable,' wrote the graduate self-confidently, 'to equate a metaphor that occurs somewhere in Aeschylus, say, with an expression from everyday life in another, arbitrary, language, that is based on the same association, and thus to show that the lyrical function is the same everywhere.'[3]

The project did not progress beyond this eloquent preamble. Yet the dissertation that he did produce would deal with the same theme, if on a more modest scale. This time, he opted for a philological subject. Following the advice of his Sanskrit teacher, Speyer, he focused on a figure from Ancient Indian drama, the jester or *vidûshaka*. His conclusion was that Indian drama was far older than the plays that were generally known. These plays, which were performed at royal courts, had evolved from popular forms of theatre. The *vidûshaka*, a prepossessing fool, was originally 'a coarse clown with childish tastes', the successor to 'an original phase in Indian stage buffoonery'.[4]

So here Huizinga does the same, as a philologist, as he had proposed to do as a linguist: he expressed the phenomenon he set out to study in terms of something more original. Both the linguist and the philologist proved to hold the historian latent within them. But with this reservation: what was more original was not necessarily what came first. Rather, it appears that what was original was also timeless. We shall frequently encounter this pattern in the following pages: initially there is a contrast between old and new, but once this contrast has been established, Huizinga places it in perspective by seeing the new as a manifestation of the old, the old in a state of permanent transformation.

Huizinga himself was now emerging from his second chrysalis, metamorphosing from a philologist to a historian. In an open lecture that he gave in his capacity as private lecturer in Ancient Indian literature in 1903, he had asserted that he set out to study subjects on the frontiers of 'the general science of civilization'. At the same time, he taught in Haarlem, where he laboured diligently on an edition of the city's mediaeval legal sources. This may sound contradictory, but it was not. The kind of history that was practised here, in these Haarlem sources, was no less visionary than his linguistic proposal. The subject at issue was nothing less than a theory about the origins of cities – we recall Huizinga's fascination with the origins of language – and it was done using philological means. This source edition owed its great success – it was this that earned Huizinga his chair in history in Groningen – to the way in which he traced the development of Haarlem's by-laws back through those of 's-Hertogenbosch to those of Leuven, in the manner of a philological genealogical tree.

But while he developed from a philologist to a historian, the DNA of his mindset, working with contrasts, was unchanged. In the mediaeval history of the city of Haarlem, old and new, origin and derivative, not only constituted the contrast that fuelled the argument, they were also the strands that, twisted together, merged cause and effect, as it were, and transformed the old into the new: 'In the fabric of the city, a development that started long ago ripens, while at the same time new life germinates for later centuries.' This was expressed pointedly in Haarlem's by-laws: Huizinga describes Haarlem as 'mother and daughter at the same time': mother of a large part of Holland, and daughter of 's-Hertogenbosch and Leuven.[5]

Once installed as a professor in Groningen, where he was given the task of writing a jubilee book to mark the university's centenary – 'A history of the university in the third century of its existence,

1814-1914' – he kept to the same pattern. In his lecture at these anniversary celebrations, in the course of which his book was launched, he said: 'In the history of science, the same cry is heard again and again; it is the cry with which ... the misers and spendthrifts clash in Dante's Hell: preserve or cast off: why do you discard what has become precious and sacred to me, and put in their place your new finds, presumptuous, impious as are all new things! And why do you hold fast to your dead doctrine, which I hate, because they seek to stifle my youthful, living thoughts! The watchwords change, but the battle remains the same.'[6]

Meanwhile, Huizinga had already been working for many years on his greatest book, *The Waning of the Middle Ages*. It was to be a book full of contrasts – body versus spirit, death versus life, dream versus reality, form versus content, image versus word – but ultimately, everything was subservient to that one great contrast: Middle Ages versus Renaissance. So here, once more, was an opposition between old and new, and once again Huizinga performed his magic trick and made the new into the old, made of the Renaissance a period that had more in common with the Middle Ages than with modern times. At the same time, the late Middle Ages were seen 'not as the herald of what is to come, but as the death throes of what is passing away'.[7]

The problem that he brought upon himself, he solved with the aid of virtuoso dialectics. The book sought to give a picture of the art of the Van Eyck brothers in the context of their time. Virtually everyone held the opinion that the realism of that art, the painfully accurate depiction of reality in all its details, should be regarded as something new, as a harbinger of the Renaissance. Huizinga saw that realism too, but in his view, it was only a question of technique. In terms of content, the Van Eycks' art was wholly attuned to the world picture of the late Middle Ages. 'With the art of the Van Eycks, the pictorial representation of holy things attained a degree of detail and naturalism that may perhaps be regarded as a beginning in strictly art-historical terms, but in terms of cultural history signifies an end.'[8]

The Waning of the Middle Ages appeared in 1919, and the strangest thing about the book, perhaps, is that it is a preface that outgrew itself. In Haarlem, Huizinga had not only become a historian, he had become a Dutchman, and from then on, his point of departure would be Dutch history, especially that of the seventeenth century. The first book that he determined to write as professor in Groningen was a history of Dutch civilization in the seventeenth century. To understand it, he delved into Burgundian culture, Modern Devotion, and humanist influence in the Netherlands. This research was the early history from which grew *The Waning of the Middle Ages*. The planned book about the Netherlands did eventually materialize too, but not until 1941. And so Huizinga's first book as a historian became his last. There can be no more fitting illustration of the unity that marked his oeuvre.

This unity did not appear to be very well served by his book *Man and the Masses in America*, for which he interrupted his work on *The Waning of the Middle Ages* and that he published a year before it, in 1918. But just as Burgundy had to do with the Netherlands, so too did America have to do with Europe: that is, the new America and the old Europe. Huizinga wrote his book out of curiosity about the country that had declared war on Germany in 1917 and thus saved Europe from its doom. And he wrote it in a way that made *Man and the Masses in America* a fully-fledged counterpart to *The Waning of the Middle Ages*.

What struck him about the United States was its people's 'tremendous acceptance of life' – their 'focus on this world and on the present time or near future'. Europe was far more preoccupied with dead cultures and old heroes. That did not alter the fact that Hawthorne reminded him of Dante. He also recognized in America's primitive religiosity and naive sentimentality the communal spirit of the Middle Ages. And how was the 'city-manager' of the United States any different, if the truth be told, from the *podestà* of the mediaeval cities of Italy? Was there not a striking similarity between 'the corporate organization of industrial capital' in America and the 'landlords and feudal system' of mediaeval Europe, between the forming of clubs and societies in the one and the foundation of religious orders in the other? Was there not a painful parallel between the way in which life in the late Middle Ages became ossified 'in the perfection and expansiveness of the all-embracing building of the Church' and the way in which modern humanity appeared to be turning into the helpless slave of 'its own perfect means of material and social technology'?[9]

Man and the Masses in America thus became not just a kind of *The Waning of the Middle Ages*, but at the same time a form of cultural criticism: 'Organization becomes mechanization,' wrote Huizinga in a tone of disquiet: 'that is the fatal moment in the development of modern civilization.' The process of mechanization first conquered the economy – transport, agriculture, management, and trust formation – and went on to pervade society, the media, the entire democratic process. Especially in his detailed account of the mechanization of politics and the commercialization of the political parties, Huizinga showed how the technology of democracy was dismantling democracy itself: 'Matter rules, the spirit has been banished.' It could have been the opening sentence of *In the Shadow of Tomorrow*.[10]

But that book would not be written until 1935. After *The Waning of the Middle Ages*, Huizinga devoted himself primarily to the Middle Ages and early modern times. He wrote about Dante and Shakespeare, Joan of Arc and Hugo de Groot. And he planned a sequel to

The Waning of the Middle Ages: a study of the twelfth century, his favourite era, the pinnacle of the Middle Ages, and possibly of European culture. He did not get much further than three studies of 'pre-Gothic minds', Alan of Lille, John of Salisbury, and Abelard. He did produce a biography of Erasmus, however, in what was proclaimed the 'Erasmus year' of 1924.

This biography, written at the request of an American, and actually not even intended for publication in Dutch, grew effortlessly from the previous work. Huizinga's interest in the transition from Middle Ages to the modern era had by no means been exhausted by his writing of *The Waning of the Middle Ages*: on the contrary, before and after this biography, he would concern himself with the sixteenth century, in essays for *De Gids* on subjects such as 'The problem of the Renaissance' (1920) and 'Renaissance and realism' (1929). The biography has a pattern that is by now familiar. Huizinga depicts Erasmus vacillating between modernity and tradition, in the hybrid form by which we have come to know him. It was the tragedy of Erasmus's life: 'He was the man who saw the new and coming things more clearly than anyone else – who must needs quarrel with the old and yet could not accept the new. He tried to remain in the fold of the old Church, after having damaged it seriously, and renounced the Reformation, and to a certain extent even Humanism, after having furthered both with all his strength.'[11]

Not for another eleven years – by which time Huizinga had published his collected essays in anthologies such as *Tien studiën* ('Ten Studies'; 1926) and *Cultuurhistorische verkenningen* ('Explorations in cultural history'; 1929) – did the book appear that would make him truly famous. While *The Waning of the Middle Ages* had really only attracted praise in the Netherlands from literary scholars, and beyond the country's borders had been celebrated mainly by the historiographical avant-garde as represented by Kantorowicz and

Bloch, *In the Shadow of Tomorrow* seemed to have been injected directly into the bloodstream of European intellectual life. Even so, for Huizinga himself it elaborated on themes he had broached in earlier studies, both linguistic and historical, and ideas he had formulated in his book about America. *In the Shadow of Tomorrow* describes the same process that he had discussed at length in *The Waning of the Middle Ages*: 'In one and the same process, modern culture both ascends to its highest peaks, and germinates the seeds of its possible decline.' What is more, he would not have undertaken this catalogue of maladies, this 'diagnosis of the spiritual suffering' of his time, had he not been convinced that here too, the old was capable of regenerating the new.[12]

Three years later, in 1938, came *Homo Ludens*. Huizinga the historian had evidently not lost sight of the philologist's explorations around the periphery of the general science of civilization. The book presents nothing less than the common denominator of culture and the stages through which it passes, from primitive to sophisticated, in East and West. The heart of culture is sought in play, in the sense that all culture is preceded by play. Culture is born as play and in play. At the same time, the book can be read as a 'prologue' to *In the Shadow of Tomorrow*, since Huizinga takes the view that the modern age had revoked the *raison d'être* of play. The book encompasses virtually all themes of his work. It not only provides the context and framework, as it were, for his cultural-historical studies of the Middle Ages and the modern era, but it also revisits his earliest work in linguistics, on the need to construe language and culture as an integrated whole.

Finally, in the war, he published his last book – that was initially to have been his first – on Dutch civilization in the seventeenth century. Here once more, we find the contrast of old versus new. The book has the same thesis as *The Waning of the Middle Ages*. Both the

Renaissance and the Dutch Republic were really modelled along mediaeval lines. The United Provinces had been forged in a 'conservative revolution'. In terms of economic structure and political system, the Dutch Republic was an anachronism, a continuation of late-mediaeval forms based on liberty, while all around the new doctrine of mercantilism and centralism was being hammered home. Yet in cultural terms, Huizinga noted, the reverse held good: 'Politically, the Louvestein system was an obsolete thing, but in terms of civilization, the exponents of that system were the most modern men of their day.'[13]

RENAISSANCES

A play of contrasts and reconciliation – that is how Huizinga's work might be defined. In him, the contrast between old and new leads naturally to the identity of old and new. The first time he presented this play with deliberation was in his public lecture 'On the study and appreciation of Buddhism' in 1903. He distinguished three ways in which history is processed by the historian: scientifically, artistically, and ethically. He then differentiated the latter two approaches in terms of renaissance and *réveil*. In the case of a renaissance, history provided inspiration for new forms of art or new thoughts, while in the case of a *réveil*, the influence of history was so strong that people sought to cast their new thoughts in old moulds. In a renaissance, the old became new, while in a *réveil*, the new became old.[14]

Was it justified, Huizinga asked himself, given the lively interest that the old India aroused in the new Europe – translations of the *Bhagavadgītā* circulated widely, while terms like 'atman' and 'karma' were on everyone's lips – to speak in this case of a renaissance, or even of a *réveil*? Did the 'idyllic-decadent wordcraft' of his day not point to creative assimilation, and the interest in contemplation and rebirth to religious inspiration? In the end, he thought not. The reception of Ancient Indian literature and philosophy was too disproportionately artistic, or rather sentimental, for this to apply. 'In truth, it is rather the hazy twilight of silent temples, and gazing at glittering snow-capped peaks, wondrously rarefied and remote, that keep our minds enthralled.' The moral aspects of Buddhism received scant attention. What had once sown fear or sorrow, and inspired pity or despair, had degenerated into pure aestheticism. 'We value for its artistic splendour what was said or built for pious edification or instruction.'[15]

For Huizinga personally, the matter was more complicated. He had initially been deeply impressed by the beauty of India's art and the depth of its mysticism. The 'ponderous grandeur' of the architecture, the 'mute pageantry' of the country's splendid stock of images, the 'ostentation and pomp' of the legends and myths had bewitched him. But as time went on he rejected it all. The underlying tone of Buddhism, in his view, 'is a dull renunciation' of everything that is 'action, beauty, and love'. Huizinga had serious ethical – as well as logical – objections to the notion of karma. A doctrine of retribution in which grace played no role struck him as belonging to a lower order – to accept the continuity of guilt while at the same time denying the continuity of the one who bears the guilt was baffling in his eyes.

Added to this was the fact that Ancient Indian art was highly formalistic; indeed, Huizinga saw formalism as one of the primary qualities of Buddhist culture. This formalism was not confined to aesthetics. A closer look showed that it had also settled into the morality and discipline of Buddhism, into its sacred teachings and philosophy. There was a certain arid quality in that 'abstract contemplation of the essence of all things'. That insubstantial abstraction was only a refined variant of a far more primitive fear of life, Huizinga concluded.

This brought him to one of the most important insights of his life: if externals, appearances, came to dominate form, this signalled a crucial phase in a culture, a phase that he also observed elsewhere. 'The development of an art of reasoning over and above the intrinsic power of thought is not an isolated phenomenon in Buddhism. It is linked to a certain level of intellectual culture; it is also found in Greek sophism and in mediaeval scholasticism. So instead of seeing it as a deliberate abuse of the power of reason, we should try to comprehend that singular phase in the evolution of human reason in the context of the cultural environment in which it occurs.' We shall see that this is precisely what Huizinga did in *The Waning of the Middle Ages*.[16]

But that is not all. Just as the formalism of karma sprang from primitive, fearful phantasms, Indian philosophy germinated in primitive, shamanistic magical rites. It was around these practices that the refined Buddhist dialectics crystallized. The germ of philosophy, Huizinga concluded, lay 'in the riddle-contests of primitive peoples'. Culture originated from competition and play. This, as we have seen, is the proposition of *Homo Ludens*. While Old Indian culture may not have been a renaissance for Huizinga, it was nonetheless certainly a form of life that fertilized his ideas.[17]

As a historian too, he continued to be fascinated by 'the problem of the Renaissance'. Was the seventeenth-century Netherlands a product of the Renaissance and Reformation, Huizinga wondered, or was the country's golden age not rather rooted in the Middle Ages? Were the Middle Ages merely a preparatory stage for the Renaissance, or was the Renaissance in fact more mediaeval than historiography supposed? And was the 'Renaissance' solely a historical concept, or did discussions about it possess a far broader significance? Were its connotations only aesthetic, or were they ethical too? Was the Renaissance not rather 'an aspect of life that extends far beyond the practice of historiography as such'?[18]

Questions of this kind illustrate Huizinga's idiosyncratic perspective in the debate. Whether the contours of the Renaissance were drawn in unduly stark terms (the dark Middle Ages, the radiant Renaissance) or sketched too loosely (the light of the Renaissance was already shining in the Middle Ages) mattered, but it mattered differently to Huizinga than to his fellow historians. In the first place, rather than bringing the Middle Ages closer to the Renaissance, he took the opposite approach, that of bringing the Renaissance closer to the Middle Ages. And in the second place, he challenged the whole notion of periodization. 'When we view the fundamental dividing-lines between the older and more recent civilizations of Western peoples, we find that some run between Middle Ages and Renaissance, others between Renaissance and seventeenth century, some cut right through the Renaissance, and more than one crosses a century as early as the thirteenth or as late as the eighteenth.'[19]

More importantly still, the history of words such as Renaissance and Reformation alerted him to 'a very ancient seed of awareness of spiritual renewal'. The origins of these concepts lay in the New Testament concept of resurrection, which in turn sprang from prospects of renewal in the Old Testament, in the Psalms and the Prophets. The humanists – whether they studied the classics or the Bible – shared a common source of inspiration. 'The idea that possessed them,' wrote Huizinga, 'bore a single mark, although one mind may have been less devout than another. All were filled with the same nostalgia for old, original purity, with the same aspiration to renew themselves from the inside. Whether these yearnings looked back to the earliest Christianity or to the noble, soundly-governed Rome of the Catos and Scipios, or to pure Latinity, with its perfect poetry, its rediscovered art, always we find a desire to go back in time: *renovatio, restitutio, restauratio.*'[20]

And that is precisely what Huizinga wanted: to go back in time. In his case, that meant above all back to the twelfth century, that other, more fascinating renaissance. In the latter half of the 1930s, he started to collect material for what might be called a pendant to *The Waning of the Middle Ages*, which would contrast the heavy, dark gold of the late Middle Ages with the light and lustre of the twelfth century. 'The twelfth century was a creative and formative era like none other,' he wrote in 1935, in a study of Abelard. It was then that Western Christian civilization assumed its definitive form. Terms such as awakening and burgeoning were far more applicable to the renaissance of the twelfth century than to that of the fifteenth. 'It is like a melody shifting into a clearer tone and a livelier rhythm, it is like the sun breaking through the clouds.'[21]

For what was not new about that age! New forms of lyrical and epic poetry, knighthood and courtly manners, a new architecture and sculpture, new monastic orders and a new mysticism, the new university and the new monarchy, feudalism and the freedom of the Church. It all cascaded together and 'sprouted into blossoming forms'. It was an age of great effervescence, restlessness and confusion. It was also an age of great creativity, in which Huizinga recognized everything that was dear to him. Everything that inspired him was offered to him here for emulation. If any particular period might be seen as exemplifying a consciousness of renewal and inspiration, it was the twelfth century.

Nothing remains of Huizinga's inspiration, as already noted, but the three portraits of Alan of Lille, John of Salisbury, and Abelard. All three had been touched by antiquity, by classical literature, and at first sight they may seem to have been early humanists. But nothing could be further from the truth. Rather, their work emphatically played down the significance of the classics. 'What was reborn? Antiquity itself? Certainly not. Classical form then? – That was dead, and should remain so. A new sense might fill it, that was all.' What united these three pre-Gothic spirits was therefore not so much classical literature as precisely their 'lack of constraints'. They possessed a freedom that no longer existed after them; they combined qualities that would later become separated.

Alan, for instance, was both poet and theologian, and these activities, or forms of creativity, were inextricably interwoven. His poetic images and doctrinal conceptions formed a single whole. John was the scholar-diplomat, the 'chivalric clerk', whose work propagated 'a noble Christianity imbued with antique liberty'. And Abelard was 'the troubadour among the schoolmen ... the knight errant', the man who linked scholasticism to chivalry and who transformed the university into a jousting field, debate into ritualized combat. These three thinkers were, above all, the embodiment of a primitive unity of faith and imagination, thinking and feeling. Old and new, strict form and passion, paganism and Christianity, all converged here. The twelfth century, for Huizinga, was both renaissance and *réveil*.

The extent to which Huizinga conceived the twelfth century in terms of emulation is also clear from his inaugural professorial address at Leiden in 1915, 'The historical ideals of life', a phrase he used to convey 'any representation[s] of excellence that men project onto the past'. One example of past perfection was the idea of a golden age. Another was that of evangelical poverty. This was a specifically twelfth-century invention: the evangelical example did not take on practical value until it acquired the dimension of real existence – when the historical as well as the holy figure of Christ was emphasized. This did not happen until the twelfth century. Only then did the parable of Jesus and the rich young man become a story of emulation. Only then did Christ's words: 'If thou wilt be perfect, go and sell that thou hast, and give to the poor' (Matt. 19:21) become a command. 'The following of Christ's example, as awakened in St Bernard, is a renaissance, and when Thomas à Kempis preaches it three centuries later, closely invoking St Bernard, it is a renaissance of a renaissance.'[22]

For Huizinga, such considerations added a separate layer of significance to the concept of renaissance. He could have called his inaugural address 'On renaissances', he wrote. And a third ideal, that of the pastoral, the glorification of rural life, developed into a 'series of renaissances': 'It is a renaissance, when the Roman poets in the days of Augustus turn bucolic, a new renaissance when the late Greek pastoral romance is born, and yet another when the rather graceless *beaux-esprits* at the court of Charlemagne drape themselves in robes as Thyrsis and Damoetas, and Alcuin exalts the cuckoo.' The pattern also proved applicable to the fourth ideal, that of chivalry. 'From its very first manifestation as a represented way of life, in the twelfth century, chivalry displays the characteristics of a renaissance, the conscious reliving of a romantic past, whether it is sought in antiquity, in the days of Charlemagne, or above all at King Arthur's round table.' Thus, the chivalric order of the fourteenth century was a deliberate recreation of that of the twelfth and thirteenth centuries, as was, in its turn, that of the fifteenth century.[23]

But what was the underlying factor that caused these ideals of life to manifest themselves as a succession of repeated renaissances? It was that form came to prevail over content. The ideal became formalistic – it became too high for the society in which it was defined. The falsehood glinted through gashes in the beautiful robes. 'The form constantly runs dry, so to speak; there are constant periods of lives lived in maximum mendacity and self-deception, each in turn followed by a reaction.' Reality became illusion. An 'unprecedented quantum of affectation' was needed to sustain the fiction of shepherd and knight in real life.

Here Huizinga reverted to his study of Buddhism, to that art of reasoning that evolved on a plane transcending the power of thought. The formalism that he had identified there, he now observed in a European context too. Still, there was a crucial difference between ancient Indian and European culture: the difference between repetition and renaissance. In Europe, the formalism was part of a movement: there, it created contrasts that demanded, as it were, to be reconciled. Only in the West did it create forms that brought forth new forms. It is in this phenomenon of the metamorphoses of forms – or in his words, of successive renaissances – that Huizinga reveals his methodological practice.

And there was something else. It was precisely in the Renaissance – that of the fifteenth century, the revival of classical antiquity in a new guise – that historical ideals of life were jettisoned. And that was because the historical aspect came to take precedence over the ideal. Here, Huizinga stumbled on a wonderful paradox. As long as Graeco-Roman antiquity was still viewed as objectively perfect, as worthy of emulation for all times, in other words, as long as that world possessed absolute authority, 'in a word, as long as it was Renaissance', the Middle Ages had essentially not ended. For that ideal was a commonplace in the Middle Ages too, although most readers necessarily had recourse to translations. But in the Renaissance, those who immersed themselves in antiquity gained a growing awareness of its historical nature: 'By and through antiquity, people learned to think historically, and once they had learned to think historically, they were compelled to abandon the notion of historical ideals of life that possessed universal value.'[24]

That may be a remarkable observation, but what is more remarkable is that Huizinga shrugged it off. He simply refused to renounce those ideals. What fascinated Huizinga was not succession and development, but repetition and renewal. That means that he only wanted to be a historian up to a certain point. Or rather: he refused to expunge the element of universal humanity from history. He refused to practise a history that could not serve at the same time as an example, an inspiration, an ideal.

His position might be summarized as follows: repetition was the law of culture, renewal was the task of man. This renewal was a rebirth of what was originally good and with God. Huizinga found this insight in the work of the greatest writer of his reading life, Dante. And in fact it permeated the entire gamut of mediaeval thought. 'The facts of the Old Testament imply, prefigure, those of the New Testament, and those of secular history reflect the same.' This was a mode of thought that enabled contrasts to be blended in a loftier harmony – one that made it possible, he wrote, to combine, in the manner of a kaleidoscope, 'the mass of unordered particles' to make 'a beautiful, symmetrical figure'.[25]

It was a mode of thought that appealed greatly to Huizinga, one that detached individual suffering and individual virtue from personal uniqueness and absorbed them into the sphere of the universal. That universality had a religious dimension, a religious inspiration that was deeply embedded in Huizinga's work. But even deeper than the religious motif lay the poetic impulse, the belief that religion was always ultimately emulation, an imitation of the nature of things. Somewhere in between imitation and emulation, between description and prescription, between what once was and what will be eternally, lay Huizinga's self-appointed mission. And that made him a poet, in the depths of his being.

READING AND WRITING

3

READING

'The things that can make life pleasurable remain the same,' wrote Huizinga in *The Waning of the Middle Ages*. 'Now, as in the past, these are reading, music, the visual arts, travel, love of nature, sport, fashion, social vanity, and the intoxication of the senses.' Clearly, there was no waning of reading habits in Huizinga's day. To him, reading was a *sine qua non*. And in his reading, the home-loving Huizinga, a man whose work centred largely on the history of his own surroundings and his own country, roamed distant frontiers. As a private lecturer on Buddhism, he avowed his preference for exploring the vast periphery of the history of civilization.[1]

But even as an explorer, he read to come home. Huizinga read in the manner of someone who is remembering something. Rudy Kousbroek observes, while discussing Baudelaire's poem *Correspondences* in his essay 'The forest of symbols',[2] that literary symbolism affects us so deeply because it has the quality of a recollection. 'Searching for repetition is perhaps our most fundamental impulse.' Reading is searching for what we already know, however veiled and encrypted. It is searching for something important that we have lost. For Huizinga – and this is his own analogy – reading evoked the emotion of an exile gazing at his mother country. Once again we encounter the central theme of his work: repetition and renewal.

Long past the middle of his journey through life, in 1932, Huizinga wrote an essay about reading. In a characteristic contrast, he saw books as 'friends and foes'. They were foes because they existed in such alarming quantities. Yet it was precisely this abundance that provided freedom of choice. 'Reading [*lezen*] is – both by the word's origin[3] and by the nature of the activity – choosing, singling out, gathering, picking. If there is one activity that expresses free will, it is reading.' Similarly, Huizinga described the writing of history as reading, gathering – picking wild flowers. The freedom of the reader-gatherer was the open context of history: each flower altered the appearance of the entire bunch.[4]

Reading, like writing, was a creative activity. If a writer succeeded in conjuring up a different reality for a reader, this was in part the reader's own achievement. That reality was not *in* but *behind* the book. 'The reader meets the writer halfway, in response to the other's call.'[5]

That is why quiet reading often contained so much passion. In the 'Dante year' of 1921, Huizinga marvelled at the fact that Dante had ever needed to be rescued, with difficulty, from a universal verdict that wavered between revulsion and oblivion. The same had happened to Shakespeare and Rembrandt, and he believed he knew why.

> The same underlying motive explains the urge to reject Shakespeare, Rembrandt, and Dante: an aversion to the extravagant, a fear of too much immediacy. 'Extravagant' should not be understood here in the attenuated sense it has acquired in everyday use, but in the concrete meaning of its Latin constituents: 'swerving outside', a roaming abroad of the

mind. The classicist centuries would not tolerate a poet suddenly transporting you, with a word, a cry, to bewilderingly remote regions, endlessly far beyond that splendid and clearly-defined circle within which they had defined life and beauty. Nor would they tolerate him breaching the distance of *wuwaardigheid* to take you by the hand, by the throat, by the heart.'[6]

This coinage *wuwaardigheid* – which is suggestive of French *vousvoyer*, denoting a formal mode of address – has not yet been recorded in any dictionary of the Dutch language. More salient here, however, is the ferocity, the directness of Huizinga's tone, in one who more usually creates the impression of delicate detachment. That also explains his choice of such a formalistic word – for its contrast with that summoning cry. It took the soft voice of the harpsichordist and conductor Gustav Leonhardt to explain precisely why Bach was far more passionate than Bono.

FAIRY TALES

Huizinga retained his childhood love of fairy tales, especially those of Hans Andersen, throughout his life. In his brief autobiography, 'My path to history', he explains, 'I enjoyed them in just the same way as I enjoy them today, the simplest most, such as "The Old House" and "The goblin and the grocer".' As a *gymnasium* pupil, he would give a talk for the school society on one of Andersen's moon tales. Even when he was working as a teacher in Haarlem, he still read a tale by his favourite story-teller before settling in for the night.

The story 'The goblin and the grocer' gives a fine picture of how Huizinga saw reading. It is about a very poor student who takes lodgings with a very rich grocer. One day, the student comes downstairs to buy a little cheese and some candles, and notices that the shopkeeper has been wrapping his wares in the pages of 'an old book, full of poetry'. So instead of cheese he buys the rest of the book and takes it up to his little room. While he is reading there, the household goblin spies on him. 'But how bright the room was! From the book a clear shaft of light rose, expanding into a stem and a tremendous tree which spread its branching rays above the student. Each leaf on the tree was evergreen, and every flower was the face of a fair lady, some with dark and sparkling eyes, some with eyes of the clearest blue. Every fruit on the tree shone like a star, and the room was filled with song.'[7]

The dream world of the fairy tale contains a number of striking constants. One is that the wish appears to be the father of the genre. Everything seems inclined towards a happy ending: the prince gains a kingdom, the young farmer marries a princess, the poor man acquires an immense fortune. There is bound to be a donkey that sneezes gold coins, a money-bag that can never be emptied, a table that lays itself, a tinderbox that fulfils your wishes. The tyrant is always punished, the harsh guardian is taught a lesson, the bad king loses his kingdom, and the cheerful farmer takes over. The weak and the oppressed, 'Jack the dullard', Cinderella, Tom Thumb and the poor mother with her infant, they are all saved and achieve notable positions in society. As if.[8]

For what really is the happy ending of Andersen's 'little mermaid' or that of 'The two brothers' in the Brothers Grimm? Or take – another tale from the Brothers Grimm – the story of the clever son who tries to teach his stupid brother how to shudder. He succeeds in the end, though not with bones and corpses, but with the aid of a bucket full of tiny wriggling minnows, emptied out over his belly. Is this a happy ending? Fairy tales are not really about the ending, the fulfilment of a wish, but about the journey to get there. They are about rising to the great challenges that are set for the hero. The hero is not intent on securing a treasure, the kingdom, his bride, but on having an adventure. On proving the purity of his heart.

That is why fairy tales are built up around the sharpest of contrasts. The fair is also the good, and triumphs, the evil is ugly and is defeated. And if the lightness of the fairy-tale world or the cheerfulness of the narrator winks a golden eye at the usual standards of conduct, the master thief or bold tailor or other unmitigated swindlers and crooks somehow manage to melt the Germanic heart such that they end up sharing the happiness of the benevolent heroes. The same applies to the cruelty of the tales. There is an astonishing amount of beating, killing, and thrusting of people into nail-studded barrels, but such goings-on never appear to impugn the moral of the tale.

The moral of the tale lies in the action, in the dangerous journey. Nothing can hurt the hero. And that is exactly what reminds the reader that events work out very differently in real life than in fairy tales. If the farmer's good-for-nothing son, or the tailor, or the merry soldier, snaps up a princess, or a kingdom, or a vast fortune, the reader's delight is not defined by a wish that things might turn out like this for everyone. It is precisely the exception that defines the fascination, the singling out of one figure that gives the tale its magic. The intensity of fairy-tale happiness is not determined by universal proclamation, but by the identification of each individual reader, by the wish harboured in seclusion, by the tree that flowers in each candlelit room.

What is more, the world is not dressed up to be a more wonderful place than it is. At its core, the harsh reality remains. The hatred and jealousy, the inconstancy of life and the cruelty of human beings are all spelled out at length, albeit primarily to contrast with their opposite poles of kindness and hospitality, the directly felt tenderness and loyalty. And it is these latter qualities that make the confused world transparent and the heaviness of human existence light. What happens, happens, but behind it lies a more poetic, a more profound world. In a fairy tale that world becomes visible, and whoever reads or hears it believes.

Fairy tales are certainly not 'implausible stories'. True, they are stories for children. Ever since fairy tales have been known, children have made up much of their audience. But what counts is not the age of these listeners or readers, but the fact that they accept these stories as true. As Wallace Stevens wrote in *The Necessary Angel*: to see the world as it truly is, we sometimes have to hold up an imaginary world before our eyes. That fantasy wears thin as time goes on, among peoples and cultures. But not for children, and not for poets. And not to readers either. How many writers are not known to have burst into tears when one of their heroes had to meet his death? How many readers do not weep with them?

This brings us to one of the primary characteristics of the fairy tale, metamorphosis. Changing from one form to another is the driving force of the story. Hands are chopped off and put back again, babies have their throats cut and are then revived. A rusty lamp becomes a powerful talisman, pestle and mortar become the winged vehicle of a sorceress, the beggar becomes a magician, the ragged wench in the filthy donkey-hide becomes a golden-haired princess, just as the ugly duckling changes into a beautiful swan. Children become ravens, the long-awaited son is as small as a thumb, the girl is as red as blood and as white as snow. In the same way, fairy tales transform adults into children. Anyone who wants to understand Huizinga must bear in mind that he was a reader of fairy tales.

READING AND HISTORY

The importance that Huizinga attached to reading shines through every page of his work. To achieve a better grasp of historical reality, he would often enlist the help of literature. In his inaugural professorial address, he counselled, 'While the historian explores the past itself in all its various expressions, to make it more vivid he must see the art of the past, he must read literature'. In his doctoral dissertation, in assessing the literary significance of ancient Indian drama, he was already considering the possibility of comparing these plays with 'an English play from Shakespeare's time'. In his professorial address, he said: 'We should consult the poets, let Shakespeare's history plays define for us the essence of majesty.'[9]

Huizinga often consulted Shakespeare. He found in Shakespeare the proof that the usual name for the Netherlands in the sixteenth century was Burgundy – 'waterish Burgundy' – and the English playwright was one of the many examples with which he added depth to his picture of the Netherlands and the Dutch in the Elizabethan period. Shakespeare can help the reader to gain a true perspective of Vondel, but he also illuminates fifteenth-century views of friendship, the parallel of courtly love. Shakespeare has the true elements of dream, which Huizinga missed in the mediaeval dream motif. 'To fully comprehend the cultural-historical significance of the concept of chivalry,' he wrote, 'one would have to follow it from the days of Shakespeare and Molière to the modern "gentleman".'[10]

The Waning of the Middle Ages as a whole is in fact a superb panoply of literary allusion. Huizinga draws freely on his familiarity with Oriental texts. To evoke the fairy-tale quality of mediaeval courtly life, he recalls the caliph from the *Thousand and One Nights*. The mediaeval fear of life puts him in mind of Buddhism. In another part of the book, his studies of Sanskrit prove their worth. 'In its motifs, the tournament is closely related to the contests in ancient Indian epics;

the *Mahâbhârata* too, revolves around the battle to win a woman.' When Dionysius the Carthusian, in his bleak cell, hears the elements calling for revenge against human injustice, it reminds him of 'the applause of celestial beings with rains of showers, flashes of light and mild quakes of the earth when a Bodhisattva performs a great deed'.[11]

On the very first page of *The Waning of the Middle Ages*, he enlists the help of 'the English novella' to clarify the mediaeval delight in a bright hearth-fire, drink and merriment, and a soft bed. He invokes a string of literary comparisons: Virgil and Ovid for courtly love, Russian literature for cruelty, Byron for lust for life paired with a cavalier contempt for life, Guy de Maupassant for the natural allure of eroticism. In a book about the Middle Ages, one may perhaps expect to find quotations from Huysmans and Hugo, but less to find that, in order to capture the flavour of a mediaeval meal, one needs to read Emile Zola or Anatole France. Nor is one particularly expecting to be despatched to the Belgian realist Camille Lemonnier to gain a better grasp of the chronicler Chastellain. And to be told that the mediaeval poem *L'amant rendu cordelier à l'observance d'amours* refers 'directly to Laforgue and Verlaine' may raise a few eyebrows. Another gem, in an essay about Abelard, is the bland assertion, 'He must have had an air of Oscar Wilde about him.'[12]

Huizinga used literature not just to add depth but also to add contrast to history. He sought appropriate writers to personify, as it were, the contrasts that he perceived in history. A case in point is his choice of Augustine and the contrast he forms with Jerome, 'two types of intellect, in mutual conflict'. By opposing these different 'religious temperaments' to each other, Huizinga sought to gain a firmer grasp of the development of Christian thought. 'Jerome is the urbane figure, for all his asceticism and reclusiveness susceptible to the products of culture; literature, relationships of intellectual sympathy, enlightened ideas, the forms of feminine thought, the needs of upbringing. Augustine... but you know him, the man of the burning heart and absolute faith.'[13]

Huizinga did the same in his biography of Erasmus. Here, he contrasted Erasmus with Luther. 'Erasmus, the man of nuance, for whom concepts endlessly modulated and shifted, whom Luther called a Proteus; Luther, the man of the disproportionate emphasis on all things. The Dutchman watching the turbulent waves as opposed to the German gazing on the fixed mountain-peaks.' It is obvious that Huizinga could identify far more easily with Jerome and Erasmus. Even so, he could not do without the passion of Augustine and Luther.[14]

Something similar recurs in the contrast between Ariosto and Rabelais. The writer of *Orlando Furioso* had stolen Huizinga's heart. In him he found 'that miraculous elevation above jest or gravity, in which the chivalric imagination found its classic expression'. In Ariosto, reality and imagination flowed together seamlessly. 'He captures everything with the primary word. He neither veils nor nuances. He neither suggests nor alludes. Everything appears in him with such clarity, such immediacy, such purity and simplicity of colour as a summer sky.'[15]

Still, Huizinga is not uncritical. Like Erasmus, Ariosto was 'never tragic, never truly heroic. Compelling, but never himself truly enthralled.' That is why Ariosto needed Rabelais, to provide balance. Rabelais was the embodiment of exaggeration, of hyperrealism, the grand personification of paradox and of laughter. This contrast was the crux of the matter. 'Rabelais and Ariosto stand at the two poles of the Renaissance. Here is harmony, serenity, and sonority, cheerful lucidity, there is the turbulent, fermenting chaos, from which, after Paracelsus, the new science will one day be born, and which still holds within it Cervantes, Ben Jonson and Rembrandt.'[16]

Huizinga was frequently not content with a single contrast, but added a third figure that linked the two opposites. 'Michelangelo's art bridged the chasm that divides Rabelais from Ariosto: the opposition between the eternal rest of the great, harmonious style and the restless, searching hyperrealism is dissolved in him.' The same applied to the difference between John of Salisbury and Abelard. Here again the customary distinction between tranquility and turbulence, balance and disharmony, nuance and the lack of it, again the wider identification with 'the time-keeping middle position' of John of Salisbury, but the eventual fascination for the passion of Abelard. Once again the 'fathoming' embrace of a third figure, in this case Thomas Aquinas. 'To the unrest and confusion of twelfth-century thought, the thirteenth brings that systematic order and that heavenly harmony, in which the age of St Thomas could envelop the mind as a diamond mounted in gold.'[17]

Huizinga took a similar approach to the contrast between Voltaire and Rousseau, writers whose thinking dominated the eighteenth century, one as an exponent of classicism, the other of incipient Romanticism. But then, 'elevated above the Voltaire-Rousseau duality was the all-fathoming' Goethe, whose 'romantic classicism' represented 'the insoluble problem of the centre'. He did the same thing with Emerson versus Whitman, America's essayist versus its poet. 'The rough, wild Walt, the Rabelaisian idler, who mingled with all sorts, and the elegant Emerson, the centre of the most refined circle of sophisticates.' The two converged in their belief in 'the unity of the world and myself', and no one expressed this notion with greater purity than Hawthorne, essayist and poet, and prose writer *pur sang*, in whom Huizinga found everything that he had loved in fairy tales and for whom he reserved the highest praise he knew: 'His view of things is almost that of Dante.'[18]

Perhaps the most important of these personifications was the dualism of Aristotle and Plato, the thinker versus the visionary. Much of what united them, their use of the mythical form, their dialogical mode of thought, their refutation of the sophists and reverence for music, was close to Huizinga's heart too. But they took very different views of the relationship between art and reality, and that was where their significance to him lay. His point of departure was Aristotle's theory of mimesis: art imitates nature. But art, in this sense, was not 'art in the modern sense', wrote Huizinga. It possessed a far wider, deeper significance and embraced 'everything that humankind shapes or makes'. And that imitation, too, was far more than representation, and rather meant 'to follow, to act in the same way'. He concluded, 'Understood thus, that principle of imitation points over Nature to God.'[19]

Plato turned matters around: it was not man but God who was the artist, and He played His game with the people that, without their knowledge, shaped His reality. The result was the same, reality, the nature of things, took on the enticing fragrance of 'higher honey' [Nijhoff]. Man was God's plaything. This meant that play was also a serious business. Luther had said something similar: all creatures were masks of God, and behind those masks, a hidden God played out the theatre of the world. 'In this profound image,' commented Huizinga, 'the contrast we were straining to define is truly and irreversibly dissolved.'[20]

The image also dissolved the contrast between Aristotle and Plato, because the accent came to lie not on the essence of things but on their description, their depiction. We would never penetrate to the bare bones of reality. The 'quality of things' was beyond our rational, logical thought. True, art was capable of imparting a certain 'sense of quality', but it remained a sense. Much of what we think we know is mere surmise, much of what we do, we do unconsciously and often against our better judgment. *How* things are, is

God's business. 'All our philosophy and science only brings us to Dante's mild exhortation, echoing Aristotle: "State contenti umana gente al quia", "Content yourselves, mortals, with the *that*".'[21]

LITERATURE AND REALITY

But how should a human being represent the *that*? Here we come to Huizinga's central question. All his reading was draped around it. 'We continue to speak of Literature, incorrigible neo-Platonists as we all are, as an essentialism, and of literary culture as a group and élite culture behind and above general civilization.' That is why Huizinga read the literature of every period, every culture or region that he studied. 'In all the major periods of civilization, literature has been the perfect expression of the prevailing ideal of life, with the exception of the Romantic period, in which we Europeans have been living for the past century and a half.'[22]

The latter exception is significant, but at least as important is the comment about the neo-Platonists. Instead of Platonists, he sometimes called them realists. Huizinga generally used the word 'realism' outside the philosophical context in which it is frequently used – in other words, not in contrast to nominalism. For him, realism was the opposite of stylization. It was found in the Egyptian world of long before the Christian era, in the Dutch painting of the seventeenth century and the French novels of the nineteenth. So it was not bound to time or civilization, rather, it was a 'fairly incidental cultured crop' that appeared here and there only to vanish again. The two other terms with which he opposed realism, Classicism and Romanticism, were similarly not so much classifying, literary, or art-theoretical concepts, but timeless terms in which Huizinga captured the central dichotomies of human representation.[23]

Consciously or unconsciously, they also determined his literary preferences. For instance, he had a penchant for sixteenth-century English and nineteenth-century French literature. It is no coincidence that these are types of representation that shared a common interface, that of rough reality and beautiful form. It was not just Shakespeare who had stolen Huizinga's heart; he also loved Marlowe and Jonson, Sidney and Gascoigne. At the same time, he had long been familiar, since his university days, with French literature by 'those who were then called new', as he wrote to Menno ter Braak: De Gourmont and Huysmans, Laforgue and Verlaine, Maeterlinck and Valéry. These literary influences determined his idiosyncratic relationship to reality, which he himself defined best in *The Waning of the Middle Ages*, when he wrote 'that every thing would be absurd, if its significance were exhausted in its immediate function and manifestations, that all things extend some distance into the world on the other side'.[24]

In *The Waning of the Middle Ages* he calls this conviction 'symbolism', like the French literature that was so dear to him. The description he gave of it was equally applicable to nineteenth-century French and sixteenth-century English literature. In both cases, the contrast between reality and ideal is central; both try to make that contrast acceptable by adopting the premise of a well-ordered cosmos in which contradictions blend harmoniously and everything is related. This relationship is not causal but symbolic: it is not about cause and effect but about meaning and purpose. Each thing possesses significance, a surplus of meaning that refers to the order of the cosmos. In that sense, each part reflects the whole. This was not only the fundamental principle underlying the mediaeval imagination; it applied equally to the Renaissance and Romanticism. The grand style of the Renaissance was predicated on the whole; the lack of style of Romanticism on the details. The Renaissance revolved around form, Romanticism around reality.

From this point of view, Huizinga actually had two reasons for reading. On the one hand, he read to familiarize himself with the conventions of the age, the fashions, the vogue, the appearances behind which contemporaries sought to conceal their bitter reality or to make it palatable. The fact that literature embellished reality also gave it its documentary character, illustrated the mentality of an age. At the same time, there was still a reality behind those forms, behind the *maniera*, behind the style, and that non-stylized reality was the second reason for his reading. That explains why Huizinga, pre-eminently a writer who knew what style was, went in search of what was styleless. However much Vermeer may have deviated from the mainstream of Dutch painting in his day, he was still a real Dutch painter, 'because he had no thesis, no idea, and in the strict sense of the word no particular style'. Huizinga was struck by the same quality in American literature in particular and Romanticism in general.[25]

This stylelessness made exotic and alien literary forms 'perfectly intelligible'. A passage from the *Hadith*, the traditional texts relating to the prophet Mohammad, had the same 'realistic effect' as one from the *Edda*. The digging of a trench around Medina under the supervision of Mohammed was accompanied by the same kind of details (the diggers' doggerel, the prophet's barley gruel) as the saga of Egill Skallagrímsson (his playing with his sword, his facial expressions). These details were 'true' in the sense that they could not have been invented, but rather sprang from a naive power of observation. Huizinga was struck by similar details in the Flemish primitives in the Quattrocento, 'the painstaking observation, the unbridled elaborateness, the meticulous rendering', 'all naively, freshly archaic'. There was nothing contrived about these representations, and nothing original. Everything seemed to have been lifted directly from reality and for that precise reason it was timeless, and pertained to what all people have in common.[26]

That was the same thing that kept his eye glued to the page in those fairy tales from long ago. That was what he found in writers such as Hawthorne, Laforgue, and Keller. Hawthorne's *Wonder-Book* and *Tanglewood Tales*, with their re-telling of old myths (Perseus, Midas, the Apples of the Hesperides, Proserpine) reminded him strongly of Jules Laforgue's *Moralités Légendaires* (Hamlet, Lohengrin, Salome) and Gottfried Keller's *Sieben Legenden*, which drew largely on the Christian heritage. Hawthorne even put him emphatically in mind of 'the childlike tenderness and naive sentimentality of Andersen'. But Huizinga went one step further in his appreciation of the writer of the *Tanglewood Tales*. 'The humour is so implicit, and there is such a fullness of profound feeling, that the old myths are radiant as if basking in a new, warm light. His view of things is almost that of Dante ... And with all this, the utterly childlike tone, which ensures that they remain real children's tales. It is as if Hawthorne already felt what modern studies of mythology have shown: that fairy tales are not cast-off myths, but myths are stylized fairy tales.'[27]

DANTE

Considering that Huizinga described Dante as the greatest reading experience of his life, he wrote surprisingly little about him. Even so, he derived his most important concepts from that reading, including that of 'a sense of place': 'No poet is so inseparable from the land and nation that brought him forth as Dante,' he wrote, in the 'Dante year' of 1921. 'He gives us a far stronger sense of Italy than Shakespeare gives us of England or even Cervantes of Spain. Is there any other poet who walks beside you in the same way, when you cross his path, as Dante does in Florence, Verona, Ravenna? Italy is the joy of the world for a thousand other things; one may become familiar with it from scores of other expressions of its rich spirit, but the deepest and strongest parts of that spirit are known only to those who love Dante.'[28]

What attracted Huizinga most was Dante's realism, which was of 'such an overwhelming insistency', 'so vibrant, so visionary, that his work provides the standard by which we may measure our concept of literary realism'. It is here that Huizinga deepens Aristotle's theory of mimesis into a theory of Christian emulation. He quotes the well-known passage from Canto XI of *Inferno*, 97-100, in which Dante gives Virgil the following lines:

'Filosofia,' mi disse, 'a chi la intende,
nota, non pure in una sola parte,
come natura lo suo corso prende
dal divino e da sua arte.'

('"Philosophy," he said, "to him who heeds it,
Noteth, not only in one place alone,
After what manner Nature takes her course
From Intellect Divine, and from its art."')[29]

This was about far more than simple artistic realism, says Huizinga. That was why Thomas Aquinas subsumed 'image' under the heading of 'representation': it was about significance as well as outward appearance. Realism – for Huizinga as well as for Dante – was meaning and reality combined, an ideal, 'but in an entirely different sense than the naive desire for deceptive imitation: a realism that incorporates the meaning of things, and that might resolve the antithesis between the scholastic concept of realism and modern aestheticism'.

As a salient example he cited the church music of Utopia, which Thomas More describes as following the natural emotions so well that it 'affects and kindles the passions, and works the sentiments deep into the hearts of the hearers'. That is precisely what Huizinga meant by dissolving the contrast between mediaeval and modern, what he meant by timeless realism: 'Behind More's beautiful and simple words, we can hear, if we will, Mozart and Beethoven, the entire music of the eternal Utopia, that is the true land of tones.' He found the same in Dürer, in what the artist referred to as 'the original face of Nature', the power to see 'in the smallest living creature its most beautiful purpose'. It was the transition from plurality to singularity, from *maniera* to simplicity, from style to stylelessness, from nature to God.[30]

And in this way all antitheses were resolved. 'It is as if, in the face of Dante's work, all the dichotomies of literary history lose their meaning, because he had already resolved them, or rather, had not known them. Whoever comes to Dante seeking to define the relationship between subject-matter and manner of treatment can save himself the trouble; they are utterly inseparable. Any distinction between reality and fiction in Dante is doomed to miscarry. One between form and content will fare no better. The different spheres of representation, Biblical, classical, romantic, between which later generations of poets would waver and choose, were not separated in Dante: his vision eclipses them all and compels them to unity.'[31]

4

WRITING

Just as there can be poetry without poems, just as landscapes, people or facts may be poetic, history appeared to Huizinga as poetry, and so he approached it as a form of literature. Historiography as a profession was of little concern to him, and language was everything. He saw language as a natural resource with an inherent poetic richness. To appreciate this is to read the unity of his work as the unity of his character. To be sure, Huizinga went through a process of development, and modified his style over the years. But that is the stuff of biography. The subject here is the enduring nature of the form; the subject is Huizinga the poet. 'Et souviens-toi qu'en nous il existe souvent,' he hummed to Alfred de Musset's lyrics, 'un poète endormi toujours jeune et vivant.'[1] His monographs and biographies, studies and essays are all part of a single endeavour; they constitute an organic whole in which style, far from being a mode of technical manipulation, is a poetic process.[2]

CONTRASTS

The most singular and striking element of Huizinga's style, perhaps, is his use of contrasting adjectives: the consistency with which he uses oppositions between, say, 'heavy' or 'black', 'sharp', and 'high' on the one hand, and 'light', 'fluid', and 'humble' on the other.[3] Or take *bont*, meaning 'colourful', 'multicoloured', 'diverse'. This is one of Huizinga's favourite words, but above all we notice the frequency with which it is opposed to *innig*, 'intimate' or 'deep'. Both *bont* and *innig* were common currency in Huizinga's day, especially in the idiom of the 1880 Movement. Still, Huizinga's idiosyncratic use of them, the way in which he contrasts and harmonizes them, exemplifies the subtle mechanics of his style.

The versatile *bont* is certainly one of Huizinga's favoured repositories for a wide spectrum of meanings. It is applied to a specific style of Sanskrit drama, 'dazzling [*bont*] with the choicest of handsome costumes'. The oldest Buddhist literature is described as 'a rich [*bont*] treasure-house of the most diverse forms and colours'. And *bont* is put to work to describe mediaeval trade, 'constrained within such a narrow framework and at the same time so rich and intricate [*bont*], so highly developed'.[4] These are all early examples, and they suffice to demonstrate Huizinga's desire to convey, within that general concept of variety, simultaneous development and *over*-development, fullness and excess, form and conventionality, approval and rejection.[5]

Innig ('intimate', 'deep') is the constant counterpart of *bont*, and its opposite. It conveys unity and simplicity. It is 'the lyrical concept of mood' as it characterized Indian drama. A work without this quality – that is not *innig* – is incapable of psychological depth. A 'boundless desire for expressiveness' is dismissed as 'vulgar and Romanesque', while a light touch or playful form can 'create an awareness of inner depths [*het innigste*]'. Huizinga uses *innig* for closeness and tact, subtlety and receptiveness; it can be expressed in lyrical or dramatic forms, and in painting too.[6]

It was its quality of 'genial neglect' that gave the Haarlemmer Wood its most 'intimate [*innigste*] charm'. But even Groningen theology possessed it, in its 'intimate [*innig*] element of emotion'. *Innig* has none of the slightly deprecatory overtones of *bont*, and in other respects too, this word is – inherently – broader and more stable. *Innig* is used as a kind of fusion that marks the flowering of a culture, an equilibrium – between earnestness and humour, for instance: 'For the unconscious ability to bring those two states into enduring union and combine them into a supremely moving expression of one's innermost [*innigste*] thoughts is what distinguishes those few who attain an equilibrium of thought and deed in the heyday of a cultural era.'[7]

It is in *The Waning of the Middle Ages*, above all, that the range of these two adjectives is exploited to the full. The 'perpetual contrast' that provides the book's basic structure is evoked on the very first pages by the 'colourful [*bonte*] forms with which everything impressed itself on the mind'. Summarizing his account of chronicles and records, Huizinga concludes, 'All this is overlaid by cries of sundry [*bonte*] sins and laments of woe.' He describes the action of wallowing in the world's 'variegated [*bonte*] beauty', he evokes the erotic culture, 'so diverse [*bont*], so dense, and so rich'. He calls the *Roman de la Rose* 'that gaudy [*bonte*], voluptuous, mediaeval work'. At the same time he alludes to the Saints Innocents Cemetery in Paris as a place of 'gloomy holiness and garish [*bonte*] gruesomeness'. We read about *bonte* colours and *bonte* imagination, the *bonte* 'flush of a courtly banquet', and figures of naive imaginings that are 'as *bont* as they appear to a child's mind'. Huizinga alludes to a '*bonte* hell' and 'the multiplicity and *bonte* quality of what is seen' – even '*bonte* crows in the snow'.[8]

Innig [with its abstract noun *innigheid*] is the opposite in every respect. From the very first use of *bont* – in connection with the 'constant contrast with which everything obtruded itself on the mind' – the subject is 'that giddy mood of raw exuberance, violent cruelty, deep [*innige*] tenderness, amid which mediaeval city life is played out'. 'The deeper the despair and despondency about the confusion of the present day,' writes Huizinga, 'the more profound [*inniger*] the yearning' for a more beautiful world. He refers to a 'deep [*innig*] belief', 'the most profound [*innigste*] emotional changes', 'an excess of intimacy [*innigheid*]', an 'overflowing ardour [*innigheid*]'. He dwells at length on the 'new form of life, that of the interiority [*innigheid*]' of Modern Devotion, and on the 'more austere unity and deeper [*inniger*] bonds' of mediaeval symbolism. He touches on 'the most profound [*innigste*] mystery, the Eucharist', and follows the mediaeval mystics into what Eckhart calls the 'Still Wilderness [*innige*] where no one is at home', whose 'highest and most profoundly [*innigst*] desired' quality may be alluded to solely in terms of double negatives. Huizinga writes of 'a treasure-house of profundity [*innigheid*]', and even 'the pathos of profundity [*innigheid*]'.[9]

You might say that *The Waning of the Middle Ages* is itself a *bont* book, given that the word *bont* occurs over forty times in it, compared to fewer than thirty uses of *innig*. In *Dutch Civilization in the Seventeenth Century*, on the other hand, *bont* scarcely puts in an appearance. Consequently, *innig* also turns up far less frequently, but it does appear at important moments. Love is *innig*, whether the reference is to Huygens's love of Nature or, by implication, to his 'profound [*innige*] mourning for his Sterre, whom he did not forget'. The Dutchman's preference for the commonplace was part of his 'deepest [*innigste*] devoutness'. His response to the joys and sorrows of family life is deeply felt [*innig*], and his experience of the sacrament is 'most profound' [*innigst*]. Drawings are in general *inniger* than paintings, while etchings are the most *innig* of all. The word appears to embrace anything that turns inward, that is tender and intimate, loving and private. It conveys precisely – in the phrase 'intimately Dutch', *innig Nederlandsch* – what Huizinga loved about his native country.[10]

It is also striking that the twofold division within *The Waning of the Middle Ages* along the fault-line between *bont* words and serene images – which works on the level of content as well – is reflected lexically in the abundant uses of *bont* in the first half and *innig* in the second. In and after Huizinga wrote *Erasmus*, his uses of *bont* became scarcer, *innig* gained the upper hand, and Huizinga's stylistic life itself branched into two parts. It is as if he evolved from a 'sublime' style that oscillates between the lofty and the intimate into one in which the *sermo humilis*, the unadorned and transparent use of language, comes to predominate. Huizinga develops from *bonte* shifts of register to *innige* simplicity.

A second stylistic device through which Huizinga sought to express contrast was the compact opposition between 'here' and 'there'. Discussing two mutually exclusive loyalties in Indian drama, Huizinga says, 'The hermits' interests lie here, the gurus' precepts there'. We encounter this device throughout his work. This is how he describes the difference between older and more recent Indian views concerning the release from the cycle of death and rebirth: 'Here is a nebulous, terror-born image ... there an avowed contempt for the world.' And when the subject shifts to the piece of the province of Drenthe that projected like a sliver of sandy soil into Friesland's clay: 'So soil types and heights differed. The population came from a different tribe. The region belonged, like the rest of Drenthe, to a different diocese: Utrecht was here, Munster there.'[11]

In *Man and the Masses in America*, Huizinga wrote: 'Here he [the condemned evolutionist] was sermonized straight to hell, while there his death was held up to the people to exemplify the avenging hand of divine retribution.' Or 'There the champagne of universal philanthropy ... here a sharp, businesslike tone.' In his nineteenth-century history of Groningen University: 'Here were Jonckbloet and De Vries, there Potgieter and Bakhuizen, the former indispensable to the university and scholarship, the latter to the nation. While the first two were unsurpassed in their knowledge of Old Dutch, the last two understood the past of the Netherlands itself.' Even later, this remained a favourite shorthand device. In his major essay 'Renaissance and realism', Huizinga defines Rabelais and Ariosto as the opposite poles of the Renaissance. 'Here reigns harmony, serenity, sonority, and frolicsome clarity, while there stretches agitated, turbulent, seething, fermenting chaos.' In his lecture on 'Ideas and moods a hundred years ago', he contrasted matter-of-factness with fanaticism, pragmatism with romanticism: 'here we find the bourgeoisie, there the artist, here the poet, there the banausians.'[12]

In *The Waning of the Middle Ages*, a study saturated in contrasts, this rhetorical figure is ubiquitous. To underscore his assertion that saints are as timeless as mystics, he writes: 'Here we find Ignatius of Loyola ... and there Bernardino of Siena ... '. He comes even closer to the book's main thesis when remarking that the accumulation of minutiae in Van Eyck's paintings does not detract from their harmony: 'There the cheerfulness of a limpid outdoor light drew one's gaze beyond the main scene into the panoramic depths, while here the enigmatic darkness of the tall church veils the whole in such a cloud of earnestness and mystery that the eye discerns only with difficulty the anecdotal details.' He goes to the heart of the book in the following contrast between courtly culture and provincialism: 'Here is the culture of the court, the nobility, and the wealthy burghers; ostentatious, ambitious and avaricious, gaudy, glowing with passion. There we see the still, plain grey air of modern devotion, the grave men and the meek burgher womenfolk, who sought refuge in friaries and with the Windesheimers.' 'There the opulent, mature life of Bruges, Ghent, Brussels, in constant contact with the court; here a remote inland city like Haarlem, in every respect far more akin to the tranquil cities of modern devotion along the river IJssel.'[13]

FORMS OF RECONCILIATION

Huizinga uses stylistic means to reconcile his contrasts as well as to evoke them. One such device is the oxymoron, yoking together two opposed concepts – a device he himself once called 'ostensible absurdity that resolves itself into irony'. The phrase 'born old' is used to describe the university, and as an epithet for literary classicism. He considers that American political parties are effectively 'vast cliques', and that the whole of American society is best characterized as 'organized individualism' and 'giant-sized parochialism'. John of Salisbury is called 'the chivalric clerk', 'the man with the serious smile'. The visual arts are 'silent speech', and printing is 'the largest and quietest revolution that the West has ever known'. Huizinga uses the phrase 'conservative revolution' while explaining both the seventeenth-century Netherlands and the modern United States. In the same context he writes of the stylelessness that becomes a style, the lack of form that is seen as form, genuine imitation, and cheating as play. We also find collocations such as 'surface civilization', 'middle-class aristocracy', and 'armchair shepherd'.[14]

A natural corollary to this rhetorical practice is his love of compound adjectives. I am not referring here to workaday compounds formed with words for 'old' or 'young', 'modern' or 'late', or obvious ones such as 'socio-economic' or 'cultural-historical', or even 'mediaeval-Western' or 'Roman-Christian' but more idiosyncratic hyphenations such as *innig-vroom* ('deeply devout'), *stemmig-vaderlandsch* ('solemnly patriotic'), *ideëel-ethisch* ('idealistically ethical'), *hoog-religieus* ('loftily religious'), *glad-middelmatig* ('glibly mediocre'), *grof-komisch* ('coarsely humorous'), and *bas-komiek* ('vulgarly humorous'). Like his preference for the adjectives *bont* and *innig*, these compounds stem from Huizinga's close association with the Movement of 1880. But he also supplied a creative 'explanation' for them in his first dissertation proposal, 'Introduction and Proposal for a Study of Light and Sound': besides indicating contrast, they also served to convey greater precision. This straining after precision sometimes went as far as to yield phrases such as *half-gedroomde, niet-scherp-omlijnde* ('half-dreamt, not sharply defined') and the *zuivere melodisch-rythmisch-harmonische*' (the 'purely melodically, rhythmically harmonic').[15]

It is delightful to see the mature historian returning to the convictions he had articulated as a young linguist regarding the origins of language, and 'proving' them in his magnum opus. For in *The Waning of the Middle Ages*, this creative compounding is carried to outré extremes. Huizinga sets up oppositions between 'formally symbolic' and 'socially realistic'; between 'causally genetic' and 'naturally genetic'; 'liturgical-sacramental' and 'symbolic-aesthetic'; 'bleakly glowing' and 'dully diverse [*bont*]'. He contrasts 'self-seeking erotic' with 'primitively romantic', 'comically erotic' with 'ecclesiastically erotic'; and adds 'lyrically erotic' to his lexicon. Other oppositions include those between 'sceptically cool' and 'cynically cruel', and between 'decoratively rhetorical' and 'pleasurably narrative'.[16]

Another frequent device is mirroring contrasts in such a way that they cancel each other out, so to speak. Using pairs of adjectives or associated nouns ('doublets' in textbook rhetoric), Huizinga sets up an equilibrium of oppositions, as it were. For instance, in *Man and the Masses in America*, he uses this device in a description of the

American Revolution: 'From small, matter-of-fact grievances came forth great passion and high-flown words.' Better still: 'There is little emphasis on the individual; the organizations – whether ecclesiastical or monastic, social or economic, feudal or guilds – are close-knit and active.' And this one: 'From the outset, economic interests, big and small, international commerce as well as local trade, permeated every fibre and tissue of America's state organism.'[17]

In Huizinga's eyes, the national consciousness that lived in the Republic, 'like the state itself, was ambivalent'. The subsequent illustration welds form to content: 'half monarchical, half republican; half Prince, half States; half The Hague, half Amsterdam.' In his biography of Erasmus, he adopts exactly the same technique when contrasting Erasmus's free will with Luther's servile will in a series of oppositions between 'sin and grace . . . redemption and the glory of God', finally concluding that 'here was waged a struggle, in words and images, that went beyond the recognizable and effable'. In his major essay 'The problem of the Renaissance', Michelangelo, 'wrathful and solitary', is opposed to Botticelli, 'yearning and languid'. 'Is that Raphael and Ariosto,' he continues, revelling in the sheer variety of the Renaissance, 'or is it Dürer and Rabelais? No, it is Ronsard, it is Hooft.'[18]

On the very first page of *The Waning of the Middle Ages*, 'calamities and want', 'more terrible and more agonizing', are contrasted with 'honour and wealth' that are enjoyed 'more deeply [*inniger*] and more eagerly'. On the miseries associated with life at court, we read: 'Bad fare and poor lodgings, endless din and mayhem, cursing and quarrelling, malice and scorn, it was a quagmire of sins, a gate of hell.' In everyday life, 'different fleeces and colours, caps and hoods, reflected the strict ordering of the estates, the flaunting of rank, the state of gladness and grief, the tender relations of friends and amorous lovers'. On the ethical content of the chivalric ideal, Huizinga explains: 'It is the veneration of superior ambition and daring alongside that of superior knowledge and talent.'[19]

Balancing antitheses in this way was embedded in Huizinga's stylistic DNA. Just how economically he expresses that is evident in an early lecture about Haarlem. 'But Haarlem, where the old that endured is squeezed, pushed aside, shouted down by the new and the big, the useful and the ugly, it vexes you at every step.' Here, the contrast between the old and the new Haarlem, presented concretely in things that endured and things that were squeezed out, is conveyed through the use of the past as opposed to the perfect tense, then by the adjective-nouns, and in 'step by step' it is repeated as it were literally, physically.[20]

The rhythm that he imparts to his prose in this way is reinforced by the use not only of the doublet, but also of the tricolon, a rhetorical term for the juxtaposition of three adjectives or nouns. 'There was a desire to enjoy the exciting, grim, and ghastly as well as the tender, sensitive, and Romanesque,' he wrote in his dissertation about the *vidûshaka*. Similarly, in *The Waning of the Middle Ages* we read: 'Thus the weary aristocracy laughed at its own ideal. When it had brought to bear all its resources of imagination, artistic skill and wealth and had embellished, coloured, and modelled into a plastic form its passionate dream of splendid life ...' 'Every historical or literary instance has a tendency to crystallize into a parable, a moral example, a piece of evidence; every statement becomes a maxim, a legend, a saying.'[21]

Erasmus appeared to be 'the harbinger of a new freedom of spirit, a new clarity, purity, and simplicity of knowledge, a new harmony of reasoned, wholesome, and good life'. In 'The problem of the Renaissance', the enumeration 'one sign', 'one nostalgia', 'one aspiration' alliterates, so to speak, with 'pure Latinity, perfect poetry, rediscovered art' and is subsequently subsumed into the full rhyme of '*renovatio, restitutio, restauratio*'. In *Homo Ludens* virtually everything appears in threes: the law in games of chance, contests, and debates, wisdom in courage, knowledge, and guile. 'Oracle, games of chance, and courts of justice' are yoked together, as are 'God's will, destiny, and outcome', and 'law, fate, and games of chance'. The rules are grammatical, poetic, or ritual, the poet is 'possessed, fervent, enraged', his play teeters on the border between 'exuberance, banter, and entertainment', 'as a miraculous feat, a festive intoxication, as ecstasy'. 'Rhyme, parallelism, distichs' incorporate the principles of 'song, music, and dance', and represent 'beauty, holiness, magical power'. All real cults are 'sung, danced, played'. 'For the spirit delights to play with the extravagant, the miraculous, the absurd.'[22]

Another striking characteristic of Huizinga's style, related to this, is his delight in alliteration, assonance, and consonance. In a treatise on Sanskrit literature he refers to 'whiling the time away with wanton women', 'mordant mountain stream-water, wild with leaves', 'the motley [*bonte*] mob of the gods'. He describes the period of the 'wishers' followed by that of the 'workers'. He notes that a Buddhist narrator gladly lingers on 'brilliants and millions'. He alludes to the 'broad [*bonte*] business of burghers' lives'. 'Shacks and sheds' nestle against the protective church wall 'like hatched chicks under the hen'. He praises Sir Philip Sidney's 'sweet and sunny song'.[23]

Man and the Masses in America even has an alliterative title. Here too we find assonance ('The man who had hacked his own path through life'), as well as alliteration ('God-fearing feminine fervour'), culminating in the 'wispy, sunny and soft salty warmth of a September day'. *The Waning of the Middle Ages* is the epitome of alliteration. Louis XI appals with his 'dreadful drollery'. The British royal court is a 'hell of hatred'. Huizinga describes waste as an alliance between avarice and arrogance. The illusory chivalric ideal has 'the value of veracity'. A book has polychrome [*bonte*] pictures; disdain for the world is 'paired with the patterns of prehistory'. Greed glimmers, old greenery runs riot. And again assonance and consonance abound: 'The great game of the fine life as a reverie of gallant valour and loyalty'; 'the sweet meanings of colours in clothing'. Or in combination: 'where mockery's bow sighs its highest notes, gushes over the gravest parts of life, love, and loss'; 'frank and free, serenity and sonority'.[24]

It is alliteration, combined with doublets and triplets, that gives the prose its rhythm. A style of architecture bursts into blossoming forms, the revival of ancient culture came to 'fertilize, free, and unfurl Western civilization'. A word 'bans and binds', plots and conspiracies are hatched in Carbonari clubs. There was a 'putative perfection in the past' to which people sought to elevate themselves or in which they lost themselves in daydreams. The humanist master in the art of living was 'gaudy and garrulous, deceitful and degenerate, a prancing peacock'. 'The poets and sages reap with a wider scythe, they harvest the new treasures riper and richer than artists and architects.' 'Renaissance, Reformation, Restoration, Risorgimento; these capital R's are the cranks with which we grind the gates of history.' 'Play binds and releases. It baits. It beguiles, bewitches.'[25]

The last of those quotations, obviously taken from *Homo Ludens*, again welds substance to form; Huizinga describes play as 'full of those two noblest of qualities, which people may observe in things and themselves express: rhythm and harmony'. In his reading too, Huizinga was highly sensitive to syntax and rhythm. Discussing the expressive powers of the poets Bredero, Hooft, Huygens and Vondel, he emphasizes that these include 'cadence, tone, and rhythm'. Consequently, his own sentences often give the impression of having been written to be recited, and in reading his work one often finds oneself involuntarily mumbling aloud.

Take the following passage from *Man and the Masses in America*, in which he evokes rich contrasts between Holland and the United States: 'When we incorrigible dreamers and silent anglers after serene beauty think of Holland, our thoughts fly first to its skies. But America booms and clangs and crashes; its thundering waterfalls roar, and its prairie grass waves in the wind.' In *The Waning of the Middle Ages* too, it is the alternation of pairs and triplets that gives our reading a metrical pace: 'Wherever we may look in the annals of that age: the historians, the poets, the sermons and religious treatises, and even the legal records, they are drenched in little other than recollections of discord, hatred and malice; greed, savagery, and misery. One wonders, did this age know no pleasures other than those of cruelty, pride, and intemperance, was there no place at all for genial joy and gentle happiness?'[26]

All this imparts an unmistakeable musical effect to Huizinga's language. Listen to the ringing sound in the name of a humble early nineteenth-century Groningen professor: 'the slender Tinga with the silvery voice'. Hear the bells pealing in his description of a poem by Vondel: 'all the chimes of Amsterdam sprinkle a shower of gold and silver over the circle dance of the new canals.' That spattering of sound, that belt of canals seen as a circle dance![27]

And listen to this: 'The bells of Ghent, which welcomed Philip the Bold of Burgundy and his consort Margaret of Flanders in January 1386, betolled more than a sealed peace and a new overlord.' In this case, a poetically lengthened word [*verwellekoomden* rather than *verwelkomden* for 'welcomed'] combines with a neologism [*begalmden*, rendered as 'betolled'] to mimic the rhythm of church bells. A splendid example in this genre is the evocation of bells at the beginning of *The Waning of the Middle Ages*: 'in everyday life, the church bells resembled kindly warning spirits, which, in their familiar voices, announced then mourning and then joy, then peace and then turmoil, then proclaiming and then admonishing.' The repetition of 'then' is the chiming of bells. This sentence is comparable to the Sanskrit mantra at the close of *The Waste Land*, 'Datta. Dayadhvam. Damyata', with which T.S. Eliot gives a voice to thunder.[28]

EXPRESSIVE POWERS

Besides these auditory qualities, Huizinga's style also possessed the compactness that he so sorely missed in Erasmus. 'The collector of the *Adagia* did not create any of his own.' Huizinga did. Some of them became, if not *gesunkenes Kulturgut*, at least the prized possessions of an élite. Every Dutch reader knows, or should know, the opening phrases of *The Waning of the Middle Ages* ('When the world was five centuries younger…') and of *In the Shadow of Tomorrow* ('We are living in a world possessed. And we know it'). The odd historian or two might also have committed to memory, 'So fierce and bright [*bont*] was life, it could endure the mingled scent of blood and roses.' And it would be an added bonus to hear the rest of this passage: 'Between hellish oppression and the most childish of pleasures, between hideous callousness and sobbing tenderness, the people veered like a giant with the head of a child.' Another well-known phrase, from *In the Shadow of Tomorrow*: 'Like the smell of asphalt and petrol lingering over a city, a cloud of circumlocution hovers over the world.'[29]

Expressive and succinct, Huizinga excels in these qualities. 'It is the fence that creates ownership, not the owner the fence,' he writes in *Man and the Masses in America*. On the public display of the eroticism of the wedding night in the Middle Ages, he writes: 'It was modern individual sentiment, which sought to cloak in silence and darkness what was of two only, that shattered these rites.' *The Waning of the Middle Ages* has armfuls of these gold nuggets. For instance, he regards the obscene jokes made at mediaeval wedding feasts as 'the remains of the phallic symbolism of primitive culture, degenerated into a social convention. In other words, as melted down mystery.' The picture of love in the woman, on the other hand, he describes as 'veiled', and as a 'more delicate and deeper secret'. The 'holy helpers' of popular religion are dubbed 'procurators of divinity'. On vulgar dealings with sacred matters, overfamiliarity with the Eucharist, he writes: 'Thirsting arms had reached out and pulled heaven downwards.' The flamboyant Gothic is 'an endless organ coda', while Bach's librettists are dismissed as 'the most provincial poetasters of a rheumatic church faith'. A bold statement – and more than that – is 'Orthodoxy and a sense of style are the nearest of kin.'[30]

Once again, such tours de force are not confined to the stylistic masterpiece that is *The Waning of the Middle Ages*. Erasmus's *Adagia* are described as 'Antiquity laid out as if in a department store, for sale by the pound.' Two pages further along: 'Could Erasmus really have believed that the next generation would play marbles in Latin?' History is referred to as an 'intellectual telescope', symbolism an 'intellectual short-circuit', mediaeval causality operates 'in the manner of a telephone exchange'. 'Clubs go with play as hats with heads.' 'Between "prized/priced" [*geprijsd*] and "praised" stretches the opposition between gravity and play.' Gijsbert Karel van Hogendorp is 'the solitary eminence', Bilderdijk 'the surly eminence'.[31]

His analogies have the same pithiness. 'Wisdom is to folly,' he remarks, in relation to *In Praise of Folly*, 'as Reason is to the Emotions.' And in a discussion of the *Enchiridion*, Huizinga writes: 'What the old philosophers called reason, Paul calls spirit, what they referred to as *affectus*, he refers to as the flesh.' This rhetorical device too recurs throughout his work. Recalling a precept of Sanskrit rhetoric, he phrases it thus: 'What in real life arouses erotic passion or some other sentiment is known as a factor in poetry and drama.' 'What in real life is known as consequence ... is called impact in discussions of poetry and drama.' History was to culture what the telescope was to astronomy. 'What is called Raphael in painting, is called Ariosto in literature.' Finally, the most marvellous and succinct example of all: 'What in the sphere of aesthetics is called style is known in ethics as loyalty and order.'[32]

CONTRAST AND HARMONY

5

CONTRAST

Huizinga's use of contrasts was a deliberate choice. History could only be perceived coherently, he wrote, 'by resolving events into a dramatic scheme'. A cultural phenomenon could only be truly comprehended 'by defining it within an equilibrium of continuing oppositions'. Huizinga used oppositions of this kind for their highly ethical as much as for their highly dramatic content. 'Dramatic – since people always perceive great tragic contrast in an inevitable lack of mutual understanding: the benightedness of the conservatives and the hubris of the innovators. Ethical – since people always share a respect for what is dead and beautiful, and a love of what is young and alive. Once an observer takes sides, the opposition is assigned a place as an episode in the cosmic struggle between light and dark, good and evil.'[1]

These contrasts were more than a way of underpinning an argument or enlivening an image. Huizinga was convinced that they were embedded in the past reality itself. That was what made history so concrete, so vivid: the fact that it almost always manifested itself in terms of oppositions. 'Clashes of arms, clashes of opinions, these are the constant themes of the historical narrative. History is essentially always epic or dramatic, however weak this potential may become.' Whether fact or fiction, historical representations did not acquire clear contours until brought into a conscious play of opposites: 'Athens does not become intelligible to us until it is contrasted with Sparta, we comprehend Rome through contrasts with Greece, Plato through Aristotle, Luther through Erasmus, Rembrandt through Rubens.'[2]

THE WANING OF THE MIDDLE AGES

The best illustration of this mode of writing is *The Waning of the Middle Ages*. This is manifest from the very first sentences: 'When the world was five centuries younger, all life events were far more sharply defined than now. The distance between suffering and joy, between calamity and happiness, seemed greater than it does to us; all human experience possessed that degree of immediacy and absoluteness that joy and suffering still have today in the mind of a child.' In the opening pages of his book, Huizinga describes the periodic system of mediaeval passion in contrasts between rich and poor, warm and cold, light and dark, tranquil and rowdy, civic and rural, happy and hopeless, tender and cruel. At the same time, he outlines the rituals through which that passion was channelled, the processions and grand entries, the executions and homilies.

All this is made tangible, as it were, by contrasting it with the present day ('more sharply defined than now'; 'greater than it does to us'), creating a seedbed of emotional receptivity in the reader. The town/country opposition contrasts with the way 'our' cities dwindle 'into slapdash suburbs of dreary factories and paltry cottages'. 'We newspaper readers' can scarcely imagine the powerful impact of the words of an itinerant preacher. 'Modern man has in general no conception of the unbridled abandon and excitability of the mediaeval temperament.' 'The Middle Ages knew none of the emotions that have made our own sense of justice fearful and faltering.'[3]

Contrasts also determine the book's broader unity, its associative cohesiveness. Although Huizinga alludes – in his very first chapter – to the harmonious potential of life, the picture he paints is of an evil world. 'Amid soaring flames of hatred and violence injustice rules, the devil spreads his black wings over the earth, darkening all below.' Still, the harshness of that reality is counterbalanced, in the second chapter, with 'the yearning for a finer life'. It is this opposition that leads him to his central line of inquiry: the contrast that he perceives between life and art. To be sure, little endured of what he calls 'the brighter half of that life'. Only painting and music remained to convey a sense of the mildness and serenity of the fifteenth century; only in farces and folk songs could its laughter still be heard. 'Anyone who has truly immersed himself in that age will often find it hard to bear that aspect of joyfulness in mind. For everywhere outside the sphere of art, darkness reigns.' The contrast is even embedded in the sources, in which the unrelieved horror stories of the chronicles stand out in black relief against the silent serenity of paintings. 'It is almost as if that century had only painted its virtues and described its vices.'[4]

The logic of Huizinga's method thus divides the book quite naturally into two halves. The first fourteen chapters depict mediaeval life by sketching contrasts between dream and reality. This part is further subdivided into two sections: one on the worldly dimension of the virtuous life, on courage and loyalty, honour and love; and one on its spiritual dimension, on death and holiness, mysticism and religious feeling. Both parts follow the same format, each starting with a black-and-white theoretical outline, after which the colourful mosaic of practice is filled in. Huizinga starts by describing the desire for beauty by invoking two cultural moulds – the ideal of chivalry, and stylized love. Both are metamorphoses, conversions of violence and sensuality into beautiful forms, both are based on unfulfilled desire, and both hold within them, as it were, their inadequacy or failure.

Each of these two cultural moulds is approached in the same dualistic way. 'As an ideal of virtuous life, the notion of chivalry is an extraordinary construction. It is an essentially aesthetic ideal, composed of vivid [bonte] imaginings and lofty emotions. Yet the ideal it strives to attain is ethical: the mediaeval mind could view an ideal of life in noble terms only in relation to piety and virtue. In that ethical function, chivalry always falls short; it is sullied by its sinful origins.' In the same way, love is divided between body and spirit, views of death are split into the elegiac and the macabre, the sacred into the supernatural and the natural, piety into feverish expression and silent introspection.[5]

After each attempted transformation, two possible avenues open up. In the case of the chivalric ideal, a prospect opened up of two roads: 'one to the real, active life and the modern spirit of inquiry, and one to a renunciation of the world. But this latter road branched like the Pythagorean letter Y into two: the main path was that of the true spiritual life, while a side path led along the edges of the world with its pleasures.' Here Huizinga is using an image from the tenth book of Plato's *Republic*, in which the Pythagorean letter Y is used to denote life after death, much as Robert Frost uses 'The road not taken' to denote life before it, as a myth for the irreconcilable duality of existence.[6]

Both these cultural moulds, the chivalric ideal and love, fall short and degenerate into empty form, mere lies. 'Neither the euphoric ideal of noble, chaste chivalric loyalty nor the brutally-refined lasciviousness of the *Roman de la Rose* – nor indeed the sickly-sweet and facile fantasy of pastoralism – could withstand the tempest of life itself.'

These remarks define the book's subsequent rationale, since the truth of life is death, and the representation of death merges into religion and mysticism. But there too, we find substance ultimately choked by outward form. And it is this that leads Huizinga to his main theme, in the second part of his book: the relationship between life and art, word and image, form and content. He observes the distinctions that are made between word and image, between reading and looking. The process he describes is the gradual ossification of representation. The degeneration of the chivalric ideal into a rigid, vacuous imagery is only one example of the overall ossification of the mediaeval power of imagination: symbols become 'fossilized flowers', the symbolic impulse becomes 'purely mechanical'. The creative principle narrows into mere allegory and personification. Mediaeval life in Europe achieves the same wealth of inane detail as ancient Indian plays.[7]

And in this respect – and here we reach the crux of the entire inquiry – the art of the Van Eyck brothers was no different from the surrounding mediaeval world. Huizinga thus comes to the central contrast of his book, between the Middle Ages and the Renaissance, with the surprising conclusion that this contrast is a fiction. Jan van Eyck's art was utterly at home in the context of the Burgundian court, and was therefore late-mediaeval art *par excellence* and not the harbinger of modern art that the entire body of art theory liked to claim. By the same token, the Renaissance was not the modern age that people had made of it, but a variant of the same late-mediaeval culture.

A TISSUE OF CONTRASTS

This contrast-based analysis is discernible throughout Huizinga's oeuvre. In his first proposal for a doctoral dissertation, his intended research project on the origins of language, he divided the sensory impressions he intended to study, tactile impressions that he saw applied to perceptions of song and light, into contrasting pairs: sharp and blunt, bright and dull, light and heavy. He focused especially on the intensity of contrasts and the resulting effect, particularly in relation to light or colour and sound. He is concerned with 'shouting colours' and 'shrill light', or – an example he calls a 'particularly finely tuned expression' – 'colours that swear at each other'. There, in that clash, says Huizinga, in those contrasts dissolved in synaesthesia, lies the key to the genesis and life of words.[8]

In the dissertation that he did go on to write, the contrast lies in the anti-hero figure of the *vidûshaka*. The fool embodies the polar opposite of the hero, the ideal. 'His matter-of-factness is the antithesis of the hero's sensitivity, his hidebound materialism the antithesis of graciousness, his ugliness and foolish behaviour the antithesis of the hero's all-encompassing harmony of being.' Drama in general, in its comical aspect, fulfils precisely the same function. Theory of Indian drama distinguished eight *rasas* or mental states. Laughter was one of these, but it also served as the counterpart to all the others.[9]

In the local studies that Huizinga wrote afterwards, on Haarlem, Groningen, and Zeeland, contrasts continued to provide the driving force behind development or image-forming. Take the following example. In his major study on the loss of the original Frisian character of the region around Groningen,[10] the Frisian/Saxon contrast provides the framework. This contrast is reduced to that between city and surrounding region, which was a matter of pure geography, a difference of soil. Into the Frisian meadows and woods jutted a diluvial tongue of Drenthe, a foothill of the Hondsrug ridge of sand. So there was a difference of soil and of altitude, the people were different, and along with the rest of Drenthe, this region belonged to a different diocese. 'Yet precisely some of these disparities fuelled exchanges and association.'[11]

His books on the nineteenth-century history of Groningen University and present-day America are both structured along similar lines. In the former, the contrast lies in the differing organizational principles of education in the different periods, *ancien régime* versus French rule, French rule versus the restoration of the Dutch monarchy, before or after the 1876 Higher Education Act. In *Man and the Masses in America*, the framework is more apparent still. This work consists of four essays that are carefully structured around binary oppositions: individualism versus collectivism, organic growth versus mechanization, politics versus economics, and 'tamed' versus 'wild'. The book is also divided into two parts, with the first two essays decidedly downbeat and the last two displaying a far more optimistic tone.

Huizinga wrote two biographies, both composed around a similar framework. In Erasmus, of course, the primary contrast was that between scholasticism and humanism. Huizinga reduces this to a largely stylistic difference: rigid logic and tight-knit syllogisms versus an idiosyncratic style and a loose, suggestive mode of writing. This stylistic disparity features on every level of the book, as philosophy versus literature, literature versus life, humanism versus Christianity. Erasmus's entire oeuvre, which is woven into the biography in brief, almost vignette-like, pieces, reveals itself to be a tissue of contrasts. From the *Enchiridion* to the *Colloquia* – and most notably *In Praise of Folly* – each of his books is based on the contrast between appearance and essence.

At the exact centre of this book, at the watershed where the discussion shifts from Erasmus as a mirror of his age to Erasmus as a catalyst of his age, Huizinga presents his real portrait. It is here that he compares Erasmus's negativity, his lack of insight, of piety, and of depth, to his positive qualities – his urge to elevate civilization, his gift for simplicity and naturalness, purity and reason. Huizinga thus paints the picture of a man who is in principle sincere and forthcoming, inexperienced and unworldly. And yet, this was not the whole man. 'He also had a deeper side, which was almost the opposite of all those characteristics, and which he himself did not know, because he did not want to know it. Perhaps because this layer concealed yet another layer, the core of his being, which was truly good.' This brings Huizinga, in the second part of his book, which revolves largely around the contrast between Erasmus and Luther, to his most important contrast, between the 'petty' and the 'great' Erasmus. 'Let us try ever to see as much of the great Erasmus' he concludes, 'as the petty one permits.'[12]

While the Erasmus biography was ultimately deeply critical of its subject, Huizinga's life of his friend, the painter and writer Jan Veth, was permeated with deep affection. Where in Erasmus he had depicted the waverer, in Veth he gave a portrait of the seeker. Painting or writing, actively engaging with the social issues of the day or artistic seclusion, these were perhaps the most important choices that Veth faced. And within these choices: portraiture or landscape, art criticism or poetry; and in addition, aesthetic socialism or patriotic art, dedication to art or a professorship. It was these choices that led Huizinga to build his biography out of chapters bearing titles like 'art and history', 'the writer-painter', 'the poet and the man'. It also inspired a twofold division of his book, in which he separated Veth's quest from its fulfilment. For that Veth would indeed discover who he was, about this we are left in no doubt from the very first pages of this book, the most harmonious of Huizinga's portraits.

Contrasts also supply the basic structure of other full-length and briefer studies. An article entitled 'Uitzichten' ('Outlooks') compares two well-known years of Dutch history, 1533 and 1584. In 'Patriotism and Nationalism in European History until 1900',[13] the contrast is even in the title. The same effectively applied to the long essay for *De Gids*, 'Two wrestlers with the angel',[14] in which Huizinga compares the views of history proposed by Spengler and H.G. Wells. In the lecture 'Ideas and moods a hundred years ago',[15] nineteenth-century culture, in the crucial year of 1840, is described as 'coupling the most matter-of-fact, banal notion of usefulness with the ecstasy of Romanticism'. Huizinga here contrasts 'widespread bourgeois complacency' with 'vehement forms of social discontent'.[16]

The pattern is repeated in his studies of the Netherlands. In *Nederlands geestesmerk* ('The national character of the Netherlands'), on a small canvas extending to less than thirty pages, he projects the country's maritime provinces as opposed to the heath-rich hinterland, the centre as opposed to the periphery. The portrait of the Dutch Republic, as Huizinga paints it in unadorned fashion in *Dutch Civilization in the Seventeenth Century*, consists of a series of contrasts, Holland versus the rest, water versus land, burghers versus nobility, trade versus industry, graduates versus those who have not attended university. He continues in the same vein when dealing with his main subject, cultural history – for instance when comparing Cats to Bredero. 'What a contrast! The lord of Zorgvliet, who had pledged his heart to poetry from childhood, and who nonetheless did not set about actually writing poetry until quite late, and who, laden with honours and official posts and earthly possessions, lived to the age of eighty-three without a moment's loss of composure, and the Amsterdam burgher boy, who, with his sparkling wit and poetic fire, survived to just thirty-three. Cats, the graduate, well versed in the classics (he had composed verse in Latin and Greek), Bredero – who, like the greatest writer of all, had small Latin and less Greek – said himself of his knowledge that "only a little school French rattled about" in his head.'[17]

Culturally too, the Dutch Republic differed sharply from the rest of Europe. In the surrounding countries, this was the age of the Baroque, which itself marked a departure from the Renaissance. 'The seventeenth century, in contrast to the sixteenth, signified a return to strict, exclusive formulas, to an austerity of line and form, the suppression of overly elaborate detail in favour of unity and compelling authority.' The 'prescription' of the Baroque, as Huizinga sees it, is based on 'conformity to established standards, whether of doctrine or dominion, plasticity or prosody. Splendour and dignity, theatrical gestures, strict rules and impregnable dogma are in the ascendancy. Dutiful respect for church and state is the ideal. The monarchy as a form of government is deified, while at the same time, each individual state holds to the fundamental rule of unrestrained national egoism and self-will. The whole of public life is conducted in forms of grandiloquent rhetoric posing as supreme seriousness. It is the heyday of pomp and parade, of overblown conventionality.' This prescription applied to papal Italy, to the England of William Laud and the Cavaliers, and to the France of the *grand siècle*, but made a sharp contrast with the Dutch civilization of the seventeenth century.[18]

DESCRIPTION OR CRITIQUE

Here we are clearly dealing with the template that defined Huizinga's experience of reality. It was contrast that gave drama and distinctiveness to history. Through contrasts, form and content blended into an ideal union, and historical narrative and historical fact, narrative principles and narrative themes, coalesced. Contrast created form and dissolved form. It was this that gave history its dynamic thrust and consolidated change into stability. And ultimately, wielding contrasts was for Huizinga himself a form, a creative principle. To make this clear, we must take a close look at the book that both contains his poetics and that seeks to outline the basic model of culture, which is simultaneously descriptive and prescriptive, the biography of a civilization but also a self-portrait: *Homo Ludens*.

Although this work is built up less systematically than most of his books, it was certainly shaped around the same principle of contrast. Play, in Huizinga's view, has contrast embedded at its core. Indeed, he even defines it in terms of contrast, as 'other than reality', as non-seriousness. He then places it alongside other 'major, categorical' binary oppositions, such as wisdom/folly, truth/falseness, good/evil, by observing that play is a completely different, autonomous category, one that cannot be reduced to something else, something more elementary. It is contrast *par excellence*, the cradle of culture. Play precedes culture, culture is born in play. In that sense, it is also the reflection of community life in ancient cultures, which tended to be based on 'an antithetical and antagonistic structure of the community itself'. The primitive dualism that divided primitive tribes into two rival phratries, the yin/yang opposition, all these are basic models that breathe a carnivalesque atmosphere of play.[19]

After a linguistic and abstract analysis of the concept of play, Huizinga takes the reader back to the earliest cultural manifestations in Africa, the Near and Far East, and America, where play takes the form of ritual and contest. In this respect, there is no difference between Native American potlatch ceremonies and Roman *ludi*. 'While in Latin the reference is to sacred contests simply as play, it provides the purest possible expression of the quality of this element of culture.' At the same time he observes that there, in those Roman games, the same mechanism applies as that which he had identified in *The Waning of the Middle Ages*, now formulated in more general terms: as a culture becomes more complex its resources grow more refined, cultural products gradually become detached from play. 'The culture becomes more and more earnest, leaving only a marginal space for play.'[20]

In consequence, play goes 'underground' into complex forms, into judicial proceedings, for instance, which have never entirely lost their flavour of contest (or indeed that of oracle or game of chance) and in other respects too have retained elements of play in their 'otherness' – a separate venue (courthouse), distinctive clothes (judge's robes), a distinctive rhetorical style. Huizinga examines a succession of forms – play and jurisdiction, play and war, play and wisdom, poetry, philosophy, art – from primitive death struggles to sophisticated cultural manifestations, before the final two chapters in which he presents his conclusions.

These two chapters both exemplify Huizinga's views of culture and display the basis for his cultural criticism. The first considers the history of civilization *sub specie ludi*, that is, it appraises diverse civilizations and periods according to their attitude to play. In this regard he finds that the declining years of the Roman Empire and the late Middle Ages have much in common: in both cases, 'civilization is overlaid by a false outer sheen'. After the renewed flowering of the Renaissance, Baroque, and Rococo, the nineteenth century allocated little room for the function of play. Gravity ruled, 'Europe donned its working clothes'. The final chapter, on play in Huizinga's own day, leads seamlessly into cultural criticism, while at the same time placing this phase in perspective, as part of a familiar process.

In these two chapters, Huizinga reflects on a crucial phenomenon. It seems to him that in the twentieth century, contrast has ceased to create form, and has led instead to formlessness. It is as if the sorcerer's apprentice had got hold of the device and sown havoc with it. *In the Shadow of Tomorrow* deals with the ensuing outcome: human thought itself has become ambivalent and 'antinomian'. Huizinga explains this view as follows: 'Antinomian, that is, the idea is suspended as it were between two opposing poles, which had previously appeared mutually exclusive. Ambivalent, that is, that the value judgment of deciding which of two opposing decisions is to be preferred vacillates like Buridan's ass.' Our power of analytical thought has been paralysed by inner conflict.[21]

This leads to a loss of judgement, a decline in the felt need for critical thought, and the eventual betrayal of the ideal of knowledge – all titles of key chapters. 'Behold the pivotal moment in the crisis of civilization: the conflict between *knowledge* and *existence*.' This was nothing new: our knowledge had always fallen short. What was new was modern man's attitude to that insufficiency, an attitude of nihilism and pragmatism. 'Truth is that which possesses essential value for those who profess it. Something is true if and insofar as it is valid for a certain period of time. The dullest of minds could easily grasp this: something applies, so it is true.' Sociology and materialism would do the rest. 'Thus the anti-noetic forces of a century gradually gathered into a mighty current, which would soon be threatening the dikes of intellectual culture that had seemed unassailable.'[22]

THE MODERN ERA

When, precisely, had this catastrophic reversal of modernity occurred? At what juncture had what had previously been superbly organic become irrationally mechanical? Huizinga must have addressed this question at an early stage and repeated it with greater urgency from the First World War onwards. While in *Homo Ludens* he defined the watershed in the nineteenth century, in *The Waning of the Middle Ages* he had placed it far earlier. There, it should be added, his decision did not hinge on some balance between play and earnestness, or on the relationship between knowledge and being, but on that between art and life. And that reversal evidently took place at some point between the Renaissance and the modern age. 'The tide turned when art and life started to diverge, when people ceased to enjoy art in the middle of life, as a noble part of *joie de vivre*, but outside life, as a lofty object of veneration, to which one turned in moments of edification or repose. The old dualism, which set God apart from the world, was thus reinstated in a different form, setting art apart from life. A line was drawn right through the pleasures of life, dividing them in two, a lower and a higher half.'[23]

In his major essay, 'The problem of the Renaissance', Huizinga continued his quest for the roots of the modern age. This essay set out to assign the fifteenth century to its rightful place between mediaeval and modern culture, but the answer was equivocal, to say the least. Huizinga saw no clear contrast between Middle Ages and Renaissance, and even the boundary between Renaissance and the modern age, he decided, was indistinct. 'When we view the fundamental dividing-lines between the older and more recent civilizations of Western peoples, we find that some run between Middle Ages and Renaissance, others between Renaissance and seventeenth century, some cut right through the Renaissance, and more than one crosses a century as early as the thirteenth or as late as the eighteenth.'[24]

Even so, the Renaissance did mark a fault-line, if only because a certain kind of open-mindedness was needed to understand it. Such understanding did not come easily, in Huizinga's view, to punctilious northerners. And this was because the Renaissance was 'one of the triumphs of the Romance spirit'. Those who wanted to comprehend it had to be receptive to that singular mix of gravity and merriment, good humour and irresponsibility, that was largely found in the south. Instead of seeking their own soul everywhere, they needed to have an eye for the things themselves, and especially 'in their finest form'. They must be able to 'see a face by Holbein or Moro and imagine Rabelaisian laughter'.[25]

To grasp the significance of Huizinga's argument here, we must recall his picture of that other renaissance, that of the twelfth century. While the fifteenth-century Renaissance was a triumph of the Romance spirit, that of the twelfth century was no less permeated with Latinism. But the twelfth century had also preserved another, primitive, aspect. And that primitive aspect, 'its Celto-Germanic or older indigenous past', had prepared the ground for the creative outburst that made that century the creator of Europe. In its feudal forms – accolades, tournaments, chivalric orders, vows – chivalry was closely related to the 'archaic' and 'the factor of play was still a vigorous and truly creative principle'. In the twelfth century, the Germanic-pagan and Romance-courtly cultures merged and produced a reformulation of Christianity.[26]

The sea-change that Huizinga identified in the fifteenth century was hence an initial parting of the ways between the two constituents of European culture, the Germanic and Romance lines. It was this that underpinned his deep concern about the First World War. In that war between France and Germany, he saw the creative contrast between Germanic and Romance that ran through the entire history of Western culture widen into an unbridgeable chasm.

In that creative contrast, his own sympathies, at the outset, were evenly divided. In his earliest reading, Huizinga had been enthralled by the richness of early Germanic narratives, from fairy tales to sagas. As a Sanskrit scholar, he praised Toorop for his work inspired by the East Indies, work 'that was so profoundly Germanic in its sentiments, that it gave the unsuspecting viewer notions of the East Indies that were half-way to Schubert'. At the same time, in that mild, sweet poetry of the East Indies, he missed 'the poet's exuberant delight in human existence'. Amid that magical mellowness, he longed for 'a northern cry of harsh melancholy'.[27]

While mellowness turned him away from India, barbarism alienated him from Germany. As a young historian, he had been relaxed about distinguishing between Germanic and Romance influences in his quest for the antecedents of the Dutch sense of national identity, but when he went to Berlin in 1933, to give a major lecture on Burgundy, he subtitled his talk 'A crisis in Romance-Germanic relations'. The phrase bore on his own time. While the Romance spirit had prevailed, politically and culturally, until the eighteenth century, this was followed by 'the great intellectual and material countermovement', in both Britain and Germany. Huizinga was referring to Romanticism, and he said that he was not yet able to envisage its lasting impact.[28]

At the end of his life, in *Geschonden wereld* ('Shattered World'), he could. Or rather, in that book, Huizinga believed – he never lost hope – that he had discovered a new connecting link. The problems facing Italy, Spain, and France were steadily eclipsing the Romance sense of community. As for the sense of Germanic cultural unity, that had already been lost, in his view, in the Migration Age. But in the Anglo-Saxon cultural type, he perceived the heir to both the Romance and the Germanic heritage. Britain appeared politically, culturally, and economically to have been endowed with 'every good fortune that the earth has to offer'. And the Netherlands obviously belonged to this same cultural type. In a number of studies of Dutch identity, he emphasized the Netherlands' in-between position, its transit culture, which had absorbed the influence of the three great cultures surrounding it and which aspired to be the cohesive element between them.

6

HARMONY

Contrast was – in Aristotelian terms – the Prime Mover of Huizinga's imagination. But its resolution, the quest for harmony, came a close second. Contrast generated tension and movement, harmony was balance and rest. Balance is perhaps the most important concept in Huizinga's entire methodological constitution. It was both prescriptive and descriptive, it applied to both scholarship and culture.

As a young linguist, he had opposed a one-sided, rational approach to language. As a historian, he argued against a one-sided emphasis on economic and quantitative history, and as a cultural critic he rejected a one-sided, materialistic development of culture. In Huizinga's world view, the creation of language was poetic impulse rather than pragmatic decision, historiography was a creative process, not a mode of bookkeeping, culture consisted of meaningful ritual, not soulless mechanisms. Throughout his life, Huizinga repudiated the separation of artistic and scientific powers. The historian's task, in his view, was, to combine 'the greatest attainable objectivity' with 'strong subjective emotion'.[1]

He sometimes described these two attitudes, objectivity and

subjectivity, academic distance and passionate involvement, as classicism versus Romanticism. One represented rationalism, the other emotion. He used these two concepts to differentiate between ideal and dream, the beautiful whole and the suggestive detail. But he also said: 'Those who go in search of the dreamland of Romantic moonshine are not infrequently the rigid rationalists of daylight.' 'Do not assume,' he wrote in his 'Brief colloquy on themes of Romanticism',[2] 'that a certain rationalism, a certain sober realism, or even a certain classicism, excludes the Romantic attitude.'[3]

Huizinga struggled with Romanticism, because both nationalism (to which he had an aversion) and history (which he loved), were its offspring. He therefore tried to distinguish the 'bad' from the 'good' Romanticism. He drew a line between pseudo-mysticism and the gentle art of lyricism; between nationalism and the rhetoric of blood and soil on the one hand, and the brotherhood of nations and supranational admiration on the other. There was the Romanticism that despised virtue and the one that venerated virtue, a Romanticism that could be seen as embracing play because it played the game of literature in all seriousness, and a Romanticism that murdered play, because it took literature too seriously.[4]

The fascination and the problem of Romanticism was that it altered one's view of reality, shifting the gaze from the perspective of the rational and moral to 'something that appeared to lie beyond'. What had once been sharply delineated now had blurred contours. 'The gaze ended up between the boundaries of the old concepts, in an atmosphere in which things moved with the nonchalance of delightful incoherence.' Images took the place of concepts here, definition was replaced by 'mood'.[5]

MOOD

The word 'mood' (*stemming*) is one of the most important concepts in Huizinga's idiosyncratic lexicon. It might be called a different word for balance. We see him wielding it in his very first dissertation proposal, 'Introduction and Proposal for a Study of Light and Sound': 'The lyrical formation of a word presupposes a mood to which the word is a fitting response.' The advantage of this term was that moods were not confined to a single sensory organ. It was precisely in that creative amalgam of impressions implicit in a mood, in the collaboration between the senses – in synaesthesia itself – that words came into being. That was why the word was so felicitous: it embraced the cohesiveness of sound and sentiment.[6]

At the same time, the word suggested an unmistakeable fragility. Huizinga emphasized that he was not using it in the sense it possessed in psychology, to denote a 'continuous mental state', but rather as a poetic concept, meaning 'immediate, momentary emotional state'. It was an instant of equilibrium, a clarity, fragile, dreamlike, full of desire. That was the sense in which he elaborated it in his dissertation about the *vidûshaka*. The drama theory from the period of the Indian plays he had discussed included the complex concept of *rasa*, a 'delightful feeling of pleasure', which possessed both a higher and lower form – a sensory and a supersensory aspect – embracing both the pleasure of 'communion of the senses with worldly matters' and 'knowledge'. The higher knowledge manifested itself in three ways: as dream, desire, and poetry. Huizinga therefore believed that the word *rasa* was best translated into Dutch as *stemming*, or mood.[7]

Whenever Huizinga describes a mood, it is in terms of harmony and disintegration, fullness and loss. This comes out well in his description of Old Dutch towns, their plain architecture, 'consisting of a *je ne sais quoi* of [architecturally] highly modest formal rhythm, and an inward-looking privacy'. The beauty of Dutch towns was not purely a matter of architecture. A town was a *Gesamttheater*, a total spectacle, comprising urban structure and the surrounding area, location and life, indeed, even the carillon sounding over the red roofs. It suggested to him nostalgic sentences about 'the inimitable air of genial neglect that gave the Haarlemmer Wood its most intimate charm', about the sad passing of the old Friesland – 'That the land of Bernlef should have been lost!'[8] – about the academic idyll of the eighteenth century – 'The Arcadia of humanity in which the spirit hovered: the world in perfect order and harmony.'[9]

A fine example is the atmosphere of the old main building of Groningen University, which is similarly described in terms of 'genial neglect': a courtyard with tiles 'between which the grass was rampant', a gallery 'covered simply with tiles, which are in plain view from below'. All that a later generation would recall of this old complex, perhaps, was the grey-plastered anatomy theatre. 'An ancient mood was caught in it, when the moon shone over the pentagonal slate roof, with the choir of the church rising behind it.' All this gave the old university the makings of 'a fine, interesting headquarters'. But the decay was too far advanced, the church of the friars had been given back to the Catholics, and in its place the university had acquired the use of the Mennonite church along with a new anatomy theatre and library. 'But it no longer had a public auditorium, and the unity of its buildings had been shattered forever.'[10]

Huizinga's work is peppered with such moods. In *Man and the Masses in America* he had called it by a different name – there it was 'insight' – but he meant the same thing, 'that immensely lucid perception of the innermost quality of things, that sense for what transcends mundane reality'. In American writers, Huizinga encountered a kind of sympathy for reality that he found deeply touching. He perceived in them a moment of insight, of inspiration, in which nature and the supernatural, physics and metaphysics, coalesced.

Like the mediaeval people of *The Waning of the Middle Ages*, they were mindful of the fact 'that all things extend some distance into the world on the other side'.[11]

Huizinga recognized this most clearly in Hawthorne. 'What chiefly lingers in the mind, after reading his fluent, unforced descriptions of nature is the impression of the hazy sunshine and soft-salty warmth of a September day, with the bronze colour and elegiac fragrance of foliage that is about to wither. But beyond simple descriptions of the natural world, Hawthorne seeks to convey the infusion of nature with spirit, the unity of spirit with its surroundings. All around him he feels that atmosphere heavy with significance, that quality that transcends the immediately discernible reality.'[12]

In *The Waning of the Middle Ages*, Huizinga explained what he meant by this 'transcendental' quality. In Van Eyck, the ability to see it had been elevated to an art, in the Arnolfini portrait, for instance: 'The tender intimacy and tranquil peace that would not reappear until Rembrandt, are encapsulated in this work as if it was Jan's own heart. Here we suddenly rediscover the twilight years of the Middle Ages, the era that we know, and that we nonetheless so frequently seek in vain in the literature, history, religious life of those times: the happy, noble, serene and simple Middle Ages of folk songs and church music. How far removed we are here from that shrill laughter and that unbridled passion!' But he also found it on the scene depicted on the back of the *Adoration of the Lamb*, in the image of a copper kettle, and the opening through which we glimpse the street. 'Here, in this silent spectacle, flowers the mystery of the mundane.'[13]

That mystery was experienced pre-eminently in the world of Modern Devotion, in friaries, and among the Windesheimers. There, in that remote and peaceful corner of the world, 'susceptibility was guided enduringly into a silent channel, normalized into a new form of life, that of intimacy'. It was in Thomas à Kempis's *Imitation of Christ*, 'the book that would comfort centuries', that Huizinga found mood in its purest form, and he described it in the same terms as in Hawthorne: 'With its jingling of sentences advancing in parallel forms, and its bland assonances, the *Imitatio* would be prose twice over, were it not that the very monotony of that rhythm recalled the sea on a mild, rainy evening, or the sighs of an autumn wind.'[14]

He encountered that same mood, the same 'realism' – 'a belief in the essence and significance of things' – in seventeenth-century Dutch culture, and he saw it heralded in Erasmus. The 'serenity and harmony' of the *Convivium religiosum*, the *Praise of Folly*, and the Colloquies made Erasmus representative of everything that appealed to Huizinga in the Renaissance. He extols the wealth of imagination in *Praise of Folly*, but what impresses him most is the austerity of line and colour, a certain restraint that gives rise to 'an image of that perfect harmony that makes up the most essential quality of the Renaissance. There is no exuberance, notwithstanding the abundance of matter and thought, but a moderation, an evenness, a lightness and a clarity, the effect of which is as gladdening as it is relaxing.' A fragile idyll is outlined here, the desire for 'a quiet, joyful and yet earnest conversation among good, wise friends, in the coolness of a house beneath the trees'. That is what linked Erasmus directly to the Netherlands of Constantijn Huygens: 'Hofwijck sprouted directly from Erasmus's desire.'[15]

In depicting the mood of the Netherlands, Huizinga applied the same 'realism' that he had called 'symbolism' in *The Waning of the Middle Ages*. The clean and polished aspect of Dutch culture, he felt, was an expression of the value that the average Dutchman attached to the things that make up everyday life. 'It corresponded to his innermost sense of piety, that all of this should be appreciated as God-given.' This was the seedbed of realism in painting, which was actually little more than a love of objects. The Dutch painters 'dressed that life in little imagination but a great deal of mystery, which is how it is'. They were realists in the philosophical sense without knowing it, 'realists in the only sense in which the word was meant to be used; in other words, firmly convinced of the utter reality of the whole of existence, and of each specific thing'.[16]

This realism not only linked the art of painting to reality, it also linked painting to literature, Rembrandt to Vondel. He was not referring here to the Vondel of saints and martyrs, but the Vondel who descended each day into 'the full reality of the present-day Netherlands, into the hectic life of Amsterdam or the mellow rusticity of the Gooi or Kennemerland regions', convinced as he was of the 'fundamental significance of all things, each in its own right, as had been the basis of St Thomas's thinking'. Nor was he thinking of the Rembrandt of the broad sweep, of the *Night Watch* and *The Oath of Claudius Civilis*, but the Rembrandt of the etchings. It was in his small-format works, in particular, that Rembrandt indulged freely in 'the enchantment of the procedure, and drew from the depths of his unfathomable genius that simplest and most convincing expression of the mystery that lies behind all things, in the swiftly drawn lines of a few human figures in a simple setting of architecture or natural scenery'.[17]

According to Huizinga, this sentiment, this mood, permeated the entire intellectual and religious life of the Republic. He situated that life in the merchants' houses in the cities and the country houses just outside them, in the atmosphere of 'the agreeable country life, celebrated by Vondel with the song of blackbirds and nightingales'. Amsterdam in particular, with its concentric canals lined on both sides with stately mansions, 'grand and yet simple', and that far outshone Versailles in architectural value, represented Dutch culture at its richest and most intimate. 'If the atmosphere of the century has been preserved anywhere, it is along the Amsterdam canals on a Sunday morning in spring, or in the late light of a summer evening.' But each of the smaller cities, too – none of which had degenerated into an imitation of Amsterdam – had its own distinctive atmosphere, down to places as small as Hoorn or Enkhuizen.[18]

And that atmosphere was being lost. Full of nostalgia, Huizinga remarks that many Dutch cities had kept the charm of their seventeenth-century history until the end of the nineteenth century. Tramlines and concrete, asphalt and motor vehicles had dispelled that atmosphere, just as the waterways had forfeited their splendour with the disappearance of typical Dutch sailing vessels such as the tjalk. 'An elegiac lament about the loss of beautiful city views and natural scenery should not be dismissed as the reactionary grumbling of an old man,' he says *en passant*. 'The younger generations do not know, nor can they know, the beauty of which they have been deprived, beauty that the older generations of today have known and enjoyed until quite recently.'[19]

The same elegiac tone characterizes *Homo Ludens*. The qualities that transcend the immediately discernible reality manifest themselves pre-eminently in play. Huizinga writes that the heart of play, the ritual act, the sacred deed, is 'more than a seeming actualization, more even than a symbolic actualization. In the spectacle, something invisible assumes an inexplicit, beautiful, actual, sacred form. The participants are convinced that the ritual brings about a certain salvation, and activates a higher order of things than the one in which they usually live.' While it was true that play was struggle and competition, 'above the participants spread the overarching notion of a community, which recognized its members as "humanity", with rights and claims to be treated as "human beings"'.[20]

The entire world of the imagination is predicated on this transcendental quality. Lyricism as such was experienced primarily in play, in dance and in music. All artistic activities – and Huizinga was primarily following the Greeks here – were intimately related to ritual, to holy feast days. 'Nowhere, perhaps, is the cohesiveness between ritual, dance, music, and play described as clearly as in Plato's *Laws*. There it is explained that the gods created thanksgiving feasts out of pity for mortals, who were doomed to suffer, to provide a little respite from their woes, and that they gave them the Muses – with Apollo, their leader – and Dionysus as companions in their festivities, so that this divine festive community might repeatedly restore the order of things among the mortals.'[21]

But play, which achieves its highest significance in such feast days, was as fragile as the mood of a beautiful Dutch city. Since the nineteenth century, the play elements of culture had gradually declined. Play had been taken over by professionals. Seriousness and levity, once integrated, had been pulled apart. On the one side was puerilism, which was having a field day in politics, since public life was ruled by coarseness and pandering to the masses. On the other side was savage seriousness, the reduction of politics to the labels 'friend' or 'foe', and the redefinition of war as *der Ernstfall* – 'things getting serious'.

RITUAL

Homo Ludens shows just how closely Huizinga identified his notion of mood with ritual. That too resurfaces in the rest of his work. On the very first page of *The Waning of the Middle Ages*, he depicts the ritualistic aspect of life in the late mediaeval period, and its 'ostentatious and hideously public' nature. 'Lepers clacked their rattles, and went about in processions, beggars wailed in the churches and displayed their deformities there. Every rank and estate, order and trade, was distinguished by its costume. The great lords never ventured forth without a grandiose display of arms and liveries, arousing awe and envy. The dispensation of justice, hawking, weddings and funerals, all was proclaimed loudly with processions, cries, wailing and music. The lover wore his lady's colours, journeymen the emblems of their fraternity, parties the colours or blazons of their lord.'[22]

What he describes in those first few pages, the 'precarious mood' of elation, cruelty, and tenderness, makes life in a mediaeval city the setting for one long ritual action, of joyous entries and executions, processions and sermons. And above all this was heard the sound of the church bells, which 'for a time suspended it all in an atmosphere of order'. Late mediaeval life was stretched on the framework of party feeling and loyalty to one's sovereign, which was expressed in colours and emblems, devices and mottoes. The royal household was marked by 'a maximum of expressiveness', its ways of life 'elevated, as it were, to mysteries'. A meal at court possessed 'almost liturgical dignity', and the totality of court etiquette was played out in a 'quasi-religious atmosphere'.

The rituals surrounding birth, marriage, and death, in particular, were rooted in primitive beliefs and cults. Huizinga dwells at length on the period's mourning pageantry, funeral services, the diverse ways of displaying grief, announcements of death. Outward shows of sorrow added beauty and sublimity to suffering. Besides mourning, the lying-in bed too afforded ample opportunity to combine a love of splendour with social distinctions. Huizinga devotes an entire chapter to 'the hierarchical conception of society', from aspects of ritual to the division into groups and classes, each with its own customs. Chivalry remained the yardstick and example, with its hero-worship and heroes' relics, tournaments and orders, crusades and duels, epithets and mottoes. But love too was stylized and dramatized, in the whole gamut from coarse sexuality to erotic imagination and courtly asceticism. 'Love formalized' is another chapter devoted entirely to ritual, the significance of colours in clothing, flowers, and jewellery, conventions in conversation and courtship.

And just as earthly matters were infused with religion, religion acquired an earthly dimension. The liturgy of church services, feast days, the multiple forms of worship, all such customs brought the sacrosanct down to earth and melted down its mystery. The literal truth with which people invested the Eucharist, robbing 'the mystery of mysteries' of its divinity, was no different from its counterpart, in which all earthly matters appeared to partake, as it were, of the sacred mysteries. Everyday life itself was ritualized. 'Everything that acquires a fixed place in life,' writes Huizinga, in a discussion of mundane everyday habits, 'that becomes a way of life, is seen as ordained, from the most trivial of habits and customs to the most exalted facets of the divine scheme.' In this world view, everything is given a name, every historical event becomes a parable, every literary episode a moral example, every utterance a dictum. And just as the distinction between religious and profane evaporated, so too did the distinction between art as spontaneous creation and art as an active part of this daily ritual.[23]

In *Homo Ludens*, Huizinga elevates a central element that in *The Waning of the Middle Ages* applies to a specific context of place and time to a universal prerequisite for culture. Culture is born as play and in play, and play is drama. 'Here lie the most crucial connections of play and ritual. That act is always in a sense a sacred act; its relationship to, or correlation with, the divine is always fundamentally present; as soon as play serves to express that relationship, it becomes a form of veneration, ritual, liturgy; it may even become *mysterium*.' And this sacred act created style, 'that indefinable, pure and sublime quality of style that art and society sometimes crave in vain.

Rhythm, repetition, cadence, refrain, closed forms, chords and harmony, all attributes of play, they are likewise all constituents of style.'[24]

This emphasis on rhythm is a key feature of his approach. In Huizinga's view, mediaeval life in its entirety, from fashions in clothing to religious art, was permeated with 'style and rhythm'. A tiny landscape in the *Très Riches Heures du Duc de Berry* struck him as 'perfect in atmosphere and rhythm'. Some subjects, such as the Lamentation of Christ, the Crucifixion, and the Adoration of the Shepherds, virtually encapsulated this rhythmic structure within them. Van Eyck's *Adoration of the Lamb* possessed 'an incomparable rhythm, a triumphant rhythm of all those processions moving with measured step towards the centre'. In ritual or veneration, life itself was governed by rhythm. The mourning traditions of the Middle Ages formalized suffering. 'They rhythmicize grief. They transpose real life to the realm of drama.' In *Homo Ludens*, play is defined with the aid of 'the noblest qualities that human beings can perceive and express in objects: rhythm and harmony'.[25]

Rhythm and harmony, proportion and balance, coincided for Huizinga. Rhythm and harmony were the meaning of life, the significance of culture, the purpose of art. But rhythm was not only drama, it could also be restraint. We have already noted Huizinga's comparison of the 'monotonous rhythm' of the prose of Thomas à Kempis with the breaking of the waves or the sighing of the wind. Fifteenth-century poetry was at its best, he felt, 'when it momentarily evokes a picture, a mood. Its influence relies on its formal elements: image, tone, rhythm. That explains why it can achieve little in works designed on a grand scale and of great length, in which the qualities of rhythm and tone are subordinate, but may be refreshing in genres in which outward form takes precedence: rondeaus and ballads, which are generally structured around a single straightforward idea, and which derive their power from vision, tone, and rhythm.'[26]

In his study of play, and later in his work of cultural criticism *In the Shadow of Tomorrow*, Huizinga used this concept to define certain prescriptive qualities: culture possessed 'a harmonious balance of spiritual and material values and an ideal that is determined primarily homogeneously, which the community's diverse activities all seek to fulfil'. He referred quite deliberately to balance, not to different 'levels'. He wanted to avoid any evaluation in terms of high or low, primitive or sophisticated, just as he wanted to avoid a one-sided emphasis on any single facet of culture, such as religion or art, law or science. 'The state of balance is characterized above all by the circumstance that each of the diverse cultural activities has as vibrant as possible a function in the cohesiveness of the whole. If such a harmony of cultural functions exists, it will manifest itself in the order, forceful articulation, style, and rhythmic life of the society concerned.'[27]

PRECEPTS

But we have moved from description to prescription here. Huizinga identified aesthetics with ethics; more specifically, he associated style with loyalty and order. This added a social dimension to his definition of culture. Culture could not be the domain of the individual, play was an activity to be shared by the community. 'For play presupposes association, in the best sense of the word.' There are three forms of association that he wanted to discuss within this framework, and he himself was intimately associated with all three of them: his country, the university, and the field of historiography. All three were ritualistic contexts, communities that were linked through tradition and ritual, loyalty and ideals.[28]

Huizinga loved the Netherlands with the affection of a vassal. In the opening sentence of 'The national character of the Netherlands',[29] he refers to his days in Haarlem, recalling that whenever he passed a certain house on Zijlstraat he would always look up at the inscriptions on its façade: 'Int soet Nederlant' ['In the dear Netherlands'] flanked by 'Ick blyf getrou' ['I will be faithful'], 'Ick wyck nyet af' ['I will not swerve']. To him, these inscriptions encapsulated the theme of 'the symphony of our own country and nation', a theme which he took up on several occasions, not just in this slim pamphlet published in 1934, but also, and most notably, in the last of his books that he would live to see in print, *Dutch Civilization in the Seventeenth Century*. The harmonious amalgam of which Dutch culture was composed in Huizinga's eyes, a fusion of disparate entities, a cohesive field of freedoms, is best expressed in this book in a production of culture that was not linked to class or riches, and in which even the illiterate masses took part.

This wide-ranging participation in the cultural process, channelled through old forms of association such as civic militias and chambers of rhetoric, and fired by an industrious classicism, imparted a 'friendly and informal' quality to that civilization. The finest example was Constantijn Huygens, a nobleman to be sure, but one who knew the people and presented them in his work. This diplomat and polyglot, well versed in the classics and a sterling musician, poet, and clerk, cast in the mould of John of Salisbury, embodied the ideal that Huizinga sought and found in Holland. 'His entire attitude to life and his clever, often rather too clever, mode of expression,' he says of Huygens 'which nonetheless remains at all times sensitive, with his good-humoured moralizing and his down-to-earth humour, they spring far more directly from the national soul than – for a patrician – one would expect.'[30]

Huizinga's image of the university has the same roots, those of chivalry. For Boucicaut, one of the purest exponents of mediaeval chivalry, the twin pillars of order in the world were chivalry and knowledge, 'chevalerie et science, qui moult bien conviennent ensemble'. Knowledge, faith, and chivalry were the three lilies of the Chapel des fleurs de lis of Philippe de Vitri. The mediaeval university, as Huizinga saw it, was 'in the full sense of the word an arena, a palaestra, entirely analogous to the lists of tournaments. It was the setting for a meaningful and often dangerous game. The actions that took place at the university, like those of chivalry, were in the nature of consecration and initiation, of wager, challenge, and battle. Constant disputes, cast in ceremonial forms, were the stuff of life at a mediaeval university. Like tournaments, they were among the significant forms of social play that bring forth culture.'[31]

Huizinga saw the Netherlands as a country able and willing to serve the world at large; it projected its internal cohesiveness externally in the form of peace. 'With the growth of international organization in the period since the war,' he wrote in 'The Netherlands as intermediary between Western and Central Europe',[32] 'our country has increasingly come to occupy a central position.' He described the university's *raison d'être*, likewise, in terms of duty. 'It is the university's task to lay foundations, to provide perspectives', he wrote in his entry on 'the University' in the fifth edition of the Winkler Prins Encyclopaedia. 'Its task is not to teach what everyone should learn himself. It should not serve "society" in the sense of the technical, economic and political machinery of present-day life, but "the community" in the most literal sense of the word.'[33]

And he viewed the discipline of historiography in the same light. For the cohesiveness and unity of that discipline were likewise based on 'association'. The historical image that a particular epoch formed of itself was never the property of a few individuals, but consisted of 'a certain catholicity of knowledge, a *consensus omnium*'. This consensus embraced the most obscure researcher of minutiae. The value of such an individual's work did not stem from the fact that he was gathering material to be used in later syntheses by greater minds; no, this 'detail worker' produced, 'by polishing one of thousands of millions of facets, the historiography of his age'. 'The researcher of even the most local form of history, together with the small group for whom his theme constitutes a living field of enquiry, is a fully-fledged association of scholarship with its own rituals.'[34]

PASSION
AND
SYNAESTHESIA

7

PASSION

It was in the multi-volume study of the French Revolution by the great Romantic historian Michelet that Huizinga read one of those anecdotes 'whose apparent triviality bears the hallmark of their high probability'. Huizinga loved trivialities of this kind. For instance, the detail that convinced him that Beatrice was a woman of flesh and blood – rather than merely a literary symbol – was that Dante called her by the pet name of Bice. Michelet's anecdote is about Robespierre. Many years after the Revolution, the aging Merlin de Thionville was asked why he had helped to secure Robespierre's conviction. The old man paused before answering, creating a brief impression of regret. Then he suddenly rose to his feet with a fierce gesture, saying: 'Robespierre! Robespierre! ... ah! si vous aviez vu *ses yeux verts*, vous l'auriez condamné comme moi.' Only those who had seen Robespierre's green eyes could understand why the man known as the 'Incorruptible' had been found guilty. 'Could anything provide a more unequivocal lesson,' concluded Huizinga, 'of true historical motivation, and of the misguided bias of an approach that reduces all those men consumed with hatred, fury and delusions to an inventory of political or economic forces? That little anecdote tells us resoundingly: Never forget passion.'[1]

FORMS OF PASSION

For Huizinga, this episode must have produced a shock of recognition. As a young Sanskrit scholar poring over his early dissertation on the *vidûshaka*, passion had already burst through his artful prose. To illustrate what he called 'the skittishness of love', he gave the following quotation: 'If you and your lover are not yet reconciled, dear lady, do cover the fresh marks of nails on your breast with your robe.' Anyone who is inclined to attribute the use of such an example to the testosterone generally associated with a young PhD student should consult the mature historian of *The Waning of the Middle Ages*, where Huizinga revels in the phallic symbolism of wedding night rituals. He describes the battle song for the hymen, the *Hymen o Hymenae*, as a 'full-bodied roar' that no church-ingrained chastity could muffle. Though his descriptions are often couched in formal and indeed at times roundly censored language, Huizinga was no stranger to passionate love, and well knew the havoc it could wreak in a human heart.[2]

His entire oeuvre is peppered with the diverse forms assumed by passion. In his study 'From the early history of our sense of national identity', for instance, passion presents itself as hatred.[3] 'Froissart tells us that when Albrecht of Bavaria landed in Friesland in 1396, a woman dressed in blue cloth suddenly burst "comme folle et esragée" ["like an enraged madwoman"] through the Frisian crowds lining the dyke waiting for the attack, towards the ships from Hainault and Holland; in full view of the enemy forces she lifted her skirts and blouse and showed them her posterior, at which she was immediately assailed by a shower of arrows and killed by the warriors who had jumped ashore.' In *The Waning of the Middle Ages* it takes the form of cruelty, in an account of the purchase of a brigand leader by the people of Bergen – 'at far too high a price' writes Huizinga, as if there were standard rates for such things – for the sheer sport of quartering him.[4]

Note the detail and feeling for burlesque in his description of the hanging of a rapacious *jonker* in Paris in 1427. 'The execution was attended by an eminent official, grand treasurer in the service of the regent, who came to vent his hatred of the prisoner; he ensured that the man's request to have his confession heard was rejected; he climbed up the ladder behind him, berating him with curses, hit him with a stick, and thrashed the executioner for admonishing the victim to think of the salvation of his soul. The executioner, startled, botched his work; the noose broke, the poor convict tumbled down, breaking his leg and some ribs, in which condition he was obliged to climb the ladder again.'[5]

Any notion that vehement passion was peculiar to Indian antiquity or the remote Middle Ages was repudiated in *Man and the Masses in America*. This book dwells on the party conventions that nominated presidential candidates, and describes the memorable convention of 1860 in Chicago at which Lincoln secured the Republican nomination. Both he and his rival, William Seward, had brought along a sizeable contingent of supporters. The convention opened in breathless silence, but no sooner was Seward's name mentioned than his supporters burst into enthusiastic applause. At the mention of Lincoln's name the response was many times louder, 'rising and raging far beyond the Seward shriek', as the chronicler reported. But the Seward faction would not be cowed, and started hollering in such an excruciating pitch that all present were forced to plug their ears. One final opportunity remained for Lincoln's supporters: could they outdo the concerted screech of Seward's supporters? They could, almost bringing the building down around their ears. 'It was in this atmosphere of heightened tension that the vote was held; amid the immediate physical intoxication of the yelling, the required number of votes accrued to Lincoln. The exhausted politicians staggered home as if drunk.'[6]

THE AESTHETIC COMPONENT

Huizinga sees passion roughly as a historical sensory organ. This may create a sense of unease in the minds of present-day readers raised on a strict diet of epistemology and objective scholarship. But Huizinga's thinking and writing sprang from a different – literary – tradition. 'Long before the historian starts hypothesizing,' he said in his inaugural address at Groningen University, 'long before the poet bends his mind to metre and rhyme, they are united by an inner predisposition.' In that address, 'On the aesthetic component of historical accounts',[7] his subject was accordingly more of a psychological than an epistemological problem. He enquired whether we had not become too docile and too humane to comprehend history. How in heaven's name was one to form a conception of the passion of centuries past, 'of barbarian pride, of the deference to divine right, of the feudal concept of bondage and loyalty'? Yet that was what Huizinga asked of the historian, that he should adopt the perspective of what he called 'the strong bias of former generations'. A historian must be capable of 'delighting simultaneously in Van Eyck and Rembrandt, the Rococo and Millet, of being a rationalist with Diderot and a Calvinist with the Beggars'.[8]

Time and again he repeated that modern man lacked the wherewithal to comprehend the past in all its passion, in its sharp contrasts. 'Modern men are generally incapable of imagining the unbridled excess and inflammability of the mediaeval mind.' Anyone studying the official sources from mediaeval times might easily conclude that the period's political transactions did not differ so very greatly from 'the politics pursued by ministers and ambassadors in the eighteenth century'. But this would be to overlook an essential quality: 'the vivid hue of the fervent passion that animated commoners and sovereigns alike.' A little later – still, needless to say, in *The Waning of the Middle Ages* – 'The Middle Ages knew none of the emotions that have made our own sense of justice fearful and faltering ... Where we, in our hesitancy and semi-contrition, apply lenient sentences, mediaeval justice knows only two extremes: the full measure of cruel punishment and clemency.'[9]

Huizinga's work abounds in such examples of the misguided and misleading subtlety we bring to sharp antitheses. One of the finest is found in the long essay he published in *De Gids* about Joan of Arc, 'Bernard Shaw's saint'. In that essay he set out to explain why Shaw does not succeed in transporting his play's audience to the Middle Ages. It is not just a lack of empathy with the period, an inability to identify with Joan of Arc's century – the century of *The Waning of the Middle Ages*. The problem is bound up with 'a dramatic failing of a far more serious kind: a lack of elevated style'. Shaw was incapable of 'transposing our spirits to an atmosphere in which all passions and emotions acquire greater potency, in which each word must go deeper and sound more solemn than in everyday life'. What he meant was that Shaw should have spent less time poring over the mediaeval chroniclers and more time reading Shakespeare.[10]

In the meantime, he had given the meek scholars of the twentieth century a few similar tips, in that inaugural address, to help bridge the chasm that separated them from passion. The historian must hone all his senses, must learn to see, hear, smell, taste. He must read literature, feast his eyes on art. Anyone who wanted to understand the demise of antiquity should go and look at the mosaics of Ravenna. 'From then on, whenever you think of those centuries, you will always see that stiff splendour, the glitter of green and gold in San Vitale, the glimmer of nocturnal blue in the burial chapel of Galla Placidia. Your historical picture of that era will have been illuminated by those memories for all time.' But books and pictures did not suffice. A historian must also explore nature, 'walk across meadows and hills, until he can also see the sun shining in the past'.[11]

There was nothing wrong with a minor anachronism here and there. We have already seen that Huizinga could look at the fifteenth century through the eyes of Guy de Maupassant or Oscar Wilde. To understand how chastity and sensuality could coexist in the Middle Ages, he urged readers to go and look at a painting by Burne Jones. Those who followed Huizinga's gaze saw a line leading straight from the calendar miniatures through Rembrandt's etchings and Murillo's street urchins to the figures in Steinlen's street scenes. Besides visiting museums, historians were also counselled to take trips abroad. Anyone who wanted to imagine the impact of itinerant preachers in the Middle Ages could drink in 'the atmosphere of Anglo-American revivalist meetings or the Salvation Army'. Certain forms of hospitality were easier to imagine by consulting 'Spanish customs', and the mediaeval sense of honour could be clarified by looking at attitudes among 'many Oriental peoples', while the way in which the Middle Ages formalized suffering could still be seen in 'relatively primitive civilizations' such as that of the Irish.[12] Seeing and touching – that was what mattered to Huizinga. For instance, he had developed his own theory about the genesis of the towns of the western Netherlands: by passing through them on his bicycle. It was that journey that had prompted his melancholy passages on the evaporating charm of the seventeenth-century town centres. These were not purely aesthetic laments; he also deplored the destruction of sources of knowledge. As a child sitting in a train near Amsterdam, he had followed his father's finger as he pointed out some hundred windmills that could still be seen in the direction of the River Zaan. That was why he fiercely opposed each fresh proposal to fill in a canal or alter the alignment of buildings. A 'genteel neglect' was what he wanted, somewhere in between the cavalier disregard of his own time and the clinical restoration practised today.[13]

It was this belief in passion that led him, in his contribution to the theory of historiography that exercised the strongest hold over the imagination of his readers – his concept of 'historical sensation' – to emphasize direct contact. A print or a notarial deed, a suit of armour 'with its fine, almost organic curves', or an old loom 'in its black oak strength', such objects gave Huizinga a sensation of 'merging' – that was what he called it – with the world they represented. He experienced such direct contact with the past as 'pathos, a moment's drunkenness'. And it was recognizable for all those 'who are familiar with the passion for the past and the charm of authenticity'.[14]

PASSION AND FORM

Huizinga's emphasis on passion is directly linked to the prominence in his work of contrasts. It also explains his preoccupation with form and ritual. Tightly-knit form is the bridle that keeps passion in check. This link between passion and form is already in evidence in his dissertation on Ancient Indian drama. He writes of a tendency to dismiss the poetry of Indian drama as 'artificial grandiloquence'. But this is to misunderstand that poetry. While it is easy to imagine that the formality of the language may pose an obstacle to appreciating its beauty, he says, 'once you have absorbed all those clichés in the full force of their significance, they come to represent emotional states. They are banal only when their use is unfounded: when embedded in the action itself, as here, they greatly intensify the emotion that is conveyed. The Indians knew this, and it is to their credit.'[15]

The best illustration, once again, is *The Waning of the Middle Ages*. The emphasis on form that characterizes that book stems from the passion that is its theme. The stronger the passion, the more constricting the forms. Huizinga wanted to provide 'forms of life and thought' where the fundamental content, passionate life itself, could hardly be apprehended. 'The passionate and violent spirit,' he wrote, 'both callous and easily moved to tears, ever fluctuating between the blackest despair at the world and delight at its dazzling beauty, could not manage without the strictest rules for life. It was essential to constrain the emotions in a fixed framework of conventional forms; that was how society acquired rules and order.'[16]

The whole book revolved around 'ceremonial form', 'the stylization of intense emotion'. 'For eroticism to be [part of] culture,' he wrote, 'it must at all costs find a style, a convention that constrained it, a mode of expression that veiled it.' (Let us not fail to note – once again – how purely this is formulated, the chastity of this 'veil'.) The cohesion of formal constraints and passion even embraces the central proposition of the book. The mediaeval ideal was encapsulated precisely in its formal features, in magnificent hyperbole. 'It is as if the mediaeval mind in its bloodthirsty passion could only be guided by setting ideals that were far too high: that was how the Church worked, that was how the notion of chivalry worked.'[17]

This unity of passion and formal constraints turns up throughout Huizinga's oeuvre. In his book on America, Huizinga traces the passion of American life back to the primitive nature of life in the wilderness. At the same time, he warns against construing the contrast between passion and form – here between individualism and conventionalism – too rigidly, 'as if the wilderness awakened personality and city living awakened the herd instinct'. 'Spontaneous intensity too can manifest itself *en masse*, a tendency that will only be enhanced by life in the wilderness. Extreme turmoil and convention are by no means mutually exclusive.' This idea is elaborated in its most extreme form in *Homo Ludens*, which describes culture as a whole as stylized zeal, as passion subdued into harmony. Play *is* passion. 'Why do players lose themselves in their passion; why does a contest drive a crowd of thousands to a frenzy? No biological analysis can explain that intensity. And yet that very intensity, that capacity to inflame, is its core, its quintessence.'[18]

PASSION AND PICTURABILITY

A lack of passion, like the absence of contrast, makes the past invisible. That explains why Huizinga shifted his focus from ancient India to the Western world. Contrast, drama, passion, they had all ostensibly been filtered out of Indian life, robbing culture of individuality and shades of nuance. 'The Indians created worlds with their minds, and illuminated them with the radiance of their wisdom, but they themselves, the people, always remain outside in the dark. We do not know a single historical Indian in the same way that we know, say, St Francis of Assisi.' The Buddhists believed that grief and distress sprang from what is precious to someone. Where nothing was precious, there was no suffering. But neither was there any action, beauty, or love. 'Does that sound like an age,' demanded Huizinga in his public lecture in 1903, 'that devotes all its great inner passion to holy works and to the beauty of all things?'[19]

Passion is a kind of 'deep freeze' that preserves all the vitamins intact. 'The great fact remains,' Huizinga remarks of Abelard, 'that a twelfth-century writer was able to understand and express love in a timbre and colour so profound and yet intense that today, eight centuries later, every reader can still feel the truth and life in it.' The particular form used by the imagination in conveying passion is therefore of lesser importance. 'Whether it is a mythical, epic, dramatic, or lyrical representation, an ancient saga or modern novel, the object, conscious or unconscious, is always to use words to generate tension, which will keep the listener (or reader) enthralled. The aim is always to move, to achieve an effect. And the substratum is always a situation involving human life, or a case of human emotion, that is suitable for conveying that tension. The number of such situations or cases, it may be added, is not very large. In the broadest sense, the vast majority are situations involving conflict or love, or a mixture of the two.'[20]

Without passion there would have been no history, and no historiography. Unreadable history, in Huizinga's view, was no history at all. And readability meant drama, it meant passion. Historiography was only readable if the history itself was readable, if the dramatic element was not just the consequence of design but an integral part of the reality itself. And this principle certainly applied to earlier eras. For the more recent past, however, Huizinga was less sure of its validity. He had the idea – oddly, for someone who had lived through the First World War – that his period lacked the element of epic drama, as a result of which recent history had acquired an amorphous quality.[21]

The main example he advanced to illustrate this eccentric view was taken from American history, but he also found evidence for it in a comparison of the French and Russian Revolutions. Whether one read the story of the French Revolution in Michelet or Carlyle, Taine or Aulard, it was always a series of lively scenes and colourful moments, 'a succession of highly striking, imaginable, to some extent distinct events full of human action and personal idiosyncrasy', 'a picture charged with epic and dramatic power'. This could hardly be said of the Russian Revolution. In fact any doctrinal Marxist would have poured scorn on such colourfulness. 'The worse for history, I reply. A history that cannot be compressed into tragedy has lost its form.'[22]

But that was precisely what had happened with American history. This could not be blamed on the faulty vision of scholars or any failure of historical imagination; it was rooted in 'a change in the components of history itself'. There was nothing intrinsically wrong with the American Revolution. The later opposition between the North and the South, combined with the fact that actions in public life were still those of an elite, involving human beings rather than mass movements, imparted to history 'its guise of epic struggle'. 'That epic is not the product of literary imagination, but inscribed in the facts themselves. Abraham Lincoln and Robert Lee are opposed in the manner of an Agamemnon and a Hector. The true heroism of the lanky lawyer from Illinois is not an effect of romantic veneration or the elegant clustering of details, it is part of the historical form of the events. Lee's surrender at Appomattox and Lincoln's death are the final act of a tragedy, in the fullest sense of the term.'[23]

But after that, American history lost its dramatic turbulence; it became impossible to paint or remember. The loss of the political divide, the growing influence of economic factors, the ultimately largely quantitative valuation of all relationships made history impossible to picture. Historiography itself, as an intellectual product, became infected with it. 'To a growing extent it is concerned with the analysis of collective variables, and number is becoming the lord and master of idea. But in numbers the story collapses and no picture is formed.' The historical concept shifted its ground from historiography itself to the periphery, to archaeology, theology, literary theory, and art history. The historical form itself disappeared.

PASSION AND HUIZINGA

That was why Huizinga assigned such a prominent role to passion in his own life, both political and personal. He wanted the political division he had witnessed in America for his own country. The unmistakeable enjoyment with which he described the party convention of 1860 indicates what he found lacking in the Dutch political culture of proportional representation. The mistake had been made with the restoration of the monarchy. The Netherlands was so eager to forget the old factions, the division into States' and stadholder's parties, that 'the tired nation had lain down to sleep, after a little cheering, in the shade of the Orange tree'. Huizinga had nothing against the House of Orange; on the contrary, he saw it as no less idyllic than his native country, with which he identified it. But politics without passion was an impossibility. 'Now that this contrast had been removed, political life scarcely bore any resemblance to the old historical constructions, any more than the new political vocabulary with its desiccated French town hall vocabulary resembled everyday speech.'[24]

If only the Netherlands had paid more attention to Van Hogendorp. 'A more centralized administration, more federalism. A truly organic nobility with entailed estates and seignorial rights.' Huizinga did not thrill to the notion of equality, nor did he welcome the bogus modernity of 1814, which he saw as mere political apathy. In the state envisaged by Van Hogendorp, 'the old élite would continue to feel more at home, and the people might have had more to hate, instead of just begging'. The system of proportional representation, which had been introduced in 1917, was the culmination of the new order. It seemed straightforward and just – with each opinion acquiring as much influence as it had support – but its net effect was to drain the life out of politics, saddling it with 'a single pudding tin with which to make the same pudding again and again for four years at a time'.[25]

He wrote those words in 1938, in an article marking the fortieth anniversary of Queen Wilhelmina's accession to the throne. Four years earlier, in 'The national character of the Netherlands', he had fulminated against what he saw as the wholly obsolete system of parties, which had been fossilized by the blunder of proportional representation. The consequence of that system was a distribution of interests enforced right down to the lowest reaches of society, which mechanized the life of the state and killed politics. He regarded it as 'an abdication of all true political principles' for the distribution of power to become a matter of parity. 'The notion of this or that post being a "Catholic vacancy" or a "liberal vacancy" should be alien to our political life.' In Huizinga's view, there should be only three parties, corresponding to the three possible political temperaments: conservative, progressive, and radical, supplemented by some kind of 'spoils system'. He favoured the Anglo-Saxon 'winner takes all' election model. That would revive passion.[26]

Yet it is in his concept of love, rather than in his political preferences, that we encounter Huizinga's blend of ardour and convention, of passion and harmony, in its purest form: in that glorious eighth chapter of *The Waning of the Middle Ages*, 'Love Formalized'. On the one hand, the whole of knighthood had acquired its knowledge and expertise from *Roman de la Rose*, that is, from an *ars amandi*, a manual for the art of love. On the other hand, Dante was the first to develop an ideal of love 'with a negative tonic' – that of loss and deprivation – which Huizinga calls 'one of the most significant changes in the mediaeval mind'. Between the *Roman de la Rose* and the *Vita nuova*, between the canonization of the female genitals and love viewed as a state of sacred knowledge, lies a dialectics that Huizinga also identified later in the oxymorons of Alan of Lille's superb cadence: 'Pax odio, fraudique fides, spes iuncta timori / Est amor et mixtus cum ratione furor': 'Love is peace joined to hatred, loyalty to treachery, / hope mixed with fear, and fury with reason'.[27]

One of the great examples of such passion was Heloise's love for Abelard: 'a wild, dark, love, a heart torn by the utterly conflicting forces of strong faith and the deepest earthly passion'. In Heloise's outpourings there is something so immediate, so extravagant, that one is driven to enquire where any parallel might be found outside Shakespeare. 'She would not hesitate to follow him, she says, if she saw him hurrying towards hell. Let him not imagine that she has regained her good health in her convent. Far from it. She is still more fearful of wounding him than of offending God.' Here too, Huizinga sought parallels in literature to tap into an older, more original, more primitive sentiment, this time in the Icelandic sagas, to enable readers to distinguish, in Heloise's love, 'an older and weightier note'.[28]

The central observation in this essay is Huizinga's assertion that the authenticity of the letters stands or falls with Heloise's contribution. 'How could Abelard have discovered the deepest notes of boundless female passion, other than by shared experience?' In much the same way, Hugo Grotius needed Mary Reigersberg. 'Mary represents that other side of the period: everything that is immediate and as warm as blood, the side of Jan Steen and Pieter de Hooch. ... In the life of this courageous and natural woman, that we see flowering in the early years of pure and joyful matrimonial love, only to wither into a sorrowful hardening of spirit over her wretched fate and the cares of the family, there was more true tragedy than in that of her great husband, that illustrious exile.' These considerations also inspired him to make his telling comparison of Grotius to Erasmus. 'Hugo was no more a born martyr than Erasmus; it was his wife who spurred him to his most vigorous actions. Ah, if only Erasmus had had a Mary Reigersberg at his side!'[29]

One of the most beautiful love stories in *The Waning of the Middle Ages* is that of Guillaume de Machaut. Just as Picasso said that Gertrude Stein would end up looking like the portrait he had painted of her, and in which she was unable to recognize herself, so Huizinga duplicated the story of Guillaume de Machaut in his second marriage. True, Huizinga was not an impoverished poet, he was neither sickly nor blind in one eye, and he did not acquire gout until later in life. But the age gap between the sixty-five-year-old historian and the twenty-eight-year-old Auguste Schölvinck, who became his wife in 1937, was large enough to remind us – and him too perhaps? – of the sixty-year-old Guillaume and his eighteen-year-old Péronelle.[30]

Huizinga tells the story in his by now familiar style. He starts by emphasizing its truth. This point is written into the very title of Machaut's poem: *Le livre du Voir Dit*, a 'true history'. In a scornful footnote he rebuts the hypothesis that the matter dealt with is not, as the text maintains, a true love story. He then goes on to discuss the story itself, the letters, the poems, the first meeting – 'full of fears regarding his shortcomings he goes to their first rendezvous, and great is his joy in discovering that his appearance does not put off his young ladylove' – the high point being a pilgrimage that gives the lovers an opportunity to spend a few days together. There is that afternoon nap, when Péronelle invites the timid poet to lay himself down to rest between her lady's maid and herself. And then comes the invitation, at the end of the journey, to awaken her to take his leave. 'And although even on this occasion [the poet] continues to use the words "honour" and "honest", it is not clear, in his fairly candid account, what she may have denied him.'

We might well bear this context in mind, when reading the letters that Huizinga wrote to his Guste in 1937. The early ones were written from Paris, where he imagined going to a beauty salon for hair transplants and to replace the grey with brown, to get his nose bleached, his spine stretched, his waist laced up. How happy Guillaume de Machaut would have been, had such modes of intervention had been available to him. And Huizinga practised the same chastity as the mediaeval poet. For abstention received just as much emphasis as passion. His beloved helped him by asserting her lack of sexual desire, and for his part he stressed that sexuality could not be the primary feature of their marriage. 'You see, our marriage will necessarily be – more than one with a more normal age difference – one of moderation and control.' And so Huizinga lived through his own middle ages, in the same pathos of intimacy that he discerned in the paintings of Van Eyck. Everything that Guste meant to him was enclosed in her 'delicious intimacy', as he called it. On 13 July 1937 he ended a letter: 'My dearest child, I hold you in my arms, and kiss you more intimately, but also with more purity – more holiness? I know no word for it – than ever.' Had he not said in *The Waning of the Middle Ages* that eroticism must always be trying to contact 'the sacred that had long been lost'?[31]

CODA

'Sixteen and sixty,' wrote Marina Tsvetaeva in her 'Moscow Diaries' about the age gap between lovers 'is not unnatural, and more importantly, there is absolutely nothing absurd about it. It is in any case less absurd than those so-called "well-balanced" marriages. It admits the possibility of true passion.' One of her poems reads as follows:

I heeded neither God nor commandment in life.
Until they sing a requiem over my grave, I will sin
As I sin – as I sinned – with passion!

The Lord has given me senses, all five.
Friends! And you accomplices, who seduce me! – Tender teachers!
Brothers in evil, one day you will all – Trees and stars and clouds and boys and girls –
Earth, stand with me at the last court before God's throne!

Huizinga did keep to God's commandments when at all feasible, and sinning was not his principal talent. But no one need be surprised if, at the gates of heaven, he did not wait with the noblemen and honourable personages of the historiographer's profession, but with the boys and girls of the poet's.[32]

8

SYNAESTHESIA

The poet Marina Tsvetaeva said that she sinned 'with all five senses'. And that is how Huizinga wrote. What he called 'aesthetic observation' was in reality *synaesthetic*. Take this sentence by Herodotus, which Huizinga quoted on numerous occasions in his work, about the battle of Salamis: 'And when [Xerxes] saw the whole Hellespont hidden by ships, and all the beaches and plains of Abydos filled with men, he called himself happy – and the moment after burst into tears.'[1] Huizinga comments: 'Instantly it appears before our eyes: the sun on the white sails, the teeming multitudes, the glint of armour and the patches of red clothing. We hear the sound of voices, and the splashing of waves, we taste the salty breeze.' In other words: 'seeing' involves all the senses at once, 'seeing' stands for synaesthesia.[2]

SIGHT

It would be hard to name a more sensual writer in the whole of Dutch literature, let alone in historiography. His strongest sense is that of sight. 'I cannot recall when the idea took root in my mind,' he writes in his memoirs, 'that historical observation is best expressed as a view of, or better still as an evocation of, certain images.' He had previously written that a historian does not just 'draw the contours around the forms he designs, but colours them in with vivid detail and lights them up with visionary suggestion'.[3]

Huizinga's visual sensitivity was highly developed, and he must have recognized a similar talent in the playwrights of ancient India. He quotes the visual metaphors he finds in their work with obvious delight: the *vidûshaka*'s bald head, like 'the knee of a young camel', or the poor man himself, 'bursting with the king's secret, like a dinner guest sated with exquisite dishes', or the moon, 'as red as the cheek of a pouting sweetheart', or a buffalo, 'its muffled snorting like that of an affronted dandy'. Then there is the butcher's boy who rinses tripe 'as if it was an old skirt'. The historian went to work in the same way. When writing his studies of Haarlem as a young man, he was already concerned with whether readers could 'form a picture of what is reconstructed historically'.[4]

Huizinga expected historiography to formulate clear and precise questions. But if these questions were not embedded in vivid descriptions of location or action, the historian had failed. So he himself took pains to make the old Haarlem almost tangible, in its picturesque judicial traditions, its bustling marketplace, and vibrant industries, conjuring up a picture of the real life of a city from the parchment world of charters. 'The city engages in a motley range of trades and businesses. Of the merchandise imported from foreign parts, we see cloth, fur goods, pedlar's wares, wine and beer, iron and steel, salt and grain. In the environs we find trade in hides, fish, butter, livestock, peat, hay, and cane. The townspeople themselves are active fishermen. There is nothing remarkable here: this is the picture of lively comings and goings we would find in any mediaeval town, however small.'[5]

This is also the power of *The Waning of the Middle Ages*, of course, in which we look over the mediaeval townsman's shoulder, as it were, as if peering through a hole in the castle or city wall, at everyday life as it is lived from the highest to the lowest circles. 'In the kitchen (let us picture here the heroic kitchen, now the only remaining part of the duke's palace at Dijon, with its seven gigantic chimneys), in the kitchen then, the presiding chef has seated himself between chimney and sideboard, from where he can survey the entire room. In his hand he would have held a large wooden spoon...' Elsewhere, we find the furious exchange between Philip the Fair and his son, the later Charles the Bold, in which the old duke flies into such a rage about his wilful son that he leaps onto his horse and roams the countryside all night in inky darkness and foul weather. 'Tired and hungry the duke roves, and his cries go unanswered. He is drawn to a river, mistaking it for a path; the horse shies away just in time. He falls, along with his horse, and is hurt. In vain he strains his ears for the crowing of a cock or the barking of a dog, which might lead him to human habitation.'[6]

While he had seen the kitchen at Dijon with his own eyes, when it came to describing the duke's wrath and his nocturnal peregrinations, Huizinga borrowed the eyes of the mediaeval chronicler Chastellain. He too was blessed with acute visual sensitivity, which Huizinga illustrates by citing the chronicler's account of Charles the Bold's first visit to Ghent. That visit coincided with the arrival of a fair or *kermis*, and ended in pandemonium: 'Again and again spontaneous details show us how clearly the writer saw all outward things. The duke confronting the insurgents sees before him 'a multitude of faces in rusty helmets, framing the grinning beards of villains, biting their lips'. The cries go from low to high. The fellow who elbows his way to the window, beside the duke, wears an iron gauntlet varnished in black, with which he strikes the window-ledge to command silence. This ability to convey such precise and immediate observations in a few simple, trenchant words is the literary equivalent of the perfect expression that Van Eyck's magnificent visual acuity achieved in painting.'[7]

And what applied to Chastellain applied to Erasmus too. 'Mark the consistency with which Erasmus describes his characters and scenes. For he sees them.' It basically applied to the whole of Dutch culture in the sixteenth and seventeenth centuries, which was pre-eminently visual in nature and which turned writers into painters. That was why it was possible to walk around Amsterdam using the writers' descriptions and really *see* the city: 'That was how Vondel saw it.' And that was Huizinga's own approach, for instance in his portrait of Johan de Witt. 'There he stands, "Long John", with his shrewd features, from which the flamboyant sensuality of Hanneman's portrait did not fade until his later years. Cheerful, lively, as strong as an ox and indefatigable, one of those delightful natures that tackle mundane affairs with vigour and élan.' And in his behaviour at the aldermen's festive dinner in Amsterdam on Christmas Day, 1668: 'Long John charms everyone with his elegant manners; he does not disdain any effect: he dances and plays the violin, indulges in card tricks and mathematical conundrums.'[8]

If no such 'picture' was formed in the mind's eye, it was generally because of a lack of affinity. That was the handicap of the historian Robert Fruin, for instance: 'In reading Erasmus and Grotius, he did not see their picture of the world.' And for the same reason, Huizinga himself could not plumb the depths of the Dutchman of around 1800. 'I can't get a picture of him,' he sighed, 'the Batavian of 1795 seems like a puppet to me, and the Restoration man a Chinese shadow.' His picture of the Batavians remained as shaky as 'the sorry chain of the Union, as oddly *vieux-neuf* as their well-groomed stage-robber formal dress. At best I can discern the dry, rarefied scent of an old chest of drawers with letters, melancholy, and snug...'.⁹

That addition of scent is noteworthy: the visual alone could sometimes be a handicap. It reduced Bredero's plays to 'painted drollery', and that was no more likely to raise a laugh than painted tragedy would move one to tears. The fact that the plays of Vondel and Bredero were predominantly visual made them essentially impossible to act. It removed the element of drama.

COLOUR AND FLAVOUR

Since looking came so naturally to Huizinga – 'zum Schauen geboren, zum Sehen bestellt'¹⁰ – what moved him most was the colour in history. Or more precisely, the colour *of* history, as he himself said of the Middle Ages: that life in that era had 'in many respects the colour of a fairy tale'. Huizinga dreamt history in colour. He describes how everything in the Middle Ages had its fixed colour and significance, the green and violet of the lying-in chambers, but also white, azure and green in clothing, flowers, and jewellery, each of which had its 'tender significance'. The 'sombre splendour' of the black of mourning stood out against the background of the 'colourful patchwork' of mediaeval life. And then the king of France was suddenly mourning in red! Or the king of Armenia, Leo of Lusignan, did so in white. Red was the most beautiful colour, and brown the ugliest, green aroused feelings of tenderness, combinations such as pale yellow and blue, orange and pink, and black and white were commended. Every colour had its own symbolic associations: green was for amorous love, blue stood for faithfulness.¹¹

These examples seem to suggest that late-mediaeval culture was pervaded by a 'thirst for colour'. The founder of a religious order dreamt of 'a feast of colours' for the garments of his Order of the

Passion, red, green, scarlet, azure, white, and black. He dwells at length on the 'magnificent display of glowing colours' in Van Eyck, green, gold, and deep red. The dominant colour in all this is red: indeed, Huizinga refers to the late Middle Ages as 'this red era'. The whole feudal age, with its love of pomp and circumstance, is 'crimson'. It is the red of passion, the image of passionate people and their 'sins flowering in red'. It is also the colour of the evening sky, 'the sunset of a culture that is expiring', accentuated by the writer's mood as he was writing the book.[12]

These same colours initially seemed to be appropriate for the book he was dreaming of writing about the seventeenth century. Huizinga imagined a book 'that would sing of those two triumphant sunsets: Rembrandt's in blood-drenched golden clouds, and Vondel's in pure celestial radiance'. Huizinga wrote this in his essay about Johan de Witt, at the same time that he was working on *The Waning of the Middle Ages*. The turning-point of De Witt's career came in 1668, 'when the failure of his life's work loomed behind him like a copper-coloured thundery sky'. Later on, he would base his picture of the Republic primarily on the first part of the seventeenth century, trying to keep the Baroque out of the picture for as long as possible.[13]

That implied that the period took on a completely different colour. From then on, the Netherlands was associated with the primary colours red, white and blue, 'so clear and simple', or with the colour orange, 'so fresh, new and beneficent'. In Huizinga's eyes, Huygens's poem *Hofwyck* mirrored the country and its people as they had been 'when all the wooden boards of boats or sheds that could be coloured were painted in cheerful green, white, red, yellow and blue'. In this respect too he was inconsistent, since Vermeer's palette was 'a symphony in blue and green and yellow. Bright, vivid red was scarcely known to Vermeer.' Indeed, to drive home the distinction between the aristocratic England and bourgeois Holland, he invokes the usual contrast between the countless applications of red in England and the Dutch 'tradition of plain grey', concluding: 'Aside from all the possible shades of grey, all we know is a great deal of green and a little blue.'[14]

In this way, every age acquired its own colour. The twelfth century was like the stained-glass windows of churches: one minute it was bright blue, then blazing red, then white. The colour of the Middle Ages was clearly bleaker, but at the same time it was 'a colour that will not stick'. The Renaissance – in the eyes of the dreamer in any case – was 'purple and gold', defined a little later as 'sunshine and the sound of brass'. Later still, but in the same piece, Huizinga refers to 'the bright sunshine of the Italian quattrocento'. With the passage of time, that brightness and that resonance only increased, at least in the surrounding countries it did, but not in Holland. The Dutch seventeenth century was not an age of 'golden lustre'. As for the Romantic period, in many respects it repeated the colours of the Middle Ages, green, red and silver, black, blue and gold.[15]

When Huizinga denied the seventeenth-century Netherlands any 'golden lustre', he added that the name 'Golden Age' was completely misplaced. 'It savours of the *aurea aetas*, that mythological paradise that we already found a little tedious as schoolboys reading Ovid. If our glorious century must have a name, then let it refer to wood and steel, pitch and tar, paint and ink, audacity and piety, spirit and imagination.' This use of smell and taste in Huizinga, while not rare – Sluter and Van Eyck could not be assigned to the Renaissance since 'they taste mediaeval' – is not very frequent. A few other examples may be cited. He referred to 'the bitter tang of the sorrow of ages', to a literature that lost its 'scent and flavour', the smell of tar that wafted up to the nostrils from a little book about Amsterdam. On Veth, he wrote: 'He savoured the quality of an age on his tongue, but took little or no interest in its ideas.' Discussing an essay by Veth about Quinten Metsys, he writes 'You see and taste Metsys.'[16]

SOUND

History possessed sound as well as colour. These two were often inextricably interwoven. Dürer's diary sometimes shifted to a different 'sound and colour'. The most elementary feature of a culture was its 'tone'. Every age had not only a colour, but also a tone. The twelfth-century Renaissance announced itself as 'a melody shifting into a brighter tone and a livelier rhythm'. The 'tone of life' of the late Middle Ages, on the other hand, was one of clashing passions and the contrast between vice and virtue. This period developed for the first time 'an ideal of love in a negative tonic'. The 'tonic' of the Renaissance and of Humanism was different again, one of balance, freedom and good cheer, 'serene and sonorous' – in a word, 'the Renaissance tone'.[17]

For Huizinga, the concept of the Renaissance retained its 'fixed form and full-bodied sound' with the 'final chord of the noble Platonism of the Florentines in the circle of Lorenzo de' Medici'. He also nuanced the contrast with the Middle Ages in tone. 'One may easily fall into the trap of imagining that the Middle Ages in their totality embraced the creed of *Contemptus mundi* [contempt of life], and with the start of the Renaissance the entire orchestra suddenly struck up the jubilant instrumentation of the theme *Juvat vivere* [It is a joy to be alive!].' But while the Renaissance sings 'the hymn of the great, new pleasure in the world', one may well discover that most of its exponents display a far darker 'tonic' than we tend to assume.[18]

Life in the seventeenth-century Netherlands, writes Huizinga, was never wholly Puritanical: 'Notwithstanding all the caprices of Protestant rigorism, the tonic of Dutch life remained the sound of

Erasmus rather than that of the reformer from Geneva.' Within the Republic, this produced a sharp contrast with the country's few exponents of the Baroque (Vondel, Sweelinck, Van Campen): 'What a difference in tone, what a difference in colour, what a different picture!' Thus, there was a clear 'difference in cultural tone between England and the Republic': the Netherlands lacked a 'courtly and chivalric element'. The Kingdom of the Netherlands in the nineteenth and twentieth centuries also, of course, had its own 'tonic'.[19]

Occasionally we even encounter nuances expressed in terms of key and musical form. 'Anyone setting out to write a history of the royal house of Burgundy must always ensure that a revenge motif resounds through the tonic of his narrative, as black as a catafalque, that will convey in every deed, whether in council or on the field, the bitter taste of spirits full of a cheerless thirst for revenge and shattered pride.' Observance of certain rules of decorum could turn attendance at church into a 'minuet'. Mediaeval symbolism was 'a veritable polyphony of ideas'. 'In a carefully-wrought symbolism, a harmonious chord of symbols is heard in every image.' The Renaissance 'rang with sonorous sounds'. Its key – to the dreamer at any rate – was C major. The Romantic period, on the other hand, had a 'minor tone'. Erasmus opened his *Colloquies* in a 'spring chord', a conversation proceeded in 'a clear adagio'. In the colloquy of 'The abbot and the bluestocking', the abbot was 'a rough bass' and the erudite woman 'a sturdy alto'. In American literature, the love of nature can be heard 'fortissimo' in Whitman, while in Hawthorne 'it sings the sweetest cantilena'. And in a discussion of Jan Veth, Huizinga writes: 'He possessed in his soul a joyful major key.' 'The tempo of his descriptive passages is adagio.' The mood of play, as described in *Homo Ludens*, was 'always in a major key'.[20]

Musical instruments are frequently named to enhance suggestiveness. The new sense of national identity in France in the early

Middle Ages sounds like a 'clarion blast'. In the fifteenth century, the sense of pride that Frenchmen felt in their country had the same sound as 'that shrill clarion timbre' that 'rang out from the army encampments of Louis XIV and from the Revolution'. Every century can be classified according to its own musical instrument. Thus 'in the sixteenth century, one sometimes heard trumpets, then violins; in the eighteenth the violins alternated with flutes. The seventeenth had the sound of an organ.'[21]

Huizinga had a special relationship with the organ. 'The flamboyant Gothic is like an endless organ coda: it resolves all the forms through self-dissolution, imparts to each detail its sustained development, to each line its counter-line.' 'The instrument of Romanticism was an organ with 1,000 registers.' History itself is linked to the organ. 'In *Hamlet*, all the tragedy is the work of the poet; anyone who chooses to dramatize *Joan of Arc* can be content if he can prevent the organ tone of history itself from sounding too off-key.'[22]

The Baroque is characterized primarily by choir and orchestra. The dedication of *De iure belli ac pacis* to Louis XIII 'is composed in the manner of a polyphonic choir, in which the word *Iustus* is taken up more and more resoundingly by each new voice'. Compare that to the Netherlands at the beginning of the nineteenth century (1813): 'Our epic voices keep cracking. The basses too lack power.' 'And suddenly a different sound is heard: Bakhuizen strikes the rumbling pot. And Potgieter joins in with a high, clear tenor, and now for the first time the old Prince's and States' tunes blend in a pure two-part harmony. Theme of our national symphony has been decided. It sounds cheerful, hopeful, a sound that evokes Old Holland. Now they stand playing it in a nearby street; now it softly fades away.'[23]

WORD AND IMAGE

Huizinga saw art as a mirror of life. That could only apply if art was intertwined with life, remaining an inextricable part of it. If the two were pulled apart, if art was separated from life, the perspective would be distorted. For instance, little had been preserved of 'the bright half of life' in the Middle Ages. As Huizinga wrote in *The Waning of the Middle Ages*, 'It is as if the joyful tenderness and serenity of the soul of the fifteenth century was buried in its painting and crystallized in the rarefied purity of its sacred music... For everywhere outside the world of art, darkness reigns.' It almost seemed 'as if that century had only painted its virtues and described its sins'. He wanted to rectify this 'false picture'. So he strove to put the ethereal art of that age back in its living context. To achieve this, he compared the chronicler's words to the painter's images.[24]

Comparisons of words and images constitute a venerable genre in literature, a genre that is as old as Homer's description of Achilles' shield (*Iliad* 18: 478-608). Art theory coined the term 'ekphrasis' for it, from the Greek for 'relate or describe in full'. Initially it was above all a rhetorical term for a lively description, later it was also used for the description of a work of art. Before long, two contrasting approaches developed. One defined literature and the visual arts as mutually dependent, each being capable of depicting ideas or evoking emotions in its own way. The other viewed the two as natural rivals that disputed each other's competency in both representation and expressiveness. The former approach saw the two arts as sisters: word and image were equated in Horace's familiar analogy *ut pictura poesis*, 'as is painting, so is poetry'. The latter led to the *paragone*, the comparison of the arts, a debate on the relative value of architecture, music, and above all of painting and poetry.[25]

Although Huizinga was mainly concerned with the similarities between word and image, he was not entirely free of the old preoccupation of the *paragone*. In those two brilliant chapters of *The Waning of the Middle Ages*, 'Image and word' and 'Word and image', he does in fact single out the areas and themes in which he regards one art as superior to another.[26] Far more important, however, was the fundamental difference in artistic method. When a poet tries to describe some visible reality, his words will 'ransack the entire treasure-house of implication'. The painter does the exact opposite. 'If the painter does nothing but simply represent an external reality in line and colour, he will nonetheless always add something implicit and ineffable to that formal imitation.' The transcendental quality was far more readily accessible in painting than in literature.[27]

This brings us back to mediaeval symbolism, which could transform every concrete thing into something abstract, hence lending an aura of holiness to mundane reality. That holiness was not alien to literature, but it was cast in a different mould there than in the visual arts. Literature had long been superior to art in terms of the capacity to depict reality. Huizinga compares conventional representations of the Passion in sculpture to accounts of it in literature. One verbal description becomes so concrete and tactile that the writer appears to know 'how he would have to press the Lord's hand to loosen the nail'. But in Van Eyck, painting achieved a wealth of detail and naturalism that greatly surpassed literature. Still, this was more a matter of technical mastery than of the art form itself. Van Eyck did not liberate himself from his age: on the contrary, he was imprisoned within it as none other.[28]

One of Huizinga's most intriguing propositions was that while Van Eyck represented a beginning within art history, he embodied an ending in terms of cultural history. Here Huizinga discusses the degeneration of symbolism into formalism, a process in which form ran riot and gradually throttled substance, in which form was drained of content, remaining behind as an empty husk. The visual arts and literature reacted to this predicament in different ways. Part of this difference is in fact a matter of perception arising from our own faulty perspective.

The faulty perspective arose from a growing emphasis on the visual, by European viewers and historians. The image of history was determined more by the visual arts than by literature. And since, unlike literature, the visual arts did not complain – 'The bitter taste of the sorrow of the times that produced them evaporates instantly' – our picture of history became more serene than corresponded to reality. More important, however, was that formalism was expressed in contrasting ways in different arts. Formalism meant that outward stylistic features gained the ascendancy, sacrificing measure and harmony. This applied in virtually all forms of artistic expression, Van Eyck's paintings being notable exceptions to the rule.

This stemmed from a difference in conventions between painting and literature concerning the representation of the main subject and secondary details. In a painting, the difference between essentials – the fitting expression of the subject – and minor details was negligible. Every aspect of a painting was essential. 'A single detail may determine, for us, the perfect harmony of a work.' And precisely in such details, the painter had a free hand. His essential task – depicting a sacred subject – was constrained by strict conventions. But in matters of detail, the painter was given, or retained, 'an unlimited field of action in which to give free rein to his creative urge'. Quite the opposite applied to poetry. In the primary matter, the thought to be expressed, the poet was free, but details – flowers, the delights of nature, joy and sorrow – were governed by standard forms of expression. And precisely here lay the concerns of late-mediaeval art. The essence of that art, the proliferation of detail, gave the painter every freedom while nailing the poet to a template. Could any insight be more brilliant?

Yes, is the answer. For Huizinga was not only concerned with the differences between painting and literature, but also with the similarities. Here too, he focused on the treatment of details. He drew attention to the 'astonishing virtuosity in the rendering of light effects' in the miniaturists, for instance (*Cuer d'amours*, *Heures d'Ailly*), and also in Geertgen tot Sint Jans's *Nativity*. The brilliance of Huizinga's insight here is that in seeking the equivalence of this treatment of light in poetry, he did not look at descriptions of lustre and light, candles and sun, but at the lively use of direct speech. That analogy must have struck him as a visual observation. For anyone reading the snatches of dialogue in Jean Meschinot, for instance: 'Sire.. – Que veux? – Entendez.. – Quoy? – Mon cas. – Or dy. – Je suys.. – Qui?' – cannot but conclude that they flash from the page like little highlights in a painting. It is too beautiful for words.[29]

We see the same thing repeated on a smaller scale in *Dutch Civilization in the Seventeenth Century*. Like our picture of the late Middle Ages, the image of the Dutch Republic has been determined by paintings. Here too we see a 'mind shift' that gave precedence to visual rather than written sources: 'our minds have gradually absorbed so much material and so many opportunities for the purely visual apperception of the past, that we are in danger of forgetting to read and think about it.' Thus, in *Dutch Civilization* Huizinga sets out, just as in *The Waning of the Middle Ages*, to correct the prevailing perspective. In this book, he plays the same game of conflating words and images.

He proposes, for instance, that Bredero's plays should be classified not as literature but as paintings. 'For Bredero's art, the metaphor of "images" is completely accurate. For that is why he is not really humorous: his words are too visual; painted comedy will no more induce laughter than painted tragedy will induce tears.' After describing the work of Vondel as 'orchestral, in the fullest sense of the word', he writes: 'The auditory imagery is immediately converted for us into visual images: Vondel's poetry is peerless in its polychromatic texture. But though polychromatic, it is never motley; it remains an iridescent play of colour. Colourfulness, richness, opulence, the metaphor that ever remains our indispensable aid, constantly leaps from the sphere of one sense to that of another, or in some cases embraces all of them at the same time.' Huizinga refers to Hals's group portrait of the regentesses of the Old Men's Almshouse in Haarlem 'as a poem from which an entire era and an entire nation speak to us'.[30]

Poetry, he asserted, was no less visual than painting. 'Bredero's comedies are scenes, and in truth so are Vondel's tragedies.' That was why they were as a rule impossible to act. And here again we find the enigma that Huizinga had already encountered in *The Waning of the Middle Ages*. At first sight, literature appears to be far less constrained than painting by stylistic rules. Painting worked for a market, and was bound by techniques and materials, professional traditions and labour relations. A poet could allow his mind to roam freely. Yet history teaches otherwise. Literature, far more than painting, adhered doggedly to 'old forms, structures, examples and authority'. It was manacled to classical blueprints. 'The outward form remained that of classicism, and the mind continued to explore the realms of Dutch meadows and dunes, the same haunts from which painters like Ruisdael and Cuyp had drawn their noblest inspiration. Vondel himself created his best poetry when least confined by classical models.'[31]

'LET US BLEND EVERYTHING TOGETHER'

This sensory sensitivity, this working with synaesthesia and mood, is a feature of Huizinga's work from the outset. The germ of this preoccupation can be found in his early explorations of the origins of language, when he was trying to locate the precise moment of linguistic creation, the spontaneous formation of the word.

Huizinga believed that language was born in a lyrical mixture of sensory impressions, in synaesthesia. To clarify his argument, he included in his proposal – to the considerable alarm of his supervising professor – a brief dialogue between a speaker arguing from erudition and one whose premises were rooted in poetry. The exponent of poetry, of course, was Huizinga himself, while the mouthpiece of scholarship was one Bechtel, an authority on modern linguistics.

In Bechtel's seminal treatise *Über die Beziehungen der sinnlichen Wahrnehmungen in den indogermanischen Sprachen* ('On the relationships between sensory perceptions in the Indo-Germanic language'; Weimar 1879), he set out to explain that colours and sounds are frequently identified with each other. To clarify his point, he cited a case in which a man who had been blind since infancy claimed to understand what the colour scarlet was: it resembled the sound of a trumpet. Bechtel asked himself what had led the blind man to make this connection. What was the common denominator of colour and sound? He concluded that both sound and colour had a penetrating quality. He separated sound from colour, and associated each of them with a third impression, in this case one of movement. And that, said Huizinga, was where he had gone wrong. Bechtel pulled apart what could only be understood as an integrated whole.

Huizinga started by dismantling Bechtel's 'proof'. The ability to permeate or penetrate was indeed applicable to both colour and sound, but in different senses. That was what he meant when he said that Bechtel had separated sound from colour: Bechtel regarded them as two different kinds of pervasiveness. Huizinga suggested adopting a different approach. He went in search of the moment at which colour and sound coincided, and suggested the emotional epithet 'intense'. He further qualified 'intense' as a 'mood word', and postulated that it is in such moods that words are born.[32]

Huizinga explained that the advantage of the term *stemming* or 'mood'[33] – the word itself expressed the intimate link between sound and emotion – was that it was not bound to a single sphere of perception. 'The same mood could be created by impressions from different spheres.' It was precisely in that creative unity of impressions that was encapsulated in mood, in the collaboration of the senses – in synaesthesia itself – that words were formed. That was why Huizinga did not use *stemming* or mood in the meaning it possessed in psychology, to denote a 'continuous mental state', but in that of poetry, as a 'momentary emotional state'. He could not suggest a better word for it: the German *Gefühlston* came closest, and that was why he used the equally synaesthetic word *stemming*.

The blind man of his example had travelled a great distance. Huizinga keeps him anonymous, but Bechtel gives his name: Saunderson. He makes his first (anonymous) appearance in Locke's *An Essay Concerning Human Understanding*, after which he takes a detour into literature as 'Mr Lock's blind man' – for instance in Fielding's *Tom Jones* – and does not acquire a name until *Corinne* by Mme De Staël. It turns out that he was the English mathematician Nicholas Saunderson, who achieved romantic immortality on the strength of this unmathematical analogy. And the provenance of the comparison, in this case, was certainly romantic. *Corinne* was written after Mme De Staël's first visit to Germany, and her book can best be called an experiment in synaesthesia: 'Laissez-nous tout confondre,' she wrote, 'let us blend everything together, love, faith, genius, and the sun, and fragrances, and music, and poetry.'[34]

That was exactly what Huizinga wanted. The motto he appended to his first proposal for a dissertation was a quotation from Jakob

Grimm's *Die V Sinne*: 'It is poetry's prerogative to guess the secret that binds things together and the people's prerogative to confirm it, following [poetry's] example in all innocence.' That was why he identified the artist and the scientist, 'künstlerisch Ahnen' ['artistic intuitive understanding'] to speak with Grimm – Huizinga's motto refers to 'intuiting secret connections'[35] – with scholarly description, discoveries and their connection with analysis and cause. Language was about lyricism. So was history.

This demonstrates yet again the great unity in his life and the literary inspiration of his work. We might say of Huizinga what Brodsky wrote about Anna Achmatova: 'She came fully equipped, and she never resembled anyone.' Huizinga came into the world as Pallas sprang from the head of Zeus, wearing a full suit of armour. He did not so much develop as grow in all directions in the manner of a crystal. And that was also how his mind worked: its modus operandi was not linear but synaesthetic, not pragmatic but poetic.[36]

METHOD AND MYSTICISM

9

METHOD

Huizinga was not a thinker. At least, that was his own view. 'My mind did not incline in general towards problems of a theoretical nature,' he wrote in his memoirs. Dabbling in theory was harmless, but he advised his students against delving too deep, since it would only distract them from the historian's real work. But on another occasion, he reflected that history without theory was inconceivable. The same man who wrote that 'a teaspoonful of theory' was enough also wrote a whole series of theoretical essays and treatises which together filled a small volume.[1]

In those essays, Huizinga tried to capture what was by definition impossible to pin down, he sought words for the mercurial. Essentially, he kept saying the same thing in different words. And naturally, he took contrasts as his point of departure. 'Again and again we are brought back to that series of oppositions between which historical thought moves. Does history set out to know the particular or the general, the concrete or the abstract, the unique occasion or the regularity of repetition? Is its knowledge that of vivid representation or is it conceptual? Is its methodological goal analysis or synthesis, is its object of study individuals or the masses, personal or collective influences?' His answers to each of these questions, of course, was: both.²

Historical consciousness had a natural tendency to focus on the specific and dramatic, the particular and unique. On the other hand, the unique could only be understood in relation to the universal. 'For someone lacking a sense of history, the assassination of Floris v and that of the De Witt brothers remain completely equivalent miscellaneous pieces of information. The particular can only be approached through abstraction. The image and the concept are not diametrically opposed. Once this polarity of historical knowledge has been properly understood, answering certain questions that have vigorously divided opinion and triggered fierce debate becomes a simple matter. All those questions that appear to have only one of two answers ("what happened here, was it this or that?") can actually be resolved in the same way: both, it was one within the other.'³

Huizinga had ample reason to concern himself with theory. He became a historian in an age in which natural science was seen as the model for all academic pursuits. History too was expected to follow that example. But Huizinga had no intention of doing any such thing. For him, history was an exercise in subtlety. You don't put imponderables on a pair of scales. Nuances must be tasted on the tongue. In addition, he placed more emphasis than fellow historians on the creative aspect of historiography. For Huizinga, history was an exercise in transformation, 'a metamorphosis of a reservoir of mental pictures into other mental pictures'. Historiography was not just representation but also an exercise in imagination, a creative leap that transformed a powerful sense of reality into an image.

THE BATTLE OF SALAMIS

To clarify his point, Huizinga repeatedly returned to the passage from Herodotus about the Battle of Salamis. 'And when [Xerxes] saw the whole Hellespont hidden by ships, and all the beaches and plains of Abydos filled with men, he called himself happy – and the moment after burst into tears.' On the one hand, a passage of this kind activates all our senses, and hence our subjectivity, but at the same time it puts us in the position of Xerxes: 'and we see all this through the king's eyes'.[4]

This latter point was the crux of the matter. For at the same time as looking through another's eyes, we experience a universal human emotion, a combination of hubris and melancholy, the belief that we can do anything combined with the realization that everything is in vain. In Huizinga's view, that was entirely different from subjectivity. He defined it, borrowing a phrase from Ranke, as *Universalität des Mitgefühls* (the universality of empathy). He gave an example of his own in his study of patriotism. He again started from the premise of a contrast, in this case the distinction between patriotism and nationalism. The former stood for brotherhood, the latter for conflict, the former was based on similarities, the latter on differences.

Huizinga believed that the sense of belonging to a particular nation took priority over most other emotions: it was one of the most deeply rooted forms of subjectivity. If one's country was in danger, everything had to be sacrificed. That was one side of the feeling. But it had a complementary side, a recognition of the beauty and value of other countries. He invited the reader to evoke the picture of one such other country that he loved. 'In your meditation, you will blend all the treasures of that foreign nation to form a single vision. You will discern the beauties of its art, the strong aspects of its way of life, you will experience the convulsions of its history and see the bewitching vistas of its landscapes, you will taste the wisdom of its maxims and hear the sounds of its immortal music, you will experience to the full the clarity of its language and the depths of its ideas, smell the aromas of its wine, you will feel at one with its courage, its strength, its vitality.'

Thus we see once more that amalgam of impressions, the synaesthesia of mood. And once again that unity of subjectivity and objectivity. 'You feel that all these things collectively bear the imprint of that indestructible hallmark of one specific nationality, one that is not yours. All this is alien to you ... and overwhelmingly precious as an abundance of riches in your life. So why should there be conflict or envy?' Huizinga was concerned with what was both alien and precious, what was remote and yet could become close. That is what made him both a historian and a writer.[5]

It was not the last time that Huizinga had recourse to the Battle of Salamis to clarify what drove him. The second time was in his major essay on Bernard Shaw's play *St Joan*, about Joan of Arc. Again he cited the description in Herodotus as a perfect example of image and reality, subjectivity and objectivity, coming together. In contrast, he argued that Joan of Arc was a subject inimical to literary treatment, especially dramatization. 'The Battle of Salamis will live on in perpetuity in the story told by Herodotus,' he wrote in *De Gids*. 'Some subjects, such as the Trojan War, find their highest form of expression in the epic, while others do not truly flourish until presented on the stage. Then there are subjects, the most profound and indissoluble nature of which is encapsulated in the historical cognitive form itself, in which the highest emotions of tragedy, empathy and catharsis, are bound up with the historical narrative as such. Just occasionally, over a period of many years, let us allow Clio to take precedence over Melpomene.'[6]

Here it may appear that Huizinga is separating literature and history and throwing his weight behind the latter. But that is not the case. In fact he is distinguishing between history and a particular kind of literary treatment of material. His point is essentially that historiography and literature both rely on the same faculty, but that certain kinds of experience or certain parts of reality are best described as historical narratives. That is clear when we see what happened to this passage, which Huizinga debated with his close friend Jolles. For you will not find the quotation in Huizinga's *Collected Works*, because the publishers did not use the original version, instead including the revised edition in *Tien Studiën* ('Ten Studies'), from which Huizinga had deleted it.

He had deleted it after a shrewd comment by Jolles, who had responded to Huizinga (also in *De Gids*) with an essay on Clio and Melpomene. A 'friend' of Jolles's (or Jolles himself, perhaps?) who was writing a book about Aeschylus had discovered that Herodotus's account of the Battle of Salamis was based on the play *The Persians* by Aeschylus. This prompted him to ask two questions: first, was the description in Aeschylus truly less immortal than that in Herodotus; and second, and most importantly: was the version in Herodotus not also a 'literary form'? Jolles maintained that the historical form of cognitive knowledge to which Huizinga alluded was a variant of the literary form, that Clio was a kind of 'Melpomene acting on her own initiative'.[7]

That was an astute observation. Huizinga had got around the argument that the historian's own subjectivity was an obstacle to contacting the past by presenting that subjectivity as universal human objectivity. But Jolles had reclassified this objectivity as literature, and the historian was once again cut off from reality, this time by literary form. Jolles claimed that an entire repertoire of genres was demonstrably present between historians and the past: from novellas and case histories to memorabilia. All these were so-called 'simple forms' – a category that included myths and fairy tales – and without them no one, historians included, could communicate anything meaningful.

Still, Huizinga did not accept defeat. In his view, Jolles had not proven that history was actually literature, but that literature was nothing other than a higher form of syntax. And that too was an apt retort. Just as he had once assumed that there was a connection between synaesthesia and the formation of words, he now posited a connection between syntax and the formation of images. Syntax, like synaesthesia, was the expression of an elementary human faculty. Syntax was 'a primordial mental function far more than an art'. And it was a function used by both the historian and the writer of literature.[8]

Of course, entire tribes existed that could not avail themselves of this function, but that was beside the point. Some people lacked a sense of smell. The function itself had two important components, one individual, the other collective. On the one hand, it presupposed a certain sensitivity to the importance of the various pieces of information. Huizinga called that a sense of discrimination, the ability to select. But there was also a collective aspect. In relation to image-forming, Huizinga's concern was not so much the individual historian or any specific description, 'but the undefined image, which – shifting, altering, sometimes blurred, sometimes sharply defined – lives in the consciousness of an entire generation'.[9]

Furthermore, selection and imagination were both suggested by the material, the sources. Inventiveness was not entirely free, but subject to certain limitations. Huizinga cited the example of the history of Venice. It presented a single cohesive picture, from the city's Byzantine origins until 1797. While the elements of the story might vary – one focused on Guardi, while another might highlight Morosini's struggle against the Turks – but the story as a whole was unequivocal, and that story could never turn into Paris. He had other examples, but the image of a city evidently sprang to mind most readily. The history of Amsterdam, for instance, consisted of an indeterminate quantity of ideas about remarkable events, as found in sources and discussed in studies. That history lay there 'like mineral ore in a mountain'. 'This aggregate of knowledge, which people call the history of Amsterdam, is in principle only potentially present, just as the mineral ore is potential metal. What matters is not what a particular scholar knows, or could know, about that history, but what a particular community, living in a particular period, has absorbed of it. What is more, this aggregate of knowledge is never identical from one moment to the next, nor is it ever a constant or sealed off in any individual mind.'[10]

In this way Huizinga triumphed over the separation between objectivity and subjectivity, between history and literature. A historical picture was not the product of an inspired individual, but that of the concerted attention of a community of people interested in history. Mood or tone [*stemming*] must become harmony [*samenstemming*]. The task of historiography was not just to induce moods, but also to clarify relationships. 'The specific subjects are uncountable, and each one is known only to a few. But the spirit of each age anew determines a certain equivalence, a harmony, a convergence in the results of research despite the apparent divergences. Each intellectual period produces its own true homogeneity of historical comprehension, even though this homogeneity is not attained in any single thinker's brain.'[11]

FORM AND FREEDOM

All this is far from simple, especially for historians who by nature shy away from theory and prefer a good story or bulging archives. The best way to explain it is by looking at what Huizinga meant by relationship, and by form. 'History sheds light on the relationships between events,' he wrote in *Man and the Masses in America*, 'by reducing the events to a dramatic pattern, by seeing them in a simple form.' This quotation reveals that Jolles's concept of 'simple forms' had inspired him from an early stage. 'Essentially, historical thinking relies on only a limited number of outlines and forms,' he wrote, and to that extent he thus concurred with Jolles.[12]

Even so, Huizinga preserved a certain distance from this view. It was not merely that the historian used these forms; history itself provided them. Between the historian and the past, the same relationship existed as that between reader and writer. Reading – *lezen* – was to choose, to gather.[13] The reality of history was formed by the historian's response to the call of the past. Literature could not dispense with certain formal rules, but neither could history, because human life could not dispense with them. They did not just impose constraints, but also gave historians their freedom of choice.

For historical relationships were primarily open forms. In his treatise on 'The pursuit of historiography',[14] the last major theoretical treatise that he published, in which he again returned to his example of the Battle of Salamis, Huizinga wrote about the historian's 'indeterministic viewpoint'. A historian must be constantly aware that he was always focusing on 'a point in the past, at which the knowable factors still seemed capable of yielding different outcomes. In the case of Salamis, it was still possible that the Persians might carry the day.'[15]

What is remarkable here is that when actually engaged in the practice of historiography, Huizinga frequently adopted the opposite point of view. Even the earliest of his historical studies reflects his sense of determinism in history, in particular the influence of geography and economics. 'Haarlem was destined to be the capital of Kennemerland,' he wrote at the beginning of his treatise. Indeed, his entire study of Haarlem is imbued with 'economic necessity': 'The old barbarian laws did not give way until economic necessity intervened.' His *Man and the Masses in America* paints a similar picture of inexorable development dictated by economic forces.[16]

This viewpoint, it should be added, was not so much materialist as it was holistic: it arose from the belief that all things are interrelated. Huizinga was convinced that culture existed 'only as a whole', unashamedly invoking the views of positivists and materialists, philosophers and system builders. 'Does not everyone feel, in history, the inner cohesiveness of all expressions and manifestations of a period that has been acknowledged by all great systems of historiography, and has been recognized – ever since Comte dubbed it *solidarité* – by Marx, Lamprecht, and Spengler? Though we may not be able to prove it, we know that Molière is unthinkable without Richelieu.' He professed a similar holistic view elsewhere too: 'That masterpiece of playful poetical ingenuity, Pope's *Rape of the Lock*, could not have been born in any other age.'[17]

Huizinga's work is indeed peppered with stark inevitabilities. He saw nationalism as rooted in 'primitive feelings of aversion between tribes and peoples, such as – inevitably, it seems – are encountered everywhere'. 'That was how it had to be,' he writes elsewhere: 'the ideal of absolute happiness necessarily transcends the limitations of life, culminating in a death wish.' And most strikingly: 'As if pulled by a gravitational force, everything in the political, social, and technical economic life tended towards an accumulation of quantity ... The world of politics is governed by the law of power, as the physical world is governed by the law of gravity.'[18]

And yet the man who wrote these things was also convinced of 'the unknowability, indeed, the impossibility, of historical laws'. History had no rigidly determined processes. Huizinga defined thoroughgoing determinism as 'a short-sighted and extremely simplistic position'. This so-called inevitability stemmed only from our way of looking at the past. 'It is so tempting,' wrote Huizinga, 'once we have arranged the historical facts into a perspective, so that we perceive intelligible relationships between them, to mistake those intelligible relationships for proven cause and effect. It is so easy to arrive at the conclusion that the two parts of the Netherlands were bound to develop independently, that it was ultimately impossible for Belgium and the Netherlands to stay together.'[19]

Suppose things had gone differently. Suppose that Flanders had imposed its strong sense of national identity on the other provinces, as the province of Holland would later do with the Republic: 'Had this happened, the Burgundian state might have become a truly national entity. But this was impossible.' This latter addition is typical of Huizinga. He told a German audience: 'From time to time, when it seems appropriate, I am in the habit of telling my listeners that there is no activity more unproductive in historiography than musing about possible outcomes that have not materialized.' Yet having issued this firm dismissal, he cheerfully proceeded to discuss three possible ways in which Burgundian history might have developed.[20]

'The most reprehensible weakness for a historian,' he called it elsewhere. 'Just imagine for a moment,' he continued, looking back at the Netherlands of the early nineteenth century, 'what might have happened if the constitution of the new state under the House of Orange had been formulated more in the spirit of Van Hogendorp's original ideas. We would have had a more antique and aristocratic state, but not the false modernity of 1814.'[21]

Huizinga could revel in these musings for pages at a time. 'What might he have achieved with a longer life?' he wondered about Hugo Grotius. Suppose Grotius had lived another three years (to 1648) or ten (to 1655); suppose he had lived to eighty-four or eighty-five, 'had he lived to ninety, he would have experienced 1672'. Much of this was wishful thinking. 'Would it all have ended differently, if the talented Sidney had stood in Leicester's shoes, as had probably once been his secret hope? – Differently without a doubt, and most probably better.' Huizinga himself referred to reasoning of this kind, when he encountered it in Erasmus, as a correlation of beliefs and inclinations. And since we are on the subject of Erasmus: if only Erasmus had had a Mary Reigersberg at his side! And if only he had written his Colloquies 'in the racy Dutch of the sixteenth century!' 'But this is an ahistorical line of argument,' he hastened to add. Still, that was evidently no reason not to indulge in it.[22]

For in Huizinga, this virtual history was merely a variant of his keenly developed visual sense. Seeing what he could not see was the driving force of his historiography. We find visual images, as speculative exercises, throughout his work. 'We are not told what they looked like, those houses that were already described in 1132 as belonging to ancient counts, but it is not too bold to imagine a lord's manor with all its accoutrements: chapel, hall, treasury, stone, nails and barns, where Kennemerland's produce was collected.' In the same way, he imagined mediaeval knights and the shape of a mediaeval city. 'We may imagine Groningen, before it became a trading city, say around 1100, as a village in Drenthe.'[23]

In the same way, he allowed himself to imagine the sacred city of Benares in India, 'the centre of the world, the holiest place on earth', as it was when Kern arrived there in 1863. 'The Indians say that anyone who dies there will go to heaven; but they also say that anyone who has nowhere else to go will always find a refuge in Benares; this is a reference to the Grande Truanderie, the floating population, who account for some one-fifth of the city's population of half a million. The city lies on the northern bank of the river Ganges, on the outer side of a wide sweep in the river, its bustling life facing the water. It is a city of temples and bazaars, of festive pageantry and ecstatic beggars. Day after day vibrant displays, fairs, processions. No more colourful or merrier hubbub is conceivable than the festive bustle of an Indian city on one of the most important days of the calendar, such as the feast of the vernal equinox.'[24]

FORM AND THEME

How does all this relate to the simple forms mentioned by Jolles? For quite aside from the fact that Huizinga had never been to Benares – but then neither had he ever been to thirteenth-century Haarlem or fourteenth-century Paris – the image he evokes has all the qualities of an elementary literary form. Thus, of Haarlem he writes: 'It is the image of a real city, isn't it, that the 1274 charter conjures up before our eyes? Anyone who wants might make a little genre painting of it; there is plenty of material: the smartly-dressed cloth merchant sitting at his table, the brewers unloading their grain at the side of the Spaarne; he can evoke for us the beating and hammering [of shipbuilding] on the Scheepmakersdijk ... but I have no wish to appropriate his task.'[25]

In *The Waning of the Middle Ages*, he would frequently appropriate it. Take this brief idyll, prompted by the poem *Regnault et Jehanneton*: 'King René provides the ingredients for a description of nature, a palette with a few colours, nothing more. A little further on, where nightfall is described, the attempt to express a mood is unmistakeable. The other birds cease their song, but the quail still calls, partridges scuttle off to their covey, deer and rabbits appear. For a brief moment, the sun lights up a steeple, then the air becomes cooler, owls and bats start to circle, and the little Ave-bell sounds from the chapel.'[26]

And what should we make of Huizinga's outpouring on contemplating the *Arnolfini Wedding* and the inscription that Van Eyck added to it, 'Johannes de Eyck fuit hic, 1434': 'Jan van Eyck was here. Just a minute ago. In the throbbing tranquillity of that room, his voice had sounded. The tender intimacy and tranquil peace that would not reappear until Rembrandt are encapsulated in this work as if it was Jan's own heart. Here we suddenly rediscover the twilight years of the Middle Ages, the era that we know, and that we nonetheless so frequently seek in vain in the literature, history, religious life of those times: the happy, noble, serene and simple Middle Ages of folk songs and church music. How far we have come now from that shrill laughter and that unbridled passion! Then our imaginations may perhaps see a Jan van Eyck, who stood outside the fierce, motley life of his time, a simple man, a dreamer, who with head bowed, his gaze turned inward, moved stealthily through life. Take care, or it may turn into an art history novella.'[27]

Nonetheless, he continues to insist that it is not the historian who determines the genre here, it is history itself, the form that people themselves chose for their mutual dealings. Life in that era had 'in many respects the colour of a fairy tale', he writes in the opening section of *The Waning of the Middle Ages*. Even erudite men such as court chroniclers could not see their kings other than in 'an archaic, hieratic guise'. Where the common people were concerned, this applied more strongly still. Huizinga gives the example of a scene from the life of young Charles the Bold, as related by the historian Chastellain. Charles is embroiled in conflict with his father, and his income has been cut off. He is forced to let his retinue go, which he does in a poignant speech that emphasizes both his respect for his misguided father and his honour and loving concern for the well-being of those close to him. His retinue reject his offer and pledge their allegiance to him. Profoundly moved, Charles accepts their pledge, at which the nobles, as if seeking to outdo him in generosity of heart, offer him all their worldly possessions.

Huizinga's main concern here is the way Chastellain shapes his narrative: 'He sees the sovereign in the simple forms of the folk ballad.' That is what the historian does, and at the same time it was the concept on which Jolles had insisted. But then Huizinga went one step further, underscoring that it is not only the historian and the writer who are indebted to that simple form, but human beings, in everything they do. 'While the mechanisms of the administration of the state and the national economy had in reality already assumed complex forms, in the minds of the people, the state's policy is projected onto a few fixed, simple figures. The political contexts within which people live are those of the folk song and the chivalric romance. People reduce the kings of their own time, as it were, into a limited number of types, each one more or less corresponding to a motif from a song or an adventure: the noble, just king, the king who is led astray by evil advisers, the king who vindicates the honour of his royal house, the king who is supported in adversity by his loyal retainers.' The whole range of politics, which was in reality complex and imbued with a sense of reality, was in the popular perception reduced to 'the cases known from tales'.[28]

The simple form was not a literary form, but a form of action. That was what Huizinga meant when he wrote, in 'The task of cultural history',[29] that history is shaped in 'ordinary life'. 'In the fact that history works with the material of spontaneous thought, lies its indissoluble connection with life itself. Historical thinking is simply an extension of the general life of the mind.' That life had an enormous range, from the most elementary of impressions to the most abstract of thoughts. But all of it crystallized into forms. There was a fundamental connection between the forms of life and the forms of historiography.[30]

Huizinga differentiated here between specific and general forms. Specific forms arose in the midst of life itself, and had their own function there. 'The subjects of cultural history are the manifold forms and functions of civilization, as reflected in the history of peoples or social groups, as condensed into cultural figures, motifs, themes, symbols, ideas, ideals, styles, or sentiments.' Each one of these had its own specialism: a literary theme, an artistic style, an intellectual idea, a sacred act.

Where a particular motif (the pastoral, say) straddled more than one field (literature and art history, intellectual and political history), one entered the domain of general forms, and of cultural history. 'Functions of civilization such as Service, Honour, Loyalty, Obedience, Emulation, Resistance, the Pursuit of Freedom, all of which are subjects of sociology', belonged pre-eminently to the field of cultural history. These included the history of vanity, of hubris, of the seven deadly sins. But they also included 'the history of the Garden as a cultural form, or of Roads, Markets, Inns, or the Horse, Dog and Falcon triad, and of the Hat and the Book in their cultural function'.[31]

Huizinga preferred to speak in terms of 'themes'. This term had the advantage of echoing its compound character, 'beings in action and in their surroundings'. 'What is more, theme should be understood here in the sense it has in music. In the great old styles of life, art, and thought, each of these themes constantly serves as affirmation, as an articulation of the underlying principle that informs the entire style. In the sculptures of cathedrals and the words of Scholasticism, the King or the Labours of the Year resonate with symbolic overtones, strictly defined according to the principles of the style in which they are inscribed. Each one speaks a single stanza in the chorus of the whole. They all speak the same language, and say the same things in different ways. All dissonants are resolved into an eternal harmony.'[32]

FORM AND LIBERATION

The latter quotation shows the extent to which Huizinga saw the coherence of history not just as form, but also as an ideal. He returned to this subject in his final theoretical deliberations, in a communication to the Dutch Academy of Arts and Sciences in 1941, 'On metamorphosis in history',[33] in which he once more invoked the description of the Battle of Salamis. The history of modern times, he said, was becoming ever harder to *assign* to a particular form because it *possessed* less and less form. As we have seen, he illustrated this proposition by reference to American history. He asked whether a presidential election conjured up in the minds of Americans 'an image of history with a similar appeal to the imagination as the Battle of Salamis possesses for us'. He thought it unlikely.[34]

Huizinga had expressed his thoughts on this matter in the past, but he had initially explained the change not in terms of the Zeitgeist but in relation to historiography itself. As early as 1915, when delivering his inaugural address 'On historical ideals of life',[35] he had maintained that history in its describable form had been dismantled by historiography itself. There was once a coherent link between ideal and form, between historical ideals of life and historical images. Historiography boosted historical factors at the expense of the ideal. 'Thus, it is history itself that has banished historical ideals of life, like ethereal phantoms.'

Those historical ideals of life had their own limited repertoire and possessed their own specific development. They began as myths, without any essential historical foundation. They were ideals of perfect happiness, very vague and remote in conception – that of the golden age, for instance. With the passage of time, the historical content increased and the ideals became more specific. People started feeling a need to actually live according to that ideal, for instance that of evangelical poverty, or the pastoral or chivalric ideal. But the last great historical ideal of life, that of classical antiquity, intensified the historical consciousness to such an extent that the ideal was recast in more relative terms. The quest for what unified led to the discovery of what divided.

In that Leiden inaugural address, delivered not long after the outbreak of the First World War, Huizinga asked what paths remained for those who were searching for ideals. The answer he gave is crucial, since it encapsulates his method and practice, his conception of history, and his cultural criticism, in a single formula. He summed up four possibilities. Three were forms of escapism: a flight into 'ancient beauty and wisdom', the realization that the passage of time eventually causes all suffering to evaporate in the same way as the Assyrian Wars, and resignation to the unavoidable fact that culture is primarily a preparation for death. But for those who did not want to renounce life itself, those who wanted to actually confront the misery of war and everything that had been destroyed, there was a fourth path: 'that of simple action, whether in the trenches or in any other kind of serious work. To give yourself is the end and the beginning of all doctrines of life. It is in the renunciation not of culture, but of the ego, that liberation is found.'[36]

10

MYSTICISM

After the death of the great Sanskrit scholar Hendrik Kern in 1917, Huizinga wrote a brief but incisive obituary in *De Gids* on the man to whom he owed such a great debt. He concluded the piece on a mild point of criticism. Huizinga shared Kern's preference for the Brahmins' strict teachings on life rather than the Buddhists' renunciation of worldly affairs. But he took a more nuanced view. Kern loathed those 'sanctimonious monks', as he called them, and freely ventilated his enlightened aversion to their religion's penchant for system. Yet behind all that superficiality and gloom, wrote Huizinga, Buddhist teachings contained a wisdom that Kern was unable to fathom: 'for that, Kern perhaps lacked that deeper irrationality, and that melancholy, that foster susceptibility to mysticism.' Susceptibility to mysticism was certainly a quality that Kern did not possess. What about Huizinga?[1]

TWO KINDS OF MYSTICISM

When Huizinga produced this portrait of Kern, he was just putting the final touches to his *The Waning of the Middle Ages*. That book dwells at length on mysticism. Chapter 16 on 'Realism and the surrender of the imagination to mysticism' distinguishes two forms: intensive and extensive, negative and positive, drunk and sober, mysticism *en gros* and mysticism *en détail*. The former was linked to the great names of Dionysius the Carthusian and Meister Eckhart, Heinrich Suso and Jan van Ruusbroec, while the latter flourished in the friaries and monasteries of the Windesheimers and gave Thomas à Kempis's *Imitatio Christi* its enduring fame.

The first variant was marked by the same contempt for the world that Huizinga had encountered in Buddhism and displayed the same signs of decadence. It sought to quantify God and salvation, and hence became enmeshed in an enumeration of immeasurable and unquantifiable properties that achieved the opposite of what was intended. The Holy Trinity was super-substantial, supremely to be worshipped, supremely good, God was 'supremely merciful, supremely compassionate, supremely praiseworthy, supremely benign, supremely glorious, supremely omnipotent, supremely wise'. And none of this helped. The effect of all these superlatives was merely to reduce the infinite to the finite. They actually attenuated and externalized the sense of eternity. 'Eternity was not immeasurable time. Every sensation that had been expressed lost its immediacy; every quality attributed to God drained Him of some of His majesty.'[2]

Since this mysticism was evidently accompanied by an awareness of such consequences, it eventually took refuge in the polar opposite, in the transformation of positive images into negative ones. Light turned to darkness, fullness to a void. At length, a series of opposites spawned a pure negation. In a poem on God, Silesius writes:

God is pure nothingness, He is not now, not here.
I reach for Him and see Him disappear.[3]

In discussing this line of thought, which Huizinga believes is timeless but also the fount of all Christian mysticism, he provides some extraordinarily beautiful examples. The finest one of all, perhaps, is a quotation from Ruusbroec, who writes that union with God will be

> Wild and desolate, an errant way ... for there is neither guide nor road, nor path, nor resting-place, nor any companion ... In it we shall find ourselves severed, plucked from earthly concerns, stripped of girth and height in an eternal dissolution from which there is no return.[4]

Huizinga had a weakness for Ruusbroec, but he himself would strike out along a different path.[5]

The difference between intensive and extensive mysticism, in his view, was only one of how rarefied the air became, how far one chose to ascend the mountain. Huizinga himself preferred to remain 'below the tree line, where mysticism did not yet make culture redundant, but contributed to it. 'There is the flowering orchard of moral perfection, a form of preparation expected of all who enter the contemplative life: tranquility and meekness, the subduing of desire, simplicity, moderation, diligence, earnestness, and an inward gaze. So it went in India, and so it went here: the initial workings of mysticism are moral and practical.' That was why Meister Eckhart elevated Martha over Mary, that was why Ruusbroec praised all simple work. 'It was in the Netherlands that mysticism's attendant qualities, of moralism, pietism, charity, and industriousness, took pride of place.' It was there that a commonplace collective mysticism developed: 'a sober mysticism, for those who are not minded to quibble over a word.'[6]

PERSONAL EXPERIENCE

If Huizinga can be called in any sense a mystic, then he became so through the circuitous route of the natural world. In his brief autobiography, he describes that even as a small boy he was highly susceptible to impressions of nature, 'a feeling that, even before adolescence, was translated into lyrical-sentimental raptures without ever seeking verbal expression'. 'I remained an incorrigible fantasist and dreamer until my late twenties,' he writes. In the afternoons, while fellow-students were absorbed in laboratory sessions, he wandered out of town on his own, not returning until the late-afternoon drinking hour. On those walks, he sometimes found himself sinking 'into a kind of trance'. 'I was not actually thinking, at least not of specific things; rather, my mind roamed almost beyond the boundaries of everyday life in a sort of ethereal pleasure, which most closely resembled the felt response to nature, but which soon faded again, surrendering to the clear light of day.'[7]

Whether that ethereal pleasure had anything to do with mysticism is a matter of definition, but that Huizinga experienced something of a 'loss of self' is clear. While staying in Zuidhorn, he could stand gazing in 'devout admiration' at a large solitary tree in a meadow by the Hoendiep canal for minutes at a time. How close all this came to melancholy is demonstrated by another memory, of his early years as a teacher. 'Aside from numerous cycling trips, my life in those years resembled that of a hermit, dominated by cheerful, slightly manic moods, which gave way at irregular intervals to depressions lasting several weeks, which to outsiders would have been perceptible at most, perhaps, in the form of a more taciturn demeanour, but which I myself experienced as highly oppressive, without it wresting me from my "normal routine".' In the original version of these memoirs, he mentions the 'taste of pennies' that such a mood would leave in his mouth.[8]

As soon as Huizinga found his young bride, his depressions vanished. But he continued to record his happiness largely in terms of responses to nature. With Mary, he saw 'much of the intimate-desolate, warm expanse of Drenthe, and much of that glorious, Van Eyck-like, sublimely simple and richly coloured Zeeland.' And describing his happiness, a moment before it was shattered, he wrote: 'A glorious sun shines over my expanse of meadows, and in everything lies the promise of spring. In the evening a moonlight such as can only be enjoyed outside.'[9]

Memories of friends were also consistently linked with responses to nature. On Kapteyn, he wrote: 'How often do I not recall that time, very early in the morning, around Whitsuntide, was it 1906 or 1907?, when I went off in the rain with Kapteyn and Swaen, after spending a restless night in his little country house in the village of Vries, to see the grouse dancing in the meadows of Zeijer.' And on De Sitter, he wrote: 'What the expansiveness and solitude of the Veluwe meant in the fabric of his being we well know, who often tried to keep up with his great strides, on long hikes over the heath and through the woodland, when he appeared to be drinking in sustenance for his mind, as if lost in cosmic exaltation.'[10]

One revealing description was entrusted to his American diary. During his travels around the United States in April to June 1926, he visited Mount Vernon. 'What a beautiful setting! The hills, the trees, the pink and white blossoms, the birds, the fragrances! The simple farmhouse with its many small rooms. And the Potomac, broad and yellowy. Later on thundery clouds gathered. I am now starting to understand, for the first time, what America is.' It is a characteristic order: first that amalgam of impressions, that synaesthetic receptivity, then the emphasis on simplicity and modesty, and eventually understanding. 'The reality of a country registers with me first through its natural scenery, or possibly through old cities. Or does it have more to do with its ideality? American history comes to life in Independence Hall, Lincoln Memorial, and Mount Vernon. The love and the memory of a great nation are concentrated in a few great men. That's how it should be. How simple America's great men are.' And then comes the epiphany, the revelation of the interrelationship between all things. 'By the Potomac I felt that while countries are separated, the water is all one. The Potomac and the Scheldt are connected.'[11]

This 'feeling for nature' was one of the factors that made Huizinga became a historian. As a young student, reading a mediaeval source – the Saxon World Chronicle – he had had an experience identical to the one he later described at the Potomac. The preface to this chronicle alludes to one 'van Repegouwe', and Huizinga had been instructed by his professor, the historian Blok, to find out whether the reference was to Eike von Repgow, a well-known jurist and advisor to the rulers of Saxony. In this chronicle, Huizinga read the account of a flood: 'In those times a great storm arose over the lake, the waters rose from the ground, as high as the mountains, so that all those living nearby were drowned.' While reading this description, he heard a chord on the piano and found himself in a trance.[12]

It was a similar experience that gave him the fundamental idea underlying *The Waning of the Middle Ages*, while he was out enjoying nature, in a place he knew extremely well. In the afternoons, Huizinga – who was by then a professor – would go for solitary walks far out of town, in the 'open, spare landscape of the Groningen countryside'. 'On one of these walks, along or near the Damsterdiep – on a Sunday I believe – it occurred to me that the late Middle Ages were not so much the harbinger of what was coming, as they were the dying breath of what was passing away.' Later on, he would note a similar combination of nature and insight in Erasmus. Twice Erasmus had a moment of inspiration in the Alps, in both cases leading to a masterpiece, first to his *Carmen*, and later to his *Praise of Folly*.[13]

In Huizinga's view, historiography itself was indebted to responses to the natural world. In his essay 'Views of nature and views of history in the eighteenth century',[14] he insisted that historiography originated, as it were, from the change that had taken place in perceptions of nature during the *Sturm und Drang* period. The natural religion of the eighteenth century had released imagination from the templates of mythology and pastoral, and following the example of Dutch painting had restored its contact with common, simple nature. *Sturm und Drang* had then sought 'to satisfy its yearning for freedom, simplicity, and nature in every sphere in what was original, powerfully sensual, graphic, real, personal, unconscious, spontaneous, instinctive, felt, in what had flourished in the wild, had become organic... and hence also in what had become historical and venerable!'[15]

Towards the end of the eighteenth century, a broader view of nature came into vogue, the light and graceful were joined by the savage and bleak; the day acquired a night side. The entire representation of nature became imbued with 'a new cosmic awareness'. There was a renewed sensitivity to lyricism and dream, and this sensitivity also revived susceptibility to the historical. 'In its view of the past, too, minds were gripped by passion. The entire focus on the past acquired a different quality: the past no longer served as a model, example, a rhetorical arsenal, or a lumber room stuffed with curiosa, it occupied the mind with a desire for the remote and alien, with the desire to relive what once had been. The historical sense filled itself with nostalgias and *hantises* [obsessive fears].' Huizinga's historical sense too was filled with nostalgia and apprehension.[16]

NATURE

Huizinga's work is full of associations with the natural world. It abounds with plants and bugs, wind and rain. In his essay about Abelard, for instance, the word for 'bloom' occurs four times on a single page, preceded by the remark: 'it is like the sun breaking through the clouds.' What might strike one as a cliché is in reality an intensely felt experience. When he describes, in relation to the mediaeval pastoral, how 'a sunny dreamland cloaks desire in a haze of flute music and birdsong', that dream stems – not just for those living in the Middle Ages, but for him too – from 'the immediate delight in sun and summer, shade and fresh water, flowers and birds'.[17]

A sense of nature, in Huizinga's view, was something that all mankind had in common. This common ground resolved, as it were, all time differences. A letter from the mediaeval monk Jean de Monstreuil had the air of one written by a modern man, when one absorbed his simple observations in the monastery of Charlieu, near Senlis: 'the sparrows sharing our food in the refectory.' 'In an account of a nocturnal journey across the fields,' writes Huizinga about *Le Jouvencel*, the biographical, chivalric romance about the nobleman Jean de Bueil, 'you can breathe night air and feel the silence.' A poem by Christine de Pisan 'begins with a clear, firm sound, like the song of a blackbird'. And then there was the bird Charadrius, to which Huizinga devoted an erudite article: was it a plover or a stone curlew? It has a penetrating call, says Aristophanes. 'This applies extremely well to the plover and the stone curlew. Everyone will recognize the wonderfully melodious, melancholy song of invisible flights of plovers on dark September evenings.'[18]

Where man simply followed nature, he could not err. That was what Huizinga found so appealing about painters: their 'respectful, stammering impersonation of nature', that he saw in Dürer, say. That is why he had such an aversion to the trend in modern art

– from Goya via Redon to Kandinsky – that completely abandoned natural forms. 'Tired to death of eternally repeated imitations of nature, profoundly oppressed by the remote greatness and beauty of Egypt and all that came after it, craving to express their deepest and most essential feelings, for which no pictorial form or word can now suffice – they reach out with trembling hands to the mystery itself. They have had enough of Nature: its forms have become shackles for them.' Thus, modern abstract art became a kind of negative mysticism.[19]

But nature took its revenge, in however mild and gentle a way, 'since it is divine'. In truth, that formlessness was actually 'the new naturalism ... primeval naturalism'. 'For it is no longer people who are stammering here, it is matter itself, the forms and colours themselves, that are doing the work.' In Huizinga's view, beauty was a question of line, colour, and form. So modern art did in fact imitate nature, though the artist might deny it. 'If you believe that it is *your* art, that *you* can take credit for the fact that rhythmically quavering lines in black on white paper, or sandalwood and silver in the play of light and shade over curves and hollows, cannot be other than beautiful – then you are whoremongers of matter, you are as Jacob stripping the peel from rods to obtain ring-streaked cattle.'[20]

The miracle of nature was the creation of forms. It was those forms that culture filled with content. The detachment and solidification of those forms provided the framework of cultural history. It was the task of art to break through that solidity. Its example was nature. For nature had no 'style', no *manièra*, and was merely itself, in a way that no human being could ever be himself. That is what Huizinga found so fascinating about the Dutch paintings of the seventeenth century, and what he looked for in the American writers of the nineteenth century.

In those American writers, Emerson, Hawthorne, Whitman, the

relationship between formless and a sense of form, nature and art, was manifest. 'Looking through nature to something that is more than nature', that was the crux. On Hawthorne, Huizinga wrote: 'What chiefly lingers in the mind, after reading his fluent, unforced descriptions of nature is the impression of the hazy sunshine and soft-salty warmth of a September day, with the bronze colour and elegiac fragrance of foliage that is about to wither.' And about Whitman: 'And all the bright joys of life and the sun, the wind and the water, float past in a chorus of raucous laughter, a modern version of St Francis's Canticle of the Sun.' It was always about that surplus of meaning, about 'insight': 'Nature always speaks of spirit, suggests the idea of the absolute.' Huizinga called it 'the purest mysticism'.[21]

It was the same mysticism that he encountered in seventeenth-century Dutch art. This is clear from his brief account of a visit that Huizinga made to an exhibition of prints by Hercules Seghers in the Rijksprentenkabinet. 'We were the only visitors there the day before yesterday, which was pleasant and disgraceful.' Still, it was mainly pleasant, since with Seghers you actually needed to be alone, 'just as you have to be alone with Meester Eckhart'. Seghers was not an imitator and not a precursor, nor did he have much affinity with the style of his own day, 'Hercules Seghers stands outside time'. But not outside Holland, for Huizinga heard the devil whisper – just before he could hush him – of associations with Van Gogh and Thijs Maris. Huizinga himself preferred to pass over such notions, instead imagining Seghers seated in Elysium, far removed from the other painters, next to Jacob Boehme and Angelus Silesius, 'in silence'.[22]

Be that as it may, Seghers could not be seated very far from Vermeer. It seemed to Huizinga as if the people in Vermeer's paintings had been placed outside the reality of everyday life, 'in an atmosphere of lucidity and harmony, where their words no longer sound and thoughts do not assume any form'. 'Their actions are full of mystery, like those that appear in a dream. The word realism is about as apt here as brushing one's teeth with a broom. The whole scene resonates with matchless poetry. If you look carefully, these are not Dutch women from sixteen hundred and something, but figures from an elegiac dream world, full of peace and tranquillity. Nor do they wear the clothes of their day, but those of a vision, it is a symphony in blue and green and yellow.' This is the passage in which Huizinga identifies Vermeer as a Dutchman because he had 'no style'.[23]

SYMBOLISM

However different the forms of mysticism may have been, they shared a common provenance, or more accurately, they represented a way of thinking or a form of knowledge that was diametrically opposed to causal or historical thinking. This way of thinking might be called by any number of names, and whether one chose to call it Indian mysticism or Platonic idealism or Mediaeval realism scarcely mattered. Its core was expressed in that little sentence of Huizinga's that I have already quoted, the belief 'that every thing would be absurd, if its significance were exhausted in its immediate function and manifestations, that all things extend some distance into the world on the other side'. 'That knowledge is also something familiar to us at every moment in time, as a nebulous feeling,' he wrote, 'whenever the sound of the rain on the leaves or the light from the lamp over the table briefly penetrates to a more profound perception than that of the practical sense of thought and action.'[24]

Once again, then, we are back to symbolic thought, a 'reflective order' that was in Huizinga's view completely different, but not for that reason any less valuable, than the historical or causal order. He was compelled to concede that from the vantage point of causal thinking, the symbolic mode could be nothing but a kind of short-circuit. 'The mind seeks the connection between two things not along the concealed convolutions of their causal relationship, but in a sudden leap, not as a relationship of cause and effect, but as one of significance and purpose. The belief in such a link can take hold as soon as two things have a single essential quality in common that can be linked to something of universal value. In other words: every association based on some kind of analogy can immediately undergo transformation into the realization of an essential, mystical connection.'[25]

So this short circuit took place only if the shared properties were experienced as essential to the things concerned. Huizinga gives the example of red and white roses, blooming amid the thorns. A denizen of the Middle Ages would immediately see the symbolic significance: virgins and martyrs, radiant amid their persecutors. For virgins and martyrs, as for roses, beauty and fragility, the white of purity and the red of blood, were fundamental. Outer appearance and inner essence touched here, creating a spark. 'But this relationship is only truly meaningful and full of mystical significance when the essence of the two terms of the symbolism is encapsulated in the connector, that is, the property; in other words, when redness and whiteness are not mere names for a physical distinction based on quantitative factors, but are seen as *Realien*, quintessentials... The property is their quiddity, the core of their being. Since beauty, fragility and whiteness are essences, they are entities: everything that is beautiful, fragile, white, must be essentially connected, has the same *raison d'être* (significance) before God.'[26]

Huizinga makes no bones about his attachment to symbolism and the relationship in society that is based on it, and since this amounts to a personal creed, I shall give the relevant quotation in full.

Symbolism created a world view of even stricter unity and close-knit cohesion than is possible within causal scientific thinking. With its strong arms, it embraced the whole of the natural world and the whole of history, creating an indissoluble hierarchy in them, an architectural subordination. For in any symbolic relationship, one element must be above and another below: equivalents cannot symbolize each other, they can only together denote a third, higher, entity. In symbolic thinking, there is room for an immeasurable multiplicity of relationships between things. For every thing has diverse properties and may thus symbolize numerous others, on the basis of its different properties, besides which a single property may signify different things; and the highest things have thousands of symbols. Nothing is too humble to signify the highest and to be singled out for glorification. The walnut tree signifies Christ: its sweet kernel is his divine nature, the fleshy outer layer is his humanity, and the wooden shell in between them is the cross. All objects provide a prop and stay enabling thoughts to ascend to eternity; each elevates the next, one step at a time. Symbolic thought provides a continuous transfusion of the sense of God's majesty and eternity into all observable and perceptible things. It keeps the mystical sense of life burning constantly. It imbues the representation of each object with heightened aesthetic and ethical value. Think of the pleasure, if every gem sparkles with the lustre of all its symbolic values, if the identification of roses with virginity is more than a lyrical Sunday best, if it conveys the essence of both. It is a veritable polyphony of thought. In a well-wrought symbolism, a harmonious chord of symbols sounds in every representation. Symbolic thinking imparts to the flush of thought, that pre-intellectual deliquescence of the boundaries of the identities of things, that moderation of rational thought which elevates the awareness of life to its highest level.[27]

Here Huizinga is describing not just a mysticism, but also a method. In several places in his theoretical writings, but first and above all in that curious essay he published in *De Gids* in 1920, 'The historical museum',[28] he discusses objects as historical resources. Objects may take any form, from tools and prints to deeds and tracts. What matters is what the object refers to, and to what state of grace it is capable of moving the viewer.

In this essay, Huizinga dissolves the distinction between the enjoyment of art and the enjoyment of history. He explains this in relation to Jan van der Velde's prints illustrating the months of the year. Clearly, these pictures cannot be classified as 'great' art. In fact they are 'clumsy', 'primitive in the baser sense of the word'. At the same time, Huizinga 'relishes' these prints with 'a childish delight'. The month of April, for instance, depicts a family moving house: the simple household effects are piled onto an open barge in a canal in the city. Father stands at the helm – 'only a separate starboard tiller' – and there are his two children, 'the boy triumphantly grasping a spanner'. Also depicted are a woman selling tulips and the inevitable young fisherman.

It is precisely details like this, historical details, here in a print but they might equally be found in a legal document, that give him a sense of 'immediate contact with the past, a sensation as deep as the purest enjoyment of art, an almost (do not laugh) ecstatic perception of no longer being myself, of flowing into the world around me, touching the essence of things, experiencing Truth through history'. Huizinga provides a similar description of this 'historical sensation' in his 'The task of cultural history'.[29] He finds it impossible to name: 'it is not enjoyment of art, not a religious feeling, not a metaphysical recognition, and yet it belongs to this chorus.' And yet it makes contact with the past, and it is accompanied 'by the utter conviction of authenticity'. Whether it is a line from a charter or a chronicle or a few sounds from an old song is irrelevant: 'Every historical given leads straight to eternity.' The 'mediaeval' quality of this notion is clear from his observation, in *The Waning of the Middle Ages*: 'Every sin, however trivial, impinges on the entire universe.'[30]

Is this mysticism? Possibly. But perhaps it is merely the kind of literary homeopathy that everyone recognizes who loves reading and who knows how texts can be time capsules, and how distant and unfamiliar authors may become friends. And how a book – and the same applies of course to a painting or a piece of music – possesses significance, in the sense that it means something to a receptive mind. It is not what we give it, but what it gives us. 'The commonplace mystery of real presence,' George Steiner called this. In its most exalted form, we might cite Proust, when he sees the entire world concentrated within a little patch of yellow in Vermeer's *View of Delft*: a door opening onto a river. Or Thomas Mann, speaking of Beethoven's Opus 111 'washing over him'. But Steiner would also include the opening bars and the raw voice of Edith Piaf, in 'Je ne regrette rien'. Steiner too tries to describe this experience in religious terms as an incarnation, with the aid of the sacrament of the Eucharist. But it is art.[31]

All this was extremely familiar to Huizinga. He experienced it with the Flemish Primitives just as strongly as when he had visited Mount Vernon on the Potomac River. Enigmatic though this feeling might be, everyone who falls in love or seals a new friendship knows what it means. It is a heightened sense of reality or truth, that many – including Huizinga – have described in religious terms, but that essentially precedes religion. There is no difference, wrote Huizinga in relation to Van Eyck's *Lamb of God*, 'between our emotional response to art when faced with the sacred image of the Worship of the Eucharist, and that aroused by Emanuel de Witte's fish stall in Museum Boymans'. He made the same point about a painting of a Dutch interior by Esaias Boursse. We see a woman at the hearthside; behind her is a box bed, with sheets and blankets toppling out. Huizinga's comment: 'Eternity depicted in a stripped bed.'³²

EXTRAPOLATION
AND
METAMORPHOSIS

11

EXTRAPOLATION

As we saw in chapter 3, fairy tales possessed an enduring appeal for Huizinga. In his memoirs he singles out for special mention the tales of Hans Andersen, most notably 'The Old House' and 'The goblin and the grocer'. But there is a third tale by Andersen with which he felt a particular connection: 'The Drop of Water', the story of an old man whom his neighbours called Kribble Krabble.[1]

The old fellow always wanted the best of everything, and if all else failed, he used magic. He liked playing with his magnifying glass, and one day he held it over a drop of ditchwater. He was shocked to see at least a thousand tiny creatures, dancing, jumping and devouring each other. 'How horrible!' cried old Kribble Krabble. 'Can't those creatures be taught to live in peace and harmony, so that each one may mind his own business?' He thought long and hard, and at length concluded that the only solution was to use magic. 'Suppose I gave them a colour,' he thought, 'then they would be able to see each other better.' So he added a tiny drop of something that looked like red wine to the drop of water, but it was really witches' blood from an earlobe, the best to be had, ten cents a drop. And now the tiny creatures were completely red, and the drop looked like a whole city of naked savages.

'What have you got there?' asked another magician.

'If you can guess what it is,' said Kribble Krabble, 'I'll give it to you.'

And the other magician looked through the magnifying glass and what he saw did indeed look like a big city with naked people, and it was horrible, horrible to see how they pushed and thrashed, bit and kicked each other. And those who were on top were pulled down, and those who were at the bottom battled their way upwards. And only one, a small girl, sat quietly begging for peace and quiet. But she too was dragged away and eaten.

'That's a funny sight,' said the magician.

'Yes, but what do you think it is?' asked Kribble Krabble.

'Oh, that's easy,' replied his friend. 'It's Copenhagen or some other city; they all look the same. It's a big city.'

'It's a drop of ditchwater,' said Kribble Krabble.

While the moral of this tale may be as obscure as witches' blood, those who read it through Huizinga's eyes saw clear water reflecting an entire world. In a lecture that Huizinga gave in Ghent in 1939, on 'Ideas and moods a hundred years ago', he said: 'Even that brief time span of just one century teems with multifarious life and toil, as in a drop of water under a microscope.'[2]

'A TEASPOON OF THEORY'

A drop of liquid reflecting an entire world is a common metaphor in literature. The Dutch poet Leopold wrote, in *Oostersch III*: 'In peering through a drop of water's gleam / I saw the oceans of the world were one / and motes of light that capered in a beam / revealed to me the essence of the sun.'[3] In the earliest known version of the poem, it is a drop of wine, which is mixed in endless dilution with the entire ocean. Of this version too, Leopold provided the canonical form in his much-discussed poem *Oinou hena stalagmon*.

the drops of wine that drizzle from the chalice
colour the Ocean; those few scattered pearls
pervade its watery transparency,
conveying their essence to the farthest shores,
the darkest deeps.[4]

This earliest version derives in turn from Chrysippus. Two of this Stoic's maxims have been preserved in the writings of Plutarch: 'there is nothing to hinder one drop of wine from being mixed with the whole sea' and 'this one drop will by mixtion extend through the whole world'. A second tradition, which is Pythagorean and hence older, seeks to give the mathematical basis for this mysticism. It focuses on the idea of a circle whose centre is everywhere and whose circumference is nowhere. Huizinga was familiar with this notion from his reading of Dante's *Vita nuova*, in which the angel says to Dante: 'I am as the centre of a circle, to the which all parts of the circumference bear an equal relation; but with thee it is not thus.'[5] He himself quoted the line in his article about Alan of Lille: 'God is an intelligible sphere, whose centre is everywhere, and whose circumference is nowhere.'[6]

It is clear from this article that Huizinga was unaware that Alan had not entirely understood the mystical principle underlying this idea. The original words were 'infinite sphere' ('sphaera infinita'). According to Alan, God was without beginning and without end, and embraced everything. This placed the emphasis on the circumference, and not simultaneously on the centre. The adjective 'intelligible' further attenuates the description into a comparison that can be visualized. The mystical unity of an unbounded vastness and a creative origin operating at every point eluded Alan. Nor did it mean very much to Huizinga – from his vantage point 'below the tree line', as he put it. When he himself invoked the figure of a circle, for instance to express what he meant by historical periods, it was therefore in the form of a serviceable image: 'a number of different-sized circles, the centres of which are grouped together in an irregular clump, such that their circumferences intersect at numerous points, and the whole has the appearance, when viewed from a distance, of a cluster or bunch'.[7]

GERM, SPARK AND DROP

To Huizinga, all this was not so much mysticism as 'a sense of quality': perceiving the importance of 'ostensible trivialities', 'an acute and apparently intuitive reaction to qualitative properties'. If it was mysticism, it was the variant with which he was familiar from modern religion: 'It was mysticism *en détail*; one had "suddenly been struck", "received a spark".' There are many such 'sparks' in Huizinga's work, where an idea is born, where people make contact, or hope is kept alive. 'The gap between existence and comprehension can only be bridged,' he wrote in *Homo Ludens*, 'by the short-circuiting spark of the imagination.'[8]

It was that spark, in Huizinga's view, that nourished historiography. No one could grasp or represent that discipline in its entirety; even the most erudite of scholars, 'to speak in the language of the ancient men of religion, had only "received a spark".' That was how he saw himself too: 'I had only, to use the words of our old Windesheimers, received a spark, which now and then glowed.'[9]

What sparked could also germinate. 'The germ of philosophy lay in the riddle contests of primitive peoples,' he had written as a young Sanskrit scholar. 'In the fabric of the city, a development that started long ago ripens, while at the same time new life germinates for later centuries,' he had written in his earliest historical study. Contemplating political factions and master-servant relations, feudal loyalties, and obedience to the God-given authorities, he saw 'the germ of an awakening awareness of the state'.[10]

He reserved his finest example for his beloved John of Salisbury. On the task of a king, this 'chivalric clerk' had written: 'To God his whole being is beholden, to his native country the largest part of himself, to his kinsmen and neighbours a great deal, to strangers very little but not nothing.' Huizinga was struck by these words, 'but not nothing' ('minimum, nonnihil tamen'), exclaiming 'Behold, a germ of international law.' He calls the expectation of salvation shared by Renaissance and Reformation 'an ancient seed of awareness of spiritual renewal'. 'Yet it is significant that certain of the ideas that inspired the standard-bearers of those great movements came from a single germ.'[11]

The germ, the spark and the drop were the faith, hope and charity of Huizinga's theory: these three, but the greatest of these was the drop. In the might of the minuscule, he sought a homeopathic alternative to everything that was too loud and over-abundant and countable. 'Behind the smallest historical entity that one may apprehend, there is always a distant horizon of human life,' he wrote. In such contexts, the drop remained his favourite metaphor. The mediaeval mind had a 'hyper-substantial conception' of the blood of Jesus: 'it was a real substance, one drop would have been enough to redeem the world'. He himself saw the salvation of Western culture in exactly the same terms: 'Compassion and justice, suffering and hope. One drop of one of these is enough to consecrate your actions and your thoughts.' 'A single drop of compassion suffices to elevate our actions above the distinctions made by the thinking mind.'[12]

ANECDOTES

In much the same way, a single drop of story sufficed to colour a sea of history. To sketch a situation, to define a period, to paint a picture of an era, Huizinga constantly resorted to anecdotes. He was already doing so as a young Sanskrit scholar. The tale of the venerable Sâriputta sitting in ecstasy with his freshly shaved head in the full moon, for instance, was a pithy example of narrative argument. One of two passing demons, 'on an errand from the Northern quarter of the heavens to the Southern quarter', is unable to suppress the urge to strike the holy man on his bald head. Even though his fellow demon warns him that this is a great monk with even greater magical powers, he deals him a blow 'with which one might fell an elephant seven or seven and a half cubits high, or one might split a mountain peak.' The outcome is that the demon is consumed by flames and tumbles into hell, and the holy man, when asked how he feels, reports having a slight headache. [13]

'Moral tales' of this kind make Huizinga's history of the University of Groningen a kind of mosaic of anecdotes. For instance, he tells the story of a physician who, as a result of financial cuts, had been appointed as a botanist, and when required to show His Majesty around the botanical gardens, had identified the plants of whose names he was ignorant in terms of parts of the human anatomy: 'deltoides, triceps, sartorius, sternocleidomastoideus'. Then there was the professor who lectured with his hat on, raising it briefly whenever he mentioned a great figure from antiquity. And poor Van Eerde, the mildest-mannered lecturer in the world, who was always relieved when the class made so much noise that he could stop trying to teach, who once snapped at a student: 'Your mother should've sent you to a kindergarten.' The student replied: 'She done that already, professor.'[14]

In *The Waning of the Middle Ages* the story of Philip the Good, duke of Burgundy, who had set his heart on having one of his knights marry the daughter of a wealthy brewer from Lille, is told three times. The first time, Huizinga mentions it to describe Philip's boundless fury when the brewer proves uncooperative, at which the duke has recourse to the Parliament of Paris. Abandoning weighty affairs of state that had been detaining him in Holland, Philip undertakes a dangerous voyage – 'moreover, in the holy days just before Easter' – from Rotterdam to Sluis, to enforce his will. The second time, the anecdote is related in rather more detail: 'The duke has the girl placed in custody; the aggrieved father moves his entire household to Tournai, so as to be outside the duke's jurisdiction and to be entitled to bring his own case before the Parliament of Paris. Endless exertions ensue; [the father] becomes sick from grief, and at the end of the story, which epitomizes Philip's impulsive character and reflects poorly on him by today's standards, when the mother comes to him as a supplicant, he sets her daughter free, but dishes out sneers and humiliation along with his pardon.' A chronicler such as Chastellain endorses these sneers, calling the aggrieved father a 'rustic rebel brewer' and a 'wayward villain'. The third time Huizinga tells the story, it is to emphasize the mendacity of chivalric honour.[15]

The point of such anecdotes is to sensitize the reader to the 'alien' quality of history, in this case to illustrate the fairy tale character of mediaeval life and to show that the ruler was more like a caliph from *One Thousand and One Nights* than a Western ruler. Thus, the duke rides out of Brussels in a white-hot rage after a row with his son, loses his way in a forest, completely disappears, and when he has finally been found, the knight Philippe Pot has the awkward task of restoring the duke's composure. Pot must have been a clever courtier, for he greets the duke with the words: 'Good day, my lord, what are you about? Are you playing King Arthur or Sir Lancelot nowadays?' When the duke's physicians advise him to shave his head, he insists on all his knights following suit. At the discovery of an unshaven knight, the barber is set to work on him without delay. And so it goes on.[16]

Equally functional is the wonderful vignette that Huizinga gives us of Erasmus, dining at Magdalen College. 'It was a meal such as gladdened his heart, of a kind that he would often describe in his *Colloquia* later on: refined table-companions, good food, moderate drinking, high-minded conversation.' After a serious discussion about Cain, Erasmus saw it as his duty to lighten the mood with a good story. To that end, he invented an old manuscript in which he had supposedly read that Cain, having frequently heard his parents talking about the remarkable heights to which the plants grew in the Garden of Eden, had gone to the angel guarding the gates of Paradise and persuaded him to give him a few seeds of that grain. Since no apples were involved, God would surely not mind? He asked the angel if he actually enjoyed standing all alone at the gate with his heavy sword, adding that on earth they had already switched to guard-dogs. Earth was doing better all the time, and with a little work it would soon be another paradise. At length, he talked the angel round, but when God saw the results of Cain's agricultural policy, swift punishment followed. 'No humanist ever thought up a more finely-tuned compromise between Genesis and the Prometheus myth,' concluded Huizinga.[17]

Unsurprisingly, Huizinga stresses Erasmus's 'lively sense of anecdote'. He himself possessed it in at least equal measure. He included one of his finest anecdotes in *Dutch Civilization in the Seventeenth Century* to depict the austerity of the Dutch Republic. 'While foreigners may not have been struck by the simplicity of life in the wealthy mercantile towns, what impression would they have gained, amid such well-being, by life in the countryside? Adriaan Leeghwater, who, with his work and plans, embodied our nation's healthy and far-sighted pragmatic vision, relates in his remarkable memoirs that in the village of De Rijp, where he was born, there were only three pairs of shoes, and that these were claimed by the magistrates when they had to go to The Hague on business relating to the States.'[18]

TYPES

This extrapolation from a single case to the whole, from the particular to the general, was called 'typism', in the historiography of the Middle Ages, but Huizinga preferred to call it idealism: 'It was less an incapacity to see the specificity of things than a conscious desire to interpret the sense of things everywhere in relation to the highest, their ethical ideality, their universal significance.' Thus, in the Middle Ages the third estate in general was personified as 'the labourer toiling in the field', 'the diligent craftsman', or 'the industrious merchant', 'as simply and concisely as a miniature in a calendar or a bas-relief depicting the weeks of the year'. With the same aim, Huizinga invoked certain typical ideals, because they were both specific and open to generalization, both imaginable and representative. Borges would refer to them as 'warm abstractions'.[19]

Examples occur throughout Huizinga's oeuvre, from his early Sanskrit studies down to his late cultural criticism. Thus, the *vidûshaka* is 'the standard comical type, who is characteristic of a particular period of literary history'. The Northern Netherlands of his early mediaeval studies exhibited 'both politically and socially, a diversity of types such as are perhaps found nowhere within such a small area in the entire German Empire'. In his book on the University of Groningen, one is left with the impression that there are as many types as there are people. Muntinge was 'a type of the day'. Van Swinderen's mind was 'typical of his circle and his period' ('No one ever walked through life with a more childlike belief in a private Providence').[20]

In his first book on the United States, every page bristles with types. From the old merchant adventurer (John Jacob Astor) to the modern captain of industry (William Duer), from the pioneering democrat (Andrew Jackson) to the pioneering entrepreneur (Jay Gould), each in turn is presented as exemplifying an essential group or layer of American society, to enable the reader to form a picture of a complex whole. Thus, Huizinga contrasts the lofty Calvinist and self-interested mercantile spirit of New England with Virginia, where aristocratic plantation-owners held sway, 'a more refined social type, but even poorer in terms of original intellectual culture than that of New England'. In short, there was 'a variegated multiplicity of types'.[21]

He approaches the history of the Netherlands in the same way. Erasmus, for example, as an 'intellectual type', belonged to the 'quite rare class of those who are both unqualified idealists and unwaveringly moderate in their views'. He sees Hugo Grotius as belonging to the same class; much of what they personify merged into 'the intellectual type of the Dutchman', which he also refers to as 'the social type of the new, free nation'. Urban life was composed of specific urban types, and even the Dutch Republic represented a specific type of government: 'an in itself weak central authority driven by the common interests of the urban oligarchies.' He also notes, 'The type of the State and the nation remained Protestant, but not exclusively Calvinist.'[22]

The best example of this kind of typism is found in Huizinga's work on the Middle Ages. *The Waning of the Middle Ages* was based to a large extent on his reading of three Burgundian chroniclers: Georges Chastellain, Olivier de la Marche, and Jean Molinet. 'Together – originating as they do from Flanders, Burgundy, and Picardy – they represent the three main elements of the Burgundian state.' He derived his image of mediaeval chivalry from three model knights, Boucicaut, Jean de Bueil, and Jacques de Lalaing. He saw the spirit of the twelfth century as encapsulated in three pre-Gothic minds: 'Abelard, whose mind I approached in the intellectual sphere, John of Salisbury, who impressed me primarily with his ethics, and Alan of Lille, that supremely apt exponent of twelfth-century aestheticism.' When Huizinga divides the nineteenth-century professors at the University of Groningen into 'three different types' – 'the versatile collector, the devoutly romantic lover of nature (and adept of rural economics), and the champion of technological advances in large-scale industry' – his approach is not that of Weberian sociology but that of mediaeval idealism.[23]

TIME WARPS

It was partly this idealism that led Huizinga to choose his subjects and sources with care. He saw Buddhism as a kind of time warp, in which the entire process whereby ideas are formed had been accelerated. 'As if the Indian mind had taken a shorter route from the fettered conceptual life of a primitive people to the higher realm of abstraction, giving the rudiments of the initial culture no time to become eroded, we see the entire gamut of primitive representations incorporated into the Indian conceptual system.' In America and the Dutch Republic too, the speed of the development had preserved the entire course from primitive beginnings to mature development in visible form in the signs of the time.[24]

On American cattle farming, he wrote 'Thus, in the space of half a century, we find it first emerging in the most primitive forms, and yet by the end of the period it has already evolved into the most modern forms of economic organization and is embroiled in the most modern of economic struggles.' 'How is it possible,' he demanded in *Dutch Civilization in the Seventeenth Century*, 'that a region as small and relatively isolated within seventeenth-century Europe as the Netherlands managed to rise to such prominence as a State, as a mercantile power, and as a centre of civilization, as the young Dutch Republic?'[25]

That is how Huizinga studied history – as a concentration of life. Dutch civilization in the seventeenth century was 'a past reality, that is, an abstract reality, but nonetheless so full of life and contours, that its representation scarcely strikes us as abstract'. That life was in the history itself, down to its very sources. The excise letter of Floris V issued on 13 December 1274, the central source for his study of Haarlem, went to the heart of civic taxation; besides, 'the entire document is plucked with such immediacy from the varied activities of burghers' lives that almost every provision sheds light on some aspect of Haarlem's business and pleasure'. 'It is as if for one brief, sharp moment, the picture of thirteenth-century Haarlem in all its teeming hustle and bustle is brightly illuminated, but as soon as we try to look more closely, the sources leave us in the dark again.'[26]

This did not mean that Huizinga could not preserve any distance from his sources, that he was too close to matters of detail and neglected questions of a more general nature. In 'The task of cultural history',[27] his very first proposition was 'Historiography suffers from the malady of an inadequate formulation of questions.' However great Huizinga's love of anecdotes may have been, history as *petite histoire* did not appeal to him. 'Here are some letters from an insignificant diplomat in a small state, there are the accounts of an impoverished little monastery'; they reduced history to 'a flow of quisquiliae'. The smaller the detail, the more general the question should be. And this was indeed always the case in Huizinga. Synaesthesia was the cradle of language (against the *Junggramatiker*), the comic figure in Indian drama personified developments in cultural history (with Levi); he defined his position on the origins of the mediaeval city (against Burdach), the origins of the nation (against Pirenne), and the origins of the modern period (against Burckhardt). Similarly, he discussed the history of the United States as a form prefiguring that of Europe: 'The argument for modern culture is being pursued more simply in America than with us. Will Europe follow?'[28]

CENTRE AND PERIPHERY

A similar device transformed periphery into centre. The follies of the *vidûshaka* reflected 'the serious matter of the play'. In Van Eyck's *Lamb of God*, it is not the protagonists who attract most attention, and the viewer's gaze wanders from the lamb itself to the depiction of nature. 'And our gaze is drawn further still to the edges: to Adam and Eve, to the donors' portraits. Although – at least in the Annunciation scene – the intimate, earnest appeal resides in the figures of the angel and the Virgin Mary, that is, in expressive piety, even there, perhaps, we delight still more in the copper kettle and the glimpse of the sunny street. It is the details, for the artist mere staffage, which cause to flower here in its silent show the mystery of the commonplace, the immediate marvel at the miracle of all things and its revelation.'[29]

Thus, Huizinga portrayed Erasmus as an outsider, as a departure from 'the general tendencies of his day'. Of Van Vollenhoven, he wrote: 'This man who lived so simply, indeed ascetically, and who was at the same time unsurpassed in his hospitality, in the quiet house in the small town, was a hub, such as no world-famous public figure in a princely state could be.' The *Einzelgänger* Jan Veth too was a 'focal point' of Dutch culture. 'A human life is a stretch of time that passes through a central point of personal consciousness. In some it seems to be but a trickling gully; in others it is as if shafts of light and vibrations from everywhere travel infinite distances, meeting and crossing there, at that centre.'[30]

He freely indulged in this game in his local historiography. The Northern Netherlands of his first mediaeval studies were characterized by 'their remarkable isolation from the old centres of civilization'. This applied most especially to Holland [the western provinces of North and South Holland – transl.], which lay, according to Herbert, the bishop of Utrecht, 'in extremo margine mundi' – 'at the extreme edge of the world'. Haarlem was 'the count's remotest little town'. Its every aspect, its economic and urban development, its ecclesiastical and political organization, exemplified the periphery. In every respect it was 'completely outside the central area of Western European civilization'. 'What was emerging in Holland,' he wrote in his biography of Erasmus, 'flowered out of sight.'[31]

At the same time, every town, whatever its size, 'was far more than now a centre of traffic, constituting together with the surrounding countryside a self-contained circle of production and consumption'. This certainly applied to Haarlem: 'Roads and waterways came together near Haarlem. All transport routes converged there.' This applied not only to its position in the Kennemerland region, but also to its significance in Dutch history. Just as the whole of Haarlem's civic life is illuminated by that single excise letter dating from 1274, Haarlem illuminated the whole of Holland. 'It did not live for itself alone, but for the whole of Holland. What other city did we know so much about – even as schoolboys, living far away in the remotest part of our country – as Haarlem? Even then we had heard of the Haarlemmer Wood, the *damiaatjes*,[32] the Blinkert [dunes] and the Manpad [castle], the ruins of Brederode, the siege, St Bavo's organ: Haarlem impinges on every part of Dutch history, and always at the most beautiful points.'[33]

This coincidence of periphery with the centre also applied to Groningen, the key to the Netherlands, the gateway to Germany, and to Zeeland, 'that most enchanting region of the Netherlands, where the lights were softer, the vistas more compelling, the meadows greener, and the villages more intimate – and where the towns were cleaner ... than elsewhere.' The same applied to Leiden and to its Relief: 'I know of no other case in history in which the fate and future of a country and a people hinged to such an extent on the outcome of a single event ... as Dutch history hinged on the relief of Leiden.' In short, it applied to all the places where Huizinga had lived and written history.[34]

He played this game most adroitly with his own country. The Netherlands, as Huizinga saw it, was a small country at the periphery of Europe. At the same time, it had assimilated the culture of the surrounding countries like none other, and was therefore pre-eminently well equipped to play a role in the concert of nations. The Netherlands' 'eccentricity' was the key qualification for its central role in Europe. 'The time may soon be ripe again, if our civilization does not sink into oblivion, for the renewed appreciation of small political entities.' The Netherlands described by Huizinga was the circle whose centre was everywhere and whose circumference was nowhere.[35]

12

METAMORPHOSIS

'A miraculous process of pupations' was how Burckhardt had described history. And that was how Huizinga had fashioned it, literally, with form as the *trait d'union* between mutable life and immutable human nature. Life existed in infinite variations, forms were limited in number, while the essence of man remained virtually constant. Somewhere in between the varicoloured variety of the day and the profound realization of eternity, between that mosaic of anecdotes and the timeless narrative, were the historical forms, which served as 'binding agents'. That was the only way to approach human identity, the true content of history. It was '*forms* of life and thought' that he presented in The Waning of the Middle Ages. 'Coming close to the essential *content* that resided in these forms – will that ever be the subject of historical research?'

Huizinga joined solid form to changing history by drawing 'lines'. 'This presages the spirit of military France,' he writes in The Waning of the Middle Ages, 'that would later yield the figures of the musketeer, the *grognard* and the *poilu.*' And further on: 'Calendar miniatures record with pleasure the threadbare knees of the little reapers in the corn, paintings capture the rags of beggars receiving charity.

This is the beginning of the line that leads through Rembrandt's etchings and Murillo's street urchins to the figures in Steinlen's street scenes.'[1]

Huizinga's concern was not to trace a linear development, but to reveal a metamorphosis of forms. These forms remained utterly constant; one age passed them on to the next, and most were as old as antiquity. 'But in Antiquity they had possessed an entirely different *significance* than in the Middle Ages. They constantly adapted to the central principle of the culture that applied them.' The Renaissance did not alter this, nor did the Baroque. It was, he said, 'a round dance of figures around the figure of the veiled goddess'.[2]

MUTABILITY

While Huizinga's observations about the way our picture of history is formed are far from systematic, the limited variation of possible forms is central to his argument. 'For the forms in which the ideal of love must necessarily cloak itself,' he wrote in *The Waning of the Middle Ages*, 'are few in number, for all time.' The same applied to dreams. Huizinga saw the aristocratic life of the later Middle Ages as an attempt to play out a dream. 'Always the same dream, that of the old heroes and sages, the knight and the maiden, the simple, contented shepherds. France and Burgundy are still repeating the play in the old style; Florence writes a new, more beautiful play on the same theme.'[3]

Huizinga then follows the pupation of these finite forms. The pastoral is a good example. 'When fifteenth-century nobles play shepherd and shepherdess, the substance in terms of a real love of nature and an admiration of simplicity and labour is still very tenuous. Three centuries later, with Marie Antoinette milking and making butter in Trianon, the ideal has been filled with the earnestness of the physiocrats: by then, nature and labour have become the great sleeping deities of time; even so, aristocratic culture still makes them into a game. When, around 1870, young Russian intellectuals mingle with the common people, to live as peasants for the peasants, the ideal has become deadly serious. And even then, its realization proved to be a delusion.'[4]

Huizinga describes this metamorphosis as 'a series of constantly repeated Renaissances'. We have already seen how he coined this idea in his inaugural address in Leiden. From pastoral to the chivalric ideal, each concept was a re-creation of existing forms, forms that slackened and then revived. The elasticity was determined by the promise of the ideal, the form slackened when the lie surpassed the inspiration. A form would die off, after which its symbols would be stored as obsolete stage props. But the intellectual need that had been visualized in this way lived on, and created for itself a different outward form.[5]

We can say that form appears like the phases of the moon, waxing and waning in relation to its distance from truth. If the moon is close to the sun, we cannot see it. That is the 'new moon'. The form is empty. As it gradually moves away from the sun, we see it more clearly. When the maximum distance is reached, it is full moon. The form too is 'full', but it has become a fiction. Huizinga had long been acquainted with this principle from ethnographic literature, and had also encountered it in his studies of ancient Indian literature. There, he had followed closely the metamorphosis of vague guilt into philosophical pessimism: 'but the outer shell of the thought, its form, has proved enduring'. As a historian he had soon observed the same phenomenon at work in the development of national identity: 'Just as in the development of religion, loftier ideas grow to maturity on the dry stem of older and cruder conceptions, the modern sense of statehood too has been grafted onto older notions that are more primitive in content.'

'Full moon', in Huizinga, is formalism. In *The Waning of the Middle Ages*, he describes this as the unwavering contours that delineated a particular form, 'isolated in a plastic form, and *it is that form that is dominant*'. But this is also the moment of reversal. An idea, a concept, can acquire such sharp contours and be so firmly entrenched in the midst of other ideas as to almost become a person. The form comes to life, as it were, but once it is incorporated into such a tightly-knit moral and religious hierarchy, its content is lost.[6]

In *The Waning of the Middle Ages*, that moment of reversal is itself the central theme. That is why Huizinga devotes so much space in it to the use of slogans and mottoes, because slogans are in a sense a compressed form of the phenomenon of externalization. 'The outward form takes the place, as it were, of the term's substance. Just as for an Indian the consciousness of his tribal attachments is translated into form and content in his totem, so it was, up to a point, in the fifteenth century. It was pre-eminently the century of mottoes and emblems, of devices and blazons.'[7]

The general rule was that as soon as a form was defined with great clarity and detail, it produced a sense of too much familiarity and predictability. 'The saints with their familiar figures possessed the reassuring characteristics of a policeman in a big unfamiliar city.' On the one hand this was a loss of style, but on the other hand, Huizinga was wary of branding it as degeneration. 'It is within one and the same process that modern culture both ascends to its highest peaks and germinates the seeds of its future decay.' In the equilibrium that ultimately constituted a culture, the process eventually signified something in the nature of shifting a weight. 'As Mary rose to greater heights, Joseph increasingly became a caricature.' What was called allegory in the Middle Ages was known in the Renaissance as mythology: 'As time went on, the Olympians and the nymphs triumphed over the Rose and the

Sinnekens [mediaeval personifications of sensual inclinations – transl.].'[8]

What was at issue here was not so much decay as a change of repertoire. The lustre of mediaeval love life could not mask the extreme coarseness of actual behaviour. 'Yet coarseness is not simply falling short of the ideal. Like rarefied love, dissipation too had a style of its own, which was truly ancient. It might be called the epithalamic style.' So here, Huizinga was harking back to a far more primitive form of eroticism – the glorification of sexual intercourse, phallic symbolism – as part of a much more formal conception of love. Thus, the very 'disruption' of form became form, just as cheating in play is also a kind of play.[9]

In Huizinga, this notion of permanent transformation, this insight into the metamorphosis of forms, stems from his earliest experiences and reading, and is essentially the world viewed in the guise of a fairy tale. 'In many respects, life still had the colour of a fairy tale,' he wrote in *The Waning of the Middle Ages*. In fact it had never really lost that colour. So the two metamorphoses that will conclude this final chapter, one psychological, the other moral, were not just history to Huizinga, they were also autobiography.[10]

THE WILD MAN, THE CHILD, THE POET, AND THE MYSTIC

At several points in his oeuvre, Huizinga combines a number of standard psychological figures. It is a curious line-up, in which he seeks to bring together everything that is original and unsullied, primitive and pure. He first does this in *The Waning of the Middle Ages*, in another passage seeking to clarify symbolism. 'Even our minds are still capable,' he writes about the capacity for seeing colours as symbolic essences, 'of seeing them like that at any time, when they briefly revert to the wisdom of the wild man, the child, the poet, and the mystic, for whom the natural constitution of things is epitomized by their general qualities.'[11]

In his major essay on Spengler and Wells, 'Two wrestlers with the angel',[12] he describes that wisdom as one of the two ways of understanding the world: 'that of the immediate awareness of things in their totality and in their interrelatedness, the apprehension of their intrinsic nature and shape, of seeing things in [the context of] time, in their supernatural fullness of significance, in their eternal motion and their tragic fatality. It is the way in which primitive man, the child and the poet understand the world.' The second way developed only at a later stage of culture: 'seeing things in their isolation, in [the context of] space, analyzing, measuring, calculating, systematizing, solving all mysteries with the category of causality'.[13]

Later still, in *Homo Ludens*, Huizinga reserves the primitive, original approach for poetry itself. 'If seriousness is interpreted as that which is capable of being fully expressed in terms of the waking life, then poetry never becomes entirely serious. It stands on the far side of seriousness, on that original side, where children, animals, primitive men and visionaries belong, in the realm of dreams, of rapture, intoxication, and laughter.' The whole text of *Homo Ludens* is geared towards dissolving the distinction between child and primitive man. The child is one with his play, just as the primitive man, in his magic dance, *becomes* the kangaroo. 'It is a mystical identity. One being becomes another.' This metamorphosis too is based on the fairy tale. It is 'the atmosphere of the sacred play, where child and poet are at home, together with the wild man'. And it is 'aesthetic sensitivity' that has 'brought modern man a little closer to that atmosphere'.[14]

He had equated the child and the wild man before, in *The Waning of the Middle Ages*. The big difference that denizens of the Middle Ages experienced between suffering and joy, between disasters and happiness, could only be measured with 'that degree of immediacy and absoluteness which joy and suffering still have now in the mind of a child'. 'In everyday life there was unlimited space for burning passion and childish imaginings.' The people's affection for their ruler was 'childishly impulsive in nature'. A child's game of forfeits was nothing but a lower form of 'the same ancient struggle and courting'. All mediaeval traditions, especially those surrounding birth, marriage, and death, had 'grown from primitive faith and cult'. Mediaeval symbolism was the quintessentially primitive mode of thought, the link that connected mediaeval thought to 'the forms of thought of a remote prehistoric age'. The entire Quattrocento was 'naive, freshly archaic'.[15]

Thus too, the poetry of Walt Whitman was 'immensely primitive and pagan'. For Huizinga, that was precisely the appeal of American literature as a whole. 'One of the most telling tests of the true humanity of a literature concerns the place that animals and children occupy in it.' Huizinga gives a splendid example in the form of an anecdote about his friend, the painter Veth, who refused to work on the basis of photographs. He knew of an exception to that rule. A fourteen-year-old boy once sent Veth a letter asking him to draw a portrait of his brother, who had died. He very much wanted to give it to his father as a present for his fiftieth birthday. 'Couldn't you draw it just as you drew Mother for him?' 'On the birthday,' Huizinga continues, 'the petitioner was able to present his father, as his own gift, a subtle, lightly elegiac drawing, a perfect image. When the father hastened to thank the real giver, the latter said, "It was such a sweet little note that I immediately said I'd do it."' That fourteen-year-old boy was Leonhard, the father was Johan Huizinga, the deceased brother was Dirk, who died young. 'Does all this – words from the mouths of babes, as it were – have too little to do with art?' demanded Huizinga. 'It is about the Meaning of art' was his answer.[16]

KNIGHT, HONNÊTE HOMME, GENTLEMAN, AND BOURGEOISIE

The second line-up is no less applicable to Huizinga himself, and connects a Greek ideal of upbringing, through a number of links, to a nineteenth-century view of the exemplary role of the upper middle classes. The ideal is *kalokagathia*, a term coined from the Greek words for good and beautiful, καλός and αγαθός. The connections are made explicit in *Homo Ludens*: 'A straight line runs from the knight through the *honnête homme* of the seventeenth century to the modern "gentleman". In its cult of the life of the noble warrior, the Latinate West also incorporated the ideal of courtship, wove it through its fabric so tightly that in the course of time, the weft concealed the warp.' Earlier, in *The Waning of the Middle Ages*, he had described chivalry as 'a social, ethical and aesthetic necessity'. The power of the ideal lay in its exaggeration, which at the same time sapped its vigour. The new era jettisoned the overly high-pitched aspirations. 'The knight becomes the French *gentilhomme* of the seventeenth century, who still upholds a set of stances and notions of honour, but no longer poses as a champion of the faith, a defender of the weak and oppressed. The French type of the nobleman is superseded by that of the gentleman, a concept derived directly from the ancient knight, but tempered and refined. With each successive transformation of the ideal, the outer layer, which had become a lie, was shed.'[17]

Huizinga shows how all this links up with the Greek ideal of upbringing in his portrait of Jean de Bueil, the model knight and a captain in Joan of Arc's army. 'What a joyful thing is war,' he quoted from a contemporary biography, commenting: 'This could just as well be said by a modern soldier as by a fifteenth-century knight. It has nothing to do with the chivalric ideal as such. It reveals the emotional foundation underlying pure martial courage itself: the shuddering shunning of narrow self-interest in the embrace of mortal peril, the deep tenderness for a comrade's bravery, the bliss of loyalty and self-sacrifice. This primitive ascetic emotion provided the basis for the cultivation of the chivalric ideal as a noble image of masculine perfection, closely related to the Greek *kalokagathia*, a powerful aspiration to live a glorious life, the energetic inspiration of the march of centuries ... and it is also the mask behind which a world of self-interest and violence could hide.'[18]

The scope of this ideal is clear from the fact that it was shared by the Brahmins of Indian antiquity and the nineteenth-century European bourgeoisie. What his teacher Kern found so congenial in the Brahmin, his ethical equanimity, moderation, composure, and forgiveness, was essentially a set of chivalric values. 'Was the attraction, for him,' Huizinga wondered, 'not related to the qualities that endeared Spaniards to him? Brahmins and Spaniards both take great pride in the *beau geste*. Spaniards too have that chivalry; bombastic perhaps, but also noble – Don Quixotes. They all possess this quality to a greater or lesser extent, and that is why Kern enjoyed associating with Spaniards just as much as reading Cervantes. When De Ruyter proclaimed in 1676: "I do not waver in offering up my life, but it grieves me that the States are offering up their flag," Kern remarks that he spoke like a Brahmin.'[19]

Huizinga himself makes the link between knight and bourgeoisie. All the higher forms of present-day bourgeois life, he asserts, are based on the emulation of aristocratic traditions. 'Just as the bread in the serviette and the very word *serviette* have their origins in the royal court of mediaeval times, the most bourgeois of wedding customs are descendants of the grand *entremets* of Lille. To fully understand the cultural significance of the chivalric ideal, one would have to follow it through the age of Shakespeare and Molière to that of the modern gentleman.' We have already seen that this conflation of knight and bourgeois gentleman has another, analogous line that is no less autobiographical: the conflation of the knight with the clerk or scholar.[20]

That Huizinga identified with this ideal can be inferred from his veneration for its great exponents, such as Alan of Lille, John of Salisbury, and Sir Philip Sidney. He writes that Alan's *Anticlaudianus* paints the portrait of the true gentleman, and describes John of Salisbury as a true 'chivalric clerk', 'positive in everything he did': 'ever serving, ever solicitous, courageous, sincere, and loyal.' Sidney, in his view, is both knight and poet, 'a poet who fell in a struggle for liberty'. 'He performed that most original and simplest act of courage, which remains eternally great, regardless of whether it is a paladin who is slain amid the full splendour of chivalric glory, or a poor Turkish solder dying of starvation behind a mound of earth.'[21]

The example they set is based on a number of special, if not cardinal, virtues, such as compassion, justice, restraint, and the willingness to serve. Huizinga places particular emphasis on loyalty, a core value of both chivalry and patriotism. Compared to 'the venality and perfidy that governed politics in the surrounding countries', he called the bourgeois politics of the seventeenth-century Netherlands 'the epitome of integrity'. And what applied in politics also applied in art. 'What in the sphere of aesthetics is called style is known in ethics as loyalty and order.'[22]

Huizinga's entire concept of play is suffused with it. 'One virtue in particular appears truly to have been born amid the noble death struggles of prehistoric warriors: loyalty. Loyalty is surrendering to person, cause, or idea, without discussing the reasons for that surrender or questioning its permanent imperative. It is an attitude closely related to that of play. It is not far-fetched to hypothesize that the origin of a virtue that has provided, in its purest form and its ghastly perversions, such a strong ferment in history, may well lie in the most primitive games.'[23]

HUIZINGA AS ANTI-MODERNIST

Ideas and ideals like these define Huizinga as someone who repudiated modernity. His cultural criticism was not a surface manifestation that deplored an incidental and temporary development: rather, it was the conclusion of someone who rejected the whole notion of irreversible progress, the acceleration of the pace of social change that had been elevated to a principle, the simplified portrayal of humankind that accompanied it. What Huizinga wanted from life was passion and repetition, but what he saw was blandness and innovation. It led him to radically reject the currents of his time, but it also gave his writings their defining timelessness.

Huizinga's anti-modernism cannot be understood without grasping his view of humanity. This view was determined in large measure by the role he accorded love and loyalty, friendship and faithfulness. To comprehend Huizinga's position, we must place his views in the context of the transformation that passion had undergone in the course of time. To put it very simply, this transformation consists of two distinct metamorphoses. The first took place in the Middle Ages, and involved an intensification that converted the passive pathos of classical antiquity into the active emulation of Christ. The second took place in the nineteenth century, and involved the scientific simplification of the Christian complex of passions into a monolithic psychology of emotions.[24]

The classical tradition of passion was that of the Stoics. Whereas Aristotle described passion in ethically neutral terms as enduring/suffering, the Stoics added the negative connotations of *perturbatio*, of vehemence and confusion. Passion was conceived as the opposite of calm and reason. The true sage was *impassibilis*, unperturbed and unmoved by the tumult of life and the struggle for existence. Under the influence of this view, many Christian authors equated *passiones* with the lusts of the flesh and with sin. At the same time, Christian ethics emphasized the *bonae passiones*, the good passions. Early Christian writers rejected the Stoics' serenity, arguing that Christians must not withdraw from the world and seek to avoid suffering and passion, but instead surrender to passion, the passion of emulating Jesus Christ, which, in the mediaeval experience, covered a huge spectrum extending from the exalted mysticism of Bernard of Clairvaux to the quiet wisdom of Thomas à Kempis.

Huizinga sought unreservedly to uphold this tradition. He wielded his oppositions for their strong ethical content as much as for their high drama. The drama of history resided in the inevitability of mutual incomprehension between blinkered conservatives and arrogant innovators. Its ethics resided in a respect for what was dead and beautiful, and the love of what was young and alive. And he aligned himself in that cosmic struggle between light and darkness, good and evil. That is why he classified periods of history according to their dominant passion, pride as the vice of antiquity, greed as the vice of modern times.

In the meantime, passion went through a second metamorphosis. After a period of germination in the eighteenth century, the first half of the nineteenth century exhibited a radical reversal in the terms in which passion was discussed. What had previously been associated with soul and conscience, sin and forgiveness, spirit and the devil, free will and dark desires, was now translated to a different idiom, full of psychology and natural laws, organism and evolution, brain and bowels, expression and behaviour. Passion became emotion, and the emotions – thoroughly secularized – were assigned a limited space in a human being's mental constitution, somewhere between feeling and understanding. Theory was that emotions originated in the brain, in the nerves, or in the bowels, from which they could be passed on to the rest of the body. In consequence, emotions reverted to the passivity they had possessed before the Christian intervention.

While Christian thought had distinguished between good and bad passions, modern science lumped them all together. While Christian psychology had distinguished between the lower passions that man shared with animals, and the higher affections that separated them, modern psychology reduced emotion to a domain of all creatures, whether animal or human. While Christian thought had prioritized the intellectual and cognitive elements of passion, modern doctrine embraced the primacy of physical reaction. Modern psychology had succeeded in becoming a true science by concentrating on observations of the activity of brain and nerves, muscles and behaviour – activity that could be described objectively. In so doing, it had diminished the range of human passion.

That was precisely what Huizinga objected to. As a philologist, he had insisted that no one could practise linguistics who did not understand poetry. As a historian, he had argued that no one could practise history who did not read literature. 'What picture would someone have of the thirteenth century,' he demanded in his 1905 inaugural address, 'if he has read all the papal registers and is unfamiliar with the *Dies Irae?*' He repeated this view in *The Waning of the Middle Ages*: 'But the history of civilization has just as much to do with people's dreams of beauty and the delusions of the noble life as it has to do with population and taxation statistics.'[25]

With its accent on the elements of emotion that were susceptible to scientific study, modern psychology had not just simplified passion, it had stripped it of its moral significance. With its own accent on official sources, modern historiography had done the same. And for Huizinga, history was 'morality in action'. In *Geschonden wereld* ('Shattered World'), discussing the system of sins and virtues, he wrote: 'Let no one sneer, "What do those familiar old abstractions have to say to us today, those general notions from a conceptual world that has long since passed away? For subjects such as these, we now have the science of psychology!" It has been my conviction for over forty years, and I have expressed this belief on more than one occasion, that these sets of virtues and vices, whether we want to count seven or eight of them, are among the most precious conceptual instruments, today just as two thousand years ago, for exploring everything relating to the emotional life and moral code of human beings.'[26]

The heart of the matter was that Huizinga loathed the standardized image of man because of its cultural implications. His passions had never become emotions, and his emotions had never become urges. His attachment to the old framework of the passions made him an anti-modernist in principle. And *Homo Ludens* was his grand response to the marshals of the modern age – Marx, Darwin, Freud – a rehabilitation of passion in all its complexity. Huizinga did not deny the applicability of the findings of the modernist trio, but he disliked the one-sidedness of the dogmas based on them. Passion was both giving and receiving, drive and restraint, conscious and unconscious.

That may be the reason – as Helmuth Plessner comments in *Die Frage nach der Conditio humana* – that precisely when science was reducing emotion to a physical substratum, literature was painting the most comprehensive physiognomy of it. At the exact moment that psychology was trying to construct a mechanical model for emotional drives and burying passion beneath terms like aggression and regression, suppression and sublimation, literature displayed a near-unquenchable thirst for personal drama. From this vantage point, history was a mere continuation of literature by other means. And that was how Huizinga saw it.[27]

CODA

13

HISTORICAL GREATNESS

The name of Huizinga refers to a place and a lineage. There is nothing uncommon about this, but in the case of Johan Huizinga it is more significant than usual. The Huizingas into which Johan was born can be traced back to the sixteenth century, to the Melkema family farm in the village of Huizinge. He was apparently not particularly proud of his name, describing it on one occasion as 'extremely common'. The Huizingas also had droves of 'Johans';[1] the name was passed on from grandfather to grandson. Johan was the most mundane of names, unless one were to associate it with the asceticism of a camel's-hair cloak and a voice crying in the wilderness – no arcane association, perhaps, in the Mennonite community.

Huizinga took a curious view of his forename. In a letter to Anna Veth, his best friend's wife, who had remarked that after all those years she still did not know exactly what he wanted to be called, he wrote: 'Oh yes, my name. I don't really have a name, I'm like Andersen's magician. I was officially registered as Johan, but only distant cousins call me that. Very early on they called me Han, but that too I only half-recognize. My name sits very loosely on me.'[2]

To understand what he meant by that, we must go back to the fairy tale 'The Drop of Water', to that exchange between Kribble Krabble and the other magician. For this second magician had no name, 'and that was the best thing about him,' added Andersen. This phrase evidently lodged in Huizinga's mind. In *Homo Ludens*, for instance, he quotes a passage from Plato about the identity of play and ritual that describes Man as God's plaything. 'And that,' added Huizinga, 'was the best thing about him.'[3]

Names play a special part in Huizinga's work. In the earliest treatise he ever published, on the *vidûshaka*, he demonstrated the character's stereotypical quality by showing that his actual name was never used. In *The Waning of the Middle Ages* he dwells at length on the primitive anthropomorphic tendency 'to name everything, even inanimate objects'. His discussion of Van Eyck's name is illustrative, since on the one hand Van Eyck signed his work with his full name, thus emphasizing his individuality, but at the same time he was famous 'only by the utterly common baptismal name' with which he signed his letters – Johannes.

It sometimes seems that Huizinga enjoyed poking fun at his own name. In the notes in his estate we find the remark: 'Geertgen's Johannes, that pensive, grey little fellow in the flower-garden, personifies the Renaissance of the Northern Netherlands!' In his major study on the loss of the original Frisian character of the region around Groningen,[4] he points out the frequency with which the Christian name of Johan appears in official records. In *The Waning of the Middle Ages*, he refers to a prior of Windesheim who bore the 'honourable nickname' of 'Jan What's-his-name'.[5]

Huizinga was acutely conscious of the link between name and personality. At one point he alludes to 'the old human habit of not attributing an essence to things until they have been named'. He also had clear views about human individuality. He disliked the repudiation of it in Buddhism and mysticism. 'The disavowal of the essence of the ego', and above all the related repudiation of the soul, which he saw as the basic principle of Buddhism, went against the grain with him. But he also rejected mediaeval mysticism, 'the sense of the complete negation of individuality'.

At the same time, he rejected what he saw as the exaggerated self-awareness of modern times, which had peaked in the Romantic era. 'We are always too concerned with personal originality,' he wrote in his 'Brief colloquy on themes of Romanticism'.[6] In a fine meditation for the Society of Dutch Literature on the contrast between originality and derivation, he referred to Huygens's correspondence with Dorothea van Dorp: how they gave each other the same pet names – Song, Songetgen. 'She is the Song, and he is the Song; she fondles the word as a caress.' Huizinga cited many earlier examples of the use of such identical pet names, for instance in the troubadour poetry of the twelfth century. He nonetheless held that the way in which Dorothea and Constantijn used them expressed an utterly individual brand of tenderness.[7]

In precisely the same way, he valued the individuality that was highlighted in biography. The two biographies he wrote, as well as the many biographical portraits that were printed in the sixth volume of his collected works, show how direct and uncomplicated, in Huizinga's view, the biographer's task was. In his biography of Jan Veth, he wanted nothing less than to portray 'the whole person, in what he meant for his country and his age', and he did so in a 'simple story of his life'. In the case of Erasmus too, the whole person is described in the context of his times, without flinching or evasion.

As for what defined that individualism, Huizinga did not see it as residing in grand gestures. To him, the depth of a human life was determined not by exorbitant claims or prizes but by a chance outcome, an oblique finger-exercise. This chimed with his preference for the 'humble' personality. 'Great men dazzle and set the norm, while humble men make it possible for that norm to be tested,' he wrote in his colloquy on Romanticism. 'Sometimes a nameless figure, whom stylistic criticism has rescued from obscurity, such as the Master of the Forties, can fascinate us more than the great men of the day,' he had said before, in *The Waning of the Middle Ages*. That is why so many of his characters are types *as well as* individuals.[8]

Also typical of Huizinga was the affinity he felt with certain characters. Indeed, he only wrote about subjects and people with whom he identified. The sympathy he felt for those pre-gothic spirits is obvious, especially for John of Salisbury, *homo plebejus*, 'the man with the serious smile'. *The Waning of the Middle Ages* refers to Jean Gerson as 'honest, pure and well-meaning, with that somewhat anxious concern for good form that in a fine mind, which has grown from humble circumstances to a truly aristocratic attitude, often betrays his origins'. And when, in his portrait of Constantijn Huygens, he writes of the man's 'deep mourning for his Sterre, whom he did not forget', he was obviously thinking of his own Mary. But with Erasmus too, for all his criticism, he displays a profound sense of affinity, for instance in his praise for Erasmus's realism and vivid detail: 'He wants to know things and their names.'[9]

It is above all in their universal human qualities, where universal and human qualities coincide, the typical with the individual, that he embraces his historical figures. John of Salisbury was 'ever serving, ever solicitous, courageous, sincere, and loyal', in Gerson he praises his compassion with the condemned and the destitute, his tenderness for children and women. It is precisely when his heroes become self-effacing that Huizinga embraces them. We have already heard him say it in 1915, at the nadir of his life – his wife dead, his culture in ruins – about the ideals that remained: 'To give yourself is the end and the beginning of all doctrines of life. It is in the renunciation not of culture, but of the ego, that liberation is found.'[10]

And here too, just as in the question of naming, the renunciation of ego was not just an individual ethical choice but also a literary-historical figure: the concealed identity of the hero. In *Homo Ludens*, in the chapter on play and poetry, Huizinga dwells at length on the anonymous hero: 'He is not recognized for who he is, either he conceals or does not know his identity, or he can vary or alter his appearance. In a word, the hero wears a mask, performs in disguise, carries a secret within him. Once again we come close to the old game of the hidden being who reveals himself to the initiate.' And it is in the knight that that hero appears in his finest guise. In the nameless knight, history meets fairy tale: 'The knight's anonymity is an entrenched fiction; he is called "le blanc chevalier", "le chevalier mesconnu", "le chevalier à la pélerine", or he acts like a hero from a romance and is called "Swan knight" or sports the arms of Lancelot, Tristan, or Palamedes.'[11]

To his second wife, Huizinga presented himself as that nameless knight. 'I'd be perfectly happy if you thought up another name for me,' he wrote to her from Paris in July 1937, in those wonderful letters that document his courting. 'I've felt little love for that name for a very long time.' He signed that letter, in anticipation of his new name, with a question-mark. He continued to beg in the following letter: 'I still haven't been given a name yet!' This time he signed with an H 'with legs and ears', which was how Guste formed the letter. Later still he resigned himself to his namelessness: 'I can't sign, I no longer have any name for you, and nor do you for me.' By then he has truly become 'le chevalier mesconnu'.[12]

His country, the Netherlands, was in effect another such 'knight'. Like the unknown knight, it had no real name. Whether the territory that would later be known as 'the Netherlands' was called 'les pays de par deça' ('the lands over there'), the Low Countries, 'ès basses régions', 'partes inferiores', or the Seventeen Provinces, it all came down to an admission that the country had no name. That number seventeen – was that not a number, as Huizinga had learned from fairy tales and children's songs, that stood for an indefinite quantity? 'Night watch, did you see the thieves? Yes sir, there were seventeen.' Seventeen was as much as to say 'untold', a nameless quantity.[13]

In the middle of his notes suggesting an outline on the history of Dutch culture in the seventeenth century, we find the disheartened sigh: 'I'm just too steeped in history. I don't see it as an academic discipline, but as life itself.' To my knowledge, there is only one other place where Huizinga makes a similar remark, and that is in his major essay on Joan of Arc for *De Gids*. There he says, of the diminutive young girl from Domrémy: 'People did not know how to deal with her, she was too real.' It seems that there was a curious parallel in Huizinga's emotional constitution between his veneration for Joan of Arc and his love of the Netherlands. Mediaevalists have often pondered the question of why the Netherlands plays such a negligible role in *The Waning of the Middle Ages*. I think that the answer lies in what Huizinga himself remarked about the absence of Joan of Arc in that book. 'Her own personality is such that, as soon as one touches her history, she commands the centre ground,' he wrote in his essay on 'Bernard Shaw's saint'. That was why he excluded her from his book. 'I knew that Joan of Arc would completely distort the context of the book I had in mind.' For the same reason, the Netherlands too was accorded very little space.[14]

In the manner of a nameless knight, Huizinga defended Joan's posthumous fame from 'her judges with their dry hearts and stiff pens'. In the same way, he staunchly defended the reputation of the Netherlands. In the 1920s and 1930s, he put himself forward as the country's 'ambassador', as Van der Lem has justly called it. He argued fervently for the mediating role of Dutch culture amid the spheres of influence of the surrounding countries, defending with unequivocal ferocity the *raison d'être* of small states. It was one of his best friends, Cornelis van Vollenhoven, who coined the enthusiastic formula for it. Van Vollenhoven's celebrated pamphlet, *De eendracht van het land* ('The unity of the nation'), called for the Dutch fleet to be placed at the disposal of an international interventionary force: he proposed that the Netherlands should assume the role of 'Joan of Arc among nations'.

In 1940, in an essay on 'Historical greatness', Huizinga drew a comparison between Carlyle and Burckhardt. In the contrast between those two – between *On Heroes, Hero-worship and the Heroic in History* on the one hand, and 'Die historische Grösse', later incorporated into *Weltgeschichtliche Betrachtungen*, on the other – Huizinga defined his own position. 'The private, remote world of a small auditorium in Basel is here contrasted with the cosmopolitan environment of Carlyle's lectures; the sober restraint of the Swiss sage, whose every word possessed and retained its value, is contrasted with the unbridled ferocity of the apocalyptic Scot. Carlyle's words immediately took flight, while Burckhardt's remained concealed for over thirty years.'[15]

Huizinga left no room for doubt as to where his sympathies lay. Much as he admired Carlyle's passion, the *Weltgeschichtliche Betrachtungen* ('Force and Freedom: Reflections on History') had always remained his vademecum, his bedside reading, the book that helped to shape his insight into history. Yet even Burckhardt (and certainly Carlyle) lacked an essential ingredient when it came to their views of historical greatness. Neither Carlyle's 'hero' nor Burckhardt's *grosse Individuum* had the contours of a real historical life. Both formulated it in largely negative terms such as unicity or irreplaceability; for both it remained a mystery, a reality perhaps, but one that was unknowable. 'If not, the only possible conclusion would be that human greatness is a mere phrase.'[16]

Although Huizinga did not disagree, he felt that there must be more. As he had done in the past, he expressed his observations in terms of contrasts. The first contrast was between logical inevitability and ethical responsibility. It seemed to be commonly believed that historical greatness conferred a kind of dispensation from the ethical dimension, as if great figures somehow transcended questions of good and evil. Huizinga rejected this notion altogether. In the second place, there was the contrast between great and small. 'The human mind appears naturally inclined to express awe, admiration, and veneration in terms of vastness.' This too was something of which Huizinga disapproved. And thirdly, he referred to the contrast between male and female. 'The popular image of greatness, heroism, is undeniably tinged with male delusion.' Together, these three fallacies meant that the concept of greatness 'always rattled a little with the tinny sound of a theatrical suit of armour'.

Considerations such as these inspired his own solution to the problem. He found it in his veneration of Joan of Arc:

> Then if greatness was too grand, and heroism too theatrical, and genius sounds too literary, and none of the three suffices to embrace the entirety of human existence, only saintliness remains. And behold, here the irreducible distinction between the concepts of the male and the female dissolves. There is no division between *Yang* and *Yin*. What is also dissolved is the link between excellence and quantity; there is no earthly measure of saintliness... The 'true greatness' of people is not, as Burckhardt believed, a mystery, but a word, a posthumous chivalric order, conferred by history. No human figure is great, any more than his country, as such, can be great. Just occasionally his works possess a quality that is best described with the imagery of the vastness of space. The quintessence of that quality lies elsewhere.'[17]

SELECT BIBLIOGRAPHY

Johan Huizinga, *Verzamelde Werken* ('Collected works'). Nine vols. (Haarlem 1948-1953)
— *Briefwisseling* ('Correspondence'). Three vols., eds. Léon Hanssen, W.E. Krul, Anton van der Lem (Utrecht 1989-1991)
— *Amerika Dagboek* ('American Diary') 14 April-19 June 1926. ed. Anton van der Lem (Amsterdam, Antwerp 1993)
— *Inleiding en Opzet voor Studie over Licht en Geluid* ('Introduction and Proposal for a Study of Light and Sound'), ed. Jan Noordegraaf, Esther Tros (Amsterdam 1996)

Léon Hanssen, *Huizinga en de troost van de geschiedenis. Verbeelding en rede* (Amsterdam 1996)

W.R.H. Koops, E.H. Kossman, Gees van der Plaat (ed.), *Johan Huizinga 1872-1972* (The Hague 1973)

W.E. Krul, *Historicus tegen de tijd. Opstellen over leven & werk van J. Huizinga* (Groningen 1990)

Anton van der Lem, *Johan Huizinga. Leven en werk in beelden & documenten* (Amsterdam 1993)
— *Het eeuwige verbeeld in een afgehaald bed. Huizinga en de Nederlandse beschaving* (Amsterdam 1997)
— *Inventaris van het archief van Johan Huizinga. Bibliografie 1897-1997* (Leiden 1998)

Christoph Strupp, *Johan Huizinga. Geschichtswissenschaft als Kulturgeschichte* (Göttingen 2000)

For a virtually complete bibliography of the secondary literature until 2000, readers are referred to Strupp.

NOTES

With very few exceptions, I refer only to works by Huizinga himself. The references are to his collected works (in Dutch), citing in each case the volume number (in Roman numerals) and page (in Arabic numerals). The same applies to the letters, which are abbreviated here as L. [WO]

Some of Huizinga's writings are available in English translation: e.g. *The Waning of the Middle Ages* (also translated as *The Autumn of the Middle Ages*), *Homo Ludens*, *Man and the Masses in America*, *In the Shadow of Tomorrow*, and *Dutch Civilization in the Seventeenth Century*. For more detailed information see Van der Lem's bibliography: *Inventaris van het archief van Johan Huizinga. Bibliografie 1897-1997* (Leiden 1998). Books available in English translation are referred to here by their English titles. Those available in Dutch only are referred to by their Dutch titles, with an English translation in parentheses: e.g. *Cultuurhistorische verkenningen* ('Explorations in cultural history') [transl.].

INTRODUCTION

1 VII, 245.
2 Jan Romein, 'Huizinga als historicus', in *Tussen vrees en vrijheid*, (Amsterdam 1950), 223.
3 VII, 244.
4 'Würde das nicht ein Conzert seyn in den schönsten Harmonie, ein Ton, ein Hauch, ein einziges Wort!'
5 VII, 246-7.

CHAPTER 1. LIFE

1 VI, 301.
2 I, 465.
3 I, 522.
4 Virtually all the biographical information provided here has been derived from Krul (1990) and Van der Lem (1993).

5 VW II, 428
6 I, 12.
7 D. Schouten, 'Huizinga's jeugdjaren', in *De Gids* III (1948) IV, 192; I, 13.
8 I, 13-4.
9 I, 15.
10 I, 19.
11 The periodical *De Nieuwe Gids* ('The New Guide') became the mouthpiece of the Movement of 1880.
12 VI, 482.
13 VI, 372-3.
14 Henriëtte Roland Holst was a late nineteenth-century socialist poet.
15 Leonhard Huizinga, *Herinneringen aan mijn vader* (The Hague 1963) 34-5.
16 II, 553.
17 L. I, 163.
18 Leonhard Huizinga, *Herinneringen aan mijn vader* (The Hague 1963), 68, 83-9.
19 Leonhard Huizinga, *Herinneringen aan mijn vader* (The Hague 1963), 98.
20 L. III, 193.

CHAPTER 2. WORK

1 Jorn Rüsen, *Konfigurationen des Historismus. Studien zur deutschen Wissen-schaftkultur* (Frankfurt am Main 1993) 278 (with thanks to Eelco Runia).
2 'Inleiding en Opzet voor Studie over Licht en Geluid'.
3 'Inleiding en Opzet voor Studie over Licht en Geluid', 51.
4 I, 111-2.

5 I, 285, 385.
6 VIII, 343-4.
7 I, 39.
8 III, 330.
9 V, 408, 388, 351, 310, 327, 335.
10 V, 290-1, 329.
11 VI, 181.
12 VII, 410.
13 II, 82.
14 I, 148-9.
15 I, 157.
16 I, 167.
17 I, 163-4.
18 IV, 242.
19 V, 274.
20 IV, 265.
21 IV, 104-5.
22 IV, 417.
23 IV, 412, 420.
24 IV, 425.
25 IV, 262-3; III, 251.

CHAPTER 3. READING

1 III, 44.
2 'Het woud der symbolen'.
3 The Dutch verb *lezen*, 'to read', can also mean 'to select', 'to gather' [transl.].
4 VIII, 495-500; VII, 56, 131.
5 VII, 72.
6 IV, 141.
7 Hans Christian Andersen, 'The Goblin and the Grocer', from *The Complete Andersen* (six volumes, New York 1949), translation by Jean Hersholt.
8 Kurt Ranke, 'Betrachtungen zum Wesen und zur Funktion des

Märchens', in Ranke, *Die Welt der Einfachen Formen. Studien zur Motiv-, Wort- und Quellenkunde* (Berlin, New York 1978) 1-31; Marina Warner, *From the Beast to the Blonde. On Fairy Tales and Their Tellers* (New York 1994); Marina Warner, *Fantastic Metamorphoses, Other Worlds. Ways of Telling the Self* (Oxford, New York 2002).
9   I, 99; VII, 23-4.
10 II, 52-3, 263, 355, 473, 501; VIIII, 524; III, 63, 386, 112.
11 III, 15, 39, 166, 96, 264.
12 III, 5, 26, 36, 112, 157, 466; IV, 112.
13 IV, 122.
14 VI, 157.
15 III, 92; IV, 293.
16 VI, 109; IV, 296.
17 IV, 110.
18 IV, 357, 558; V, 410, 408.
19 IV, 286.
20 V, 25.
21 VII, 219.
22 V, 437.
23 VII, 38.
24 L. III, 269; III, 246.
25 II, 487.
26 V, 280-1, 289.
27 V, 408.
28 IV, 142-3.
29 IV, 283; Dante Alighieri, *The Divine Comedy*, translation by Henry Wadsworth Longfellow (Chartwell 2006).
30 IV, 287-81, 291, 327.
31 IV, 142.

CHAPTER 4. WRITING

1   'Remember that within us often slumbers / A poet ever vibrant, ever young'.
2   IV, 402.
3   Most of Huizinga's words are translated into English here. Occasionally, most notably in the case of the pervasive *bont* and *innig* – which Huizinga employs in a wide variety of meanings – the original Dutch words are given or added [transl.].
4   The original Dutch quotations are: 'bont van keur van fraaien dos'; 'een bonten schat van de meest uiteenlopende vormen en kleuren'; and 'tegelijk binnen zoo geringe afmetingen beperkt en toch zoo rijk en bont, zoo intensief ontwikkeld'.
5   I, 63, 107, 167, 255.
6   I, 96, 140.
7   I, 405; VIII, 147; I, 126.
8   III, 6, 29, 57, 135, 139, 176, 198, 214, 297, 306, 332, 363.
9   III, 6, 34, 181, 200, 213, 244, 231, 250, 186, 271-2, 275, 305, 330.
10 II, 446, 466, 465, 475, 477, 500.
11 I, 67, 160, 475.
12 V, 488, 253; VIII, 253; IV, 296, 399.
13 III, 219, 348, 325-7.
14 II, 467; VII, 222; III, 402; V, 272, 283, 383; IV, 85, 90, 390; VIII, 496; IV, 391; V, 210; II, 443; IV, 425.
15 III, 328, 448; VI, 419, 436; III, 267, 351, 375, 436; IV, 404.
16 III, 212, 259, 275, 338, 90, 132-3, 571, 136, 366, 372.
17 V, 260, 257, 339.

18 II, 536; V, 156-7; IV, 231, 240.
19 I, 365; III, 5, 322, 55, 64, 75.
20 I, 100; III, 110, 281.
21 I, 100; III, 110, 281.
22 VI, 96; IV, 265; V, 107-9, 149, 151, 172, 190, 201.
23 I, 71, 73, 151, 144, 169, 219, 270, 365-6; IV, 327.
24 V, 267, 288, 409; III, 8, 17, 30, 67, 199, 266, 372, 389, 98, 144, 338, 375, 389.
25 IV, 105, 107, 115, 544, 412, 425; III, 451; IV, 341; V, 38.
26 II, 531; V, 374; III, 34.
27 VIII, 90, 532.
28 II, 97; III, 6.
29 VI, 102; III, 28; VII, 412.
30 V, 255; III, 131-2, 90, 206, 330, 312, 345, 234.
31 VI, 40, 42; V, 384; III, 247, 293; V, 40, 79; II, 528, 530.
32 VI, 68, 224; I, 91, 96, 98; IV, 352, 293; V, 7.

CHAPTER 5. CONTRAST
1 V, 251-2, 378.
2 VII, 137; IV, 397.
3 III, 19, 26.
4 III, 28, 345.
5 III, 78.
6 III, 152.
7 III, 161, 252.
8 'Inleiding en Opzet voor Studie over Licht en Geluid', 57.
9 I, 57.
10 'Hoe verloren de Groningsche Ommelanden hun oorspronkelijk Friesch karakter'.
11 I, 475.

12 VI, 117, 125.
13 'Patriottisme en nationalisme in de Europeesche geschiedenis tot het einde der 19e eeuw'.
14 'Twee worstelaars met den engel'.
15 'Denkbeelden en stemmingen van voor honderd jaar'.
16 IV, 397.
17 II, 469.
18 II, 416-7.
19 V, 34, 81-2.
20 V, 103.
21 VII, 340-1.
22 VII, 358-9.
23 III, 44.
24 IV, 274.
25 IV, 275.
26 V, 211.
27 I, 144, 147.
28 II, 242-3.

CHAPTER 6. HARMONY
1 VII, 21.
2 'Kleine samenspraak over de thema's der Romantiek'.
3 IV, 385.
4 VII, 273, 375; V, 221-3; VII, 434.
5 IV, 385.
6 These remarks are more pertinent to the Dutch word *stemming*, translated here as 'mood', since *stemming* contains the root *stem*, meaning 'voice' [transl.].
7 I, 89; Krul (1990) 133 ff.
8 Bernlef was a blind Frisian poet who lived in the 8th century, the first known poet of the Low Countries.
9 I, 405, 522; VIII, 85.

10 VIII, 73, 83-4.
11 IV, 406; III, 246.
12 V, 409.
13 III, 324-5, 453.
14 III, 231, 278.
15 VI, 67, 100. *Hofwijck* is a poem by Huygens.
16 II, 465, 485.
17 II, 474, 492.
18 II, 441.
19 II, 441-2.
20 V, 41-2, 118.
21 V, 190.
22 III, 5.
23 III, 279.
24 V, 5, 7.
25 III, 64, 361, 384, 60; V, 38.
26 III, 278, 366.
27 VII, 329.
28 V, 7.
29 *Nederlands geestesmerk*.
30 II, 445-7.
31 III, 74-5; VII, 35.
32 'Die Mittlerstellung der Niederlande zwischen West- und Mitteleuropa'.
33 II, 302; VIII, 13.
34 VII, 40, 44.

CHAPTER 7. PASSION

1 VII, 17.
2 I, 107; III, 131.
3 'Uit de voorgeschiedenis van ons nationaal besef'.
4 II, 104.
5 III, 26.
6 V, 288.
7 'Over het aesthetisch bestanddeel van geschiedkundige voorstellingen'.
8 VII, 14, 23, 21.
9 III, 19, 26.
10 III, 534.
11 VII, 23-4.
12 III, 89, 360, 374, 10, 39, 54, 60.
13 II, 428, 441-2.
14 II, 566.
15 I, 135.
16 III, 57.
17 III, 11, 134, 127.
18 V, 386, 30.
19 I, 196, 152.
20 IV, 113; V, 162.
21 VII, 196-7.
22 VII, 197-8.
23 VII, 201.
24 II, 537.
25 II, 538, 551.
26 VII, 299.
27 III, 128-9; IV, 36.
28 IV, 113-4.
29 II, 391.
30 III, 147-8.
31 L. III, 201, 213, 208, 193; III, 134.
32 Marina Tsvetaeva, *Earthly Signs. Moscow Diaries, 1917-1922* (New Haven, London 2002) 87.

CHAPTER 8. SYNAESTHESIA

1 Herodotus, *The Histories*, translation by Aubrey de Sélincourt, Penguin Classics 1954.
2 VII, 25.
3 I, 35; VII, 76.
4 I, 60-1, 132-3, 236.
5 I, 281.

6 III, 48; IV, 466-7.
7 III, 357.
8 VI, 109-10; I, 412; II, 75, 84.
9 II, 391, 529, 86-7.
10 Goethe, *Faust* II: 'Born to look, pre-ordained to see'.
11 III, 12, 62, 144, 58, 337-339.
12 III, 216, 348, 459, 338, 30, 216, 3; II, 101.
13 II, 74, 84.
14 II, 389; VIII, 85; II, 468, 487; III, 537.
15 IV, 19, 38; III, 77; IV, 231, 240, 248, 383.
16 II, 507; III, 342-3; I, 412; VI, 439, 429.
17 IV, 319, 105; III, 12, 31, 128, 389.
18 IV, 242, 247, 271.
19 II, 455, 389, 381, 549; VII, 316.
20 III, 19-20, 54, 250-1; IV, 231, 240; VI, 243, 245; V, 409; VI, 446, 430; V, 49.
21 II, 111, 390.
22 III, 312; IV, 385; III, 531.
23 II, 395, 528, 542.
24 III, 28, 345.
25 James A.W. Heffernan, *Museum of Words. The Poetics of Ekphrasis from Homer to Ashbery* (Chicago, London 1993); Roberto E. Campo, *Ronsard's Contentious Sisters: The Paragone between Poetry and Painting in the Works of Pierre Ronsard* (Chapel Hill 1998).
26 In the Hopman translation, these chapters are entitled 'Verbal and Plastic Expression Compared' (I and II) [transl.].
27 III, 343.
28 III, 330.
29 III, 358-9.
30 II, 470, 472, 486.
31 II, 501.
32 'Inleiding en Opzet voor Studie over Licht en Geluid', 56.
33 See chapter 6, note 6 on the Dutch word *stemming* [transl.].
34 Fritz Bechtel, *Über die Beziehungen der sinnlichen Wahrnehmungen in den indogermanischen Sprachen. Ein Beitrag zur Bedeutungsgeschichte* (Weimar 1879) 94; John Locke, *Philosophical Works*, II (London 1875) 26; Henry Fielding, *Tom Jones* (Penguin 1966) 152; Mme de Stael, *Corinne* (Paris 1807) 36; Erica von Erhardt-Siebold, 'Harmony of the Senses in English, German, and French Romanticism', in *Publications of the Modern Language Association of America* XLVII (1932) 577-592.
35 Huizinga refers to the *ahnen* of *geheime bezüge*.
36 Joseph Brodsky, *Less Than One* (New York 1986) 35.

CHAPTER 9. METHOD

1 I, 35.
2 VII, 143.
3 VII, 144.
4 VII, 25.
5 IV, 553-4.
6 *De Gids* 89 (1925) II, 120.
7 *De Gids*, 89 (1925) III, 386-400.
8 VII, 29.
9 VII, 30.
10 VII, 193.
11 VII, 73, 40.
12 V, 251.

13 See chapter 3, note 2 on the meanings of *lezen*.
14 *De wetenschap der geschiedenis*.
15 VII, 137.
16 I, 210, 241.
17 VII, 450; IV, 486; V, 218.
18 IV, 509, 415, 543.
19 VII, 128; IV, 525; VI, 479; II, 97.
20 II, 139, 240.
21 II, 537-8.
22 II, 401-2; VI, 331, 113; II, 391; VI, 42.
23 I, 212, 216, 370-1, 238, 427-8.
24 VI, 291-2.
25 I, 381.
26 III, 362.
27 III, 324-5.
28 III, 13-4.
29 'De taak der cultuurgeschiedenis'.
30 VII, 76.
31 VII, 83-4.
32 IV, 384.
33 'Over vormverandering der geschiedenis'.
34 VII, 192-206.
35 'Over historische levensidealen'.
36 IV, 431.

CHAPTER 10. MYSTICISM

1 VI, 319-20.
2 III, 269.
3 Gott ist ein lauter Nichts, ihn rührt kein Nun noch Hier
Je mehr du nach ihm greifst, je mehr entwird er dir.
4 'Wilt ende woeste, alse een verdolen,' ... 'want daer en is wise, noch wech, noch pat, noch zate, noch mate.' 'Daer in selen wi sijn ons selven onthoecht, ontsonken, ontbreit ende ontlangt in ene ewighe verlorenheit sonder wederkeer.'
5 III, 272-3.
6 III, 276-7.
7 I, 18-9.
8 Van der Lem (1993) 34; I, 31.
9 I, 44, 130.
10 VI, 337, 499-500.
11 Huizinga, *Amerika Dagboek* ('American Diary'), 48-9.
12 Krul (1990) 100; Van der Lem (1993) 30-34; Van der Lem (1997) 197-8.
13 I, 39; VI, 59, 65.
14 'Natuurbeeld en historiebeeld in de achttiende eeuw'.
15 IV, 356.
16 IV, 356-7.
17 IV, 105; III, 157-8.
18 III, 391, 86, 369; I, 184.
19 IV, 327-9.
20 VIII, 488.
21 V, 409, 414, 417.
22 VIII, 490.
23 II, 487.
24 III, 246.
25 III, 247.
26 III, 248.
27 III, 250-1.
28 'Het historisch museum'.
29 'De taak der cultuurgeschiedenis'.
30 VII, 146; III, 264.
31 George Steiner, 'Real presences', in Steiner, *No Passion Spent* (London, Boston 1996) 20-40; George Steiner, *Real Presences. Is there anything in what we say?*

(London, Boston 1989).
32 Van der Lem (1997) 76.

CHAPTER 11. EXTRAPOLATION

1 Hans Andersen, 'the Drop of Water', in *Complete Andersen's Fairy Tales*, Wordsworth Library Collection.
2 'Denkbeelden en stemmingen van voor honderd jaar'; IV, 393.
3 'Des waterdruppels helderte doorturend/besefte ik den wereldoceaan/en zonnestofjes in hun spel beglurend/heb ik het wezen van de zon verstaan.' J.H. Leopold, *Verzen* (Amsterdam 1967) 200, 116; English translation by David McKay.
4 '... daar kleurt de druppel uit de kelk gevloten den Oceaan; een enkle pereling doordringt de gansche helderheid en deelt haar wezen mede aan de verste stranden, den diepsten bodem;...' English translation by David McKay.
5 'Ego tamquam centrum circuli, cui simili modo se habent circumferentiae partes; tu autem non sic.' Dante, *La Vita Nuova*, 37, English translation by Dante Gabriel Rossetti.
6 'Deus est sphaera intelligibilis cuius centrum ubique circumferentia nusquam.' *La vita nuova*, 53; Dietrich Mahnke, *Unendliche Sphäre und Allmittelpunkt. Beiträge zur Genealogie der mathematischen Mystik* (Halle, Saale 1937); IV, 10.
7 VII, 90-1; Mahnke, 173.
8 VI, 436; V, 163.
9 I, 420.
10 I, 164, 285; II, 110.
11 IV, 99, 261-2.
12 V, 24.
13 I, 161.
14 VIII, 60, 134, 187.
15 III, 15, 70, 123.
16 III, 15; see also II, 226.
17 VI, 33.
18 VI, 111; II, 464.
19 III, 262, 14; Borges, *A History of Eternity*.
20 I, 57, 203; VIII, 87-8, 91.
21 V, 385.
22 VI, 181; II, 386, 437, 441, 434, 453.
23 II, 99; III, 84-7; IV, 85; VIII, 103.
24 I, 159.
25 V, 256; II, 414.
26 II, 414; I, 264, 270, 375.
27 'De taak der cultuurgeschiedenis'.
28 VII, 37; V, 418.
29 I, 134; III, 350.
30 VI, 25, 171-2, 179, 497, 479.
31 I, 203, 204, 337, 368, 206, 367; VI, 5-6.
32 The *damiaatjes* are the small bells in the belfry of St Bavo's Church, which according to tradition were donated by William I, count of Holland, the Crusader.
33 I, 373, 369, 366.
34 I, 476; II, 50.
35 VII, 509.

CHAPTER 12. METAMORPHOSIS

1 III, 86, 374.
2 IV, 384.
3 III, 162, 46.

4 III, 157; 217.
5 I, 160; II, 105.
6 III, 290, 296-6.
7 II, 131.
8 III, 202; VII, 410; III, 203, 258.
9 III, 130, 56; V, 39, 80.
10 III, 13.
11 III, 248.
12 'Twee worstelaars met den engel'.
13 IV, 446.
14 V, 148, 53-4.
15 III, 5, 12, 21, 96, 57, 59, 249, 266; IV, 289, 296.
16 V, 415, 408-9; VI, 397.
17 V, 133; III, 127.
18 III, 87.
19 VI, 302.
20 III, 112; see also IV, 422.
21 IV, 72, 86; VI, 327.
22 II, 81; V, 7.
23 V, 133.
24 Erich Auerbach, 'Passio als Leidenschaft', in Auerbach, *Gesammelte Aufsätze zur romanischen Philologie* (Bern, Munich 1967) 161-176; Thomas Dixon, *From Passions to Emotions. The Creation of a Secular Psychological Category* (Cambridge 2003).
25 VII, 24; III, 111.
26 VII, 574.
27 Helmuth Plessner, 'Die kategorische Konjunktive. Ein Versuch über die Leidenschaft' and 'Trieb und Leidenschaft', in Plessner, *Die Frage nach der Conditio Humana. Aufsätze zur philosophischen Anthropologie* (1976) 124-138 and 159-170.

CHAPTER 13. HISTORICAL GREATNESS

1 It should be noted that 'Johan', 'Johannes' and 'Han' are all Dutch equivalents of the English name of 'John' [transl.].
2 Letters II, 158; Léon Hanssen (1996) 23 ff.
3 V, 46.
4 'Hoe verloren de Groningsche Ommelanden hun oorspronkelijk Friesch karakter'.
5 Van der Lem (1997) 113; I, 496, III, 232.
6 'Kleine samenspraak over de thema's der Romantiek'.
7 IV, 383; VIII, 482-3.
8 IV, 383; III, 516-7.
9 VI, 110.
10 IV, 431.
11 V, 162; III, 96-7.
12 Letters III, 189 (and 209-10 and 224), 203, 208, 212, 258.
13 II, 125, 141.
14 III, 562.
15 VII, 212.
16 VII, 214.
17 VII, 217.

INDEX OF PERSONS

Abelard, Peter 48, 54, 55, 68, 70, 139, 144, 193, 215
Aeschylus 43, 173
Alan of Lille 48, 54, 143, 207, 215, 229
Albrecht, Duke of Bavaria 132
Alcuin (of York) 56
Allen, P.S. 37
Andersen, Hans 63, 64, 75, 205, 237, 238
Anrooy, Peter van 34, 35, 37
Aristophanes 193
Ariosto, Ludovico 69, 83, 86, 93
Aristotle 70, 71, 76, 98, 230
Arnolfini, Giovanni 117, 180
Asser, Tobias 35
Astor, John Jacob 214
Augustine 68, 69
Aulard, Alphonse 140

Bach, Johann Sebastian 34, 63, 92
Bakhuizen van den Brink, R.C. 83, 157
Bechtel, Fritz 163, 164
Beethoven, Ludwig van 34, 77, 200
Bernlef 116

Beuil, Jean de 193, 215, 227
Bilderdijk, Willem 92
Bloch, Marc 49
Bloem, J.C. 40
Blok, P.J. 191
Boehme, Jacob 195
Borges, Jorge Luis 213
Botticelli, Sandro 86
Boucicaut 127, 215
Boursse, Esaias 201
Braak, Menno ter 33, 73
Brahms, Johannes 34
Bredero, Gerbrand Adriaensz. 89, 105, 152, 161, 162, 218
Burckhardt, Jacob 41, 217, 220, 243, 244
Burdach, Konrad 217
Buridan, Jean 109
Burne-Jones, Edward 136
Byron, George Gordon 68

Caesar 14, 22
Campen, Jacob van 156
Carlyle, Thomas 16, 140, 243

Cats, Jacob 105
Cervantes, Miguel de 69, 75, 228
Charlemagne 56
Charles IV 16
Charles the Bold 150, 181
Chastelleain, Georges 68, 150, 151, 181, 182, 211, 214
Clairvaux, Bernard of 56, 231
Chrysippus 207
Comte, Auguste 177
Cuyp, Albert 162

Dante 30, 33, 45, 47, 58, 62, 70, 71, 75-77, 131, 143, 207
Darwin, Charles 233
Diderot, Denis 134
Dionysius (the Carthusian) 67, 187
Dorp, Dorothea van 239
Duer, William 214
Dürer, Albrecht 77, 86, 155, 193

Eckhart, (Meister) 81, 187, 188, 195
Edzard (count of Friesland) 27
Emerson, Ralph Waldo 70, 194
Erasmus, Desiderius 37, 38, 69, 86, 87, 91, 92, 98, 103, 104, 118, 144, 151, 156, 179, 191, 212, 214, 217, 239, 240
Eyck, Jan van 45, 83, 101, 117, 124, 134, 146, 151, 153, 154, 159, 160, 180, 181, 190, 200, 217, 238

Fielding, Henry 164
Floris V 27, 170, 216
France, Anatole 68
Francis of Assisi 34, 139, 195
Freud, Sigmund 233
Froissart, Jean 131
Fruin, Robert 151

Gascoigne, George 73
Geertgen tot St. Jans 161, 238
Gerson, Jean 240
Geyl, Pieter 14
Goethe, Johann Wolfgang von 70
Gogh, Vincent van 195
Gourmont, Remy de 73
Goya, Francisco 194
Grimm, Jacob 29, 165
Grimm, Wilhelm 64
Groot, Hugo de (Grotius) 35, 47, 144, 151, 178, 214
Guardi, Francesco 174

Hals, Frans 162
Hawthorne, Nathaniel 17, 47, 70, 74, 75, 117, 118, 156, 194, 195
Heering, G.J. 14
Helouïse (abbesse) 144
Herodotus 148, 171-173
Hogendorp, Gijsbert Karel van 92, 142, 178
Homer 28, 158
Hooft, P.C. 86, 89
Huisinga Bakker, Pieter 28
Huizinga, Dirk (father) 23, 24, 26
Huizinga, Dirk (son) 36, 226
Huizinga, Herman (half-brother) 26
Huizinga, Jakob (grandfather) 23-26
Huizinga, Jakob (brother) 24, 28
Huizinga, Johan,
Books:
Introduction and Proposal for a Study of Light and Sound (1896) 42, 85, 115
The vidûsaka in Indian Theatre (1897) 43, 87, 102, 115, 132, 238

Man and the Masses in America (1918) 42, 46, 47, 82, 85, 88, 90, 91, 103, 116, 133, 176, 177
The Waning of the Middle Ages (1919) 13, 35, 42, 45-49, 52, 54, 61, 67, 68, 73, 80-83, 85-88, 90-92, 98, 107, 109, 117, 118, 121, 123, 132, 135, 138, 143, 144, 146, 150, 153, 158, 159, 161, 162, 180, 181, 186, 191, 200, 210, 214, 220, 221, 223-225, 227, 232, 238, 240, 242
Erasmus (1924) 13, 48, 69, 82, 86, 104, 218
Ten Studies (1926) 48, 173
Extrapolations in Cultural History (1929) 48
Homo Ludens (1938) 13, 40, 42, 49, 52, 88, 89, 107, 109, 120, 121, 123, 124, 139, 156, 208, 225, 227, 233, 238, 241
Dutch Civilization in the Seventeenth Century (1941) 24, 42, 46, 49, 81, 105, 126, 161, 212, 215
In the Shadow of Tomorrow (1935) 13, 42, 47, 49, 91, 108, 125
Shattered World (1945) 40, 112, 232
My Path to History (1947) 33, 63
Essays:
'On the study and appreciation of Buddhism' (1903) 50
'On the aesthetic component of historical accounts' (1905) 134
'The historical museum' (1920) 199
'The problem of the Renaissance' (1920) 48, 52, 86, 87, 110
'Two wrestlers with the angel' (1921) 195, 225
'Bernard Shaw's saint' (1925) 135, 172, 242

'Brief colloquy on themes of Romanticism' (1929) 114, 239
'Renaissance and realism' (1929) 48, 83
'The task of cultural history' (1929) 182, 199, 216
'Views of nature and views of history in the eighteenth century' (1933) 192
'Outlooks: 1533, 1584' (1933) 103
'The national character of the Netherlands' (1934) 105, 126, 143
'Ideas and moods a hundred years ago' (1939) 83, 105, 206
'On metamorphosis in history' (1941) 184
Huizinga, Leonhard (son) 34, 36, 37, 226
Huizinga-de Cock, Manna (stepmother) 27
Huizinga-Schölvinck, Auguste (second wife) 39, 145, 146, 241
Huizinga-Schorer, Mary Vincentia (first wife) 33, 35, 36, 190, 240
Hugo, Victor 68
Huygens, Constantijn 81, 89, 118, 126, 153, 239, 240
Huysmans, Joris-Karl 68, 73

Jackson, Andrew 214
Jean Paul 42
Jerome 68, 69
Joan of Arc 47, 135, 157, 172, 227, 242-244
Jolles, André 37, 173, 174, 176, 180, 182
Jonson, Ben 69, 73
Jonckbloet, W.J.A. 83

Kaegi, Werner 28
Kandinsky, Wassily 194
Kantorowicz, Ernst 48
Kapteyn, J.C. 190
Keller, Gottfried 74, 75
Kern, Hendrik 21, 179, 186, 198, 228

Lalaing, Jacques de 215
Laforgue, Jules 68, 73-75
Lamprecht, Karl 177
Lee, Robert 141
Leers, Johann von 38
Leeghwater, Adriaan 212
Leicester (Earl of) 179
Lemonnier, Camille 68
Leopold, J.H. 206
Lévy, Sylvain 37
Lincoln, Abraham 132, 134, 141, 191
Locke, John 164
Louis XI 88
Louis XIII 157
Louis XIV 157
Louis the Pious 28
Lusignan, Leo of 152
Luther, Martin 69, 71, 86, 98, 104

Machaut, Guillaume de 145, 146
Maeterlinck, Maurice 73
Malinowski, Bronislaw 37
March, Olivier de la 214
Marie Antoinette 221
Maris, Mattijs 195
Marlowe, Christopher 72, 73
Marx, Karl 177, 233
Maupassant, Guy de 68, 136
Merlin de Thionville, Antoine 130
Meschinot, Jean 161
Metsys, Quentin 155

Michelangelo 69, 86
Michelet, Jules 16, 131, 140
Millet, Jean François 133
Mohammad (prophet) 74
Molière 67, 177, 228
Molinet, Jean 214
Monstreuil, Jean de 193
Mor, Antonis 111
More, Thomas 76, 77
Morosini, Francesco 174
Mozart, Wolfgang Amadeus 34, 77
Musset, Alfred de 78

Nietzsche, Friedrich 26

Ovid 68, 154

Paul (apostle) 92
Philip the Bold 90
Philip the Fair 150
Philip the Good 210, 211
Pisan, Christine de 193
Plato 70-72, 98, 100, 121, 238
Plessner, Helmuth 233
Pope, Alexander 177
Pot, Philippe 211
Potgieter, E.J. 83, 157

Rabelais, François 69, 70, 83, 86, 111
Ranke, Leopold von 14-16, 171
Raphael 86, 93
Redon, Odilon 194
Reigersberg, Mary 144, 179
Rembrandt 62, 69, 98, 117, 119, 134, 136, 153, 181, 221
Repgow, Eike von 191
Robespierre, Maximilien de 131
Roland Holst, Henriëtte 32, 37

Roland Holst, Richard 32, 37
Romein, Jan 14
Ronsard, Pierre de 86
Rousseau, Jean-Jacques 70
Rubens, Peter Paul 98
Ruisdael, Jacob van 162
Ruusbroec, Jan van 187, 188

Salisbury, John of 48, 54, 70, 84, 126, 209, 215, 229, 240
Saunderson, Nicholas 164
Schubert, Franz 34, 111
Seghers, Hercules 195
Seward, William 132
Shakespeare, William 30, 47, 62, 72, 75, 135, 144, 228
Shaw, George Bernard 135, 172, 242
Silesius, Angelus 187, 195
Sitter, Willem de 190
Sitter, Bine de 36
Sluter, Claus 154
Spengler, Oswald 105, 177, 225
Speyer, J.S. 30, 43
Staël, Mme de 164
Steiner, George 200
Suso, Heinrich 187
Sydney, Philip 73, 88, 179, 229
Sijmons, B. 42
Sweelinck, J.P. 156
Swinderen, Th. van 213

Taine, Hippolyte 140
Thomas Aquinas 70, 76
Thomas à Kempis 56, 118, 124, 187, 231

Toorop, Jan 111
Tsvetaeva, Marina 146, 148

Valéry, Paul 73
Valkenburg, C.T. van 14, 37
Velde, Jan van de 199
Verlaine, Paul 68, 73
Vermeer, Johannes 74, 153, 195, 196, 200
Veth, Anna 237
Veth, Jan 31, 33, 37, 104, 154-156, 217, 226, 237, 239
Virgil 33, 68, 76
Vitri, Philip de 127
Vollenhoven, Cornelis van 35, 37, 217, 243
Voltaire 70
Vondel, Joost van den 67, 89, 90, 119, 151-153, 156, 161, 162
Vries, Matthias de 83

Wells, H.G. 105, 225
Whitman, Walt 70, 156, 194, 195, 226
Wilde, Oscar 68, 136
Wilhelmina (queen) 32, 35, 143
Willem I (king) 33
Wilson, Edmund 17
Winkel, Jan te 29
Witt, Johan de 151, 153, 170
Witte, Emanuel de 200

Xerxes 148, 171

Zola, Emile 68